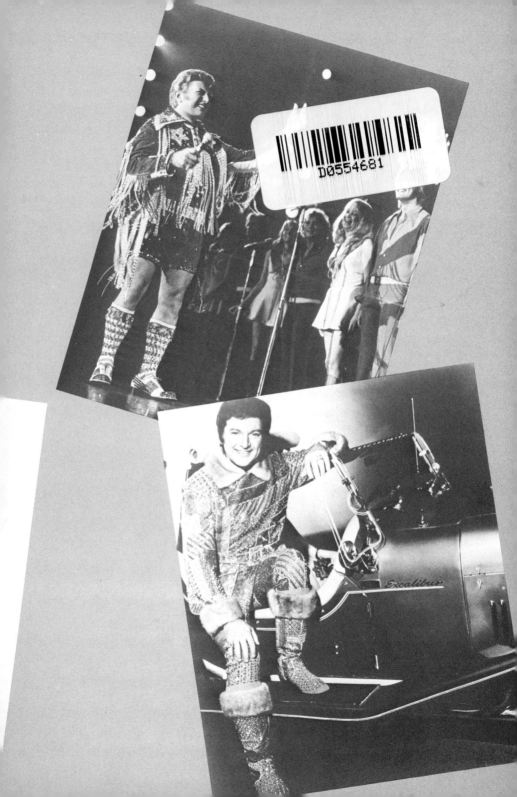

LIBERACE

LIBERACE

AN AUTOBIOGRAPHY

 Longman Canada Limited

Longman Canada Limited
55 Barber Greene Road
Don Mills, Ontario
M3C 2A1

SBN: 399-11229-4

My sincerest and deepest thanks to Carroll Carroll for his editorial assistance in the preparation of this manuscript.

LIBERACE

Illustrations will be found following pages 128 and 256.

Introduction

When you're young, starting out on a career, your hopes are high. But so are your apprehensions. The possibility of failure can't be accepted. But it can't be ignored. Your mind is dominated by the will to win; but at the same time you're haunted by the fear of failure. These are the conflicts that control everything you do.

Some men grow old never having been able to overcome their inner conflicts. No matter what they accomplish they continue to question their worth. They live with fear of failure or rejection and so all the success in the world doesn't bring them peace of mind or happiness.

Some men, on the other hand, are lucky as I was, to come upon a solution to their uncertainties, something that makes them realize who they are and have confidence in the validity of their instincts.

For me all this happened when I found a book called *The Magic of Believing* by Claude M. Bristol. Reading Mr. Bristol's book taught me the true meaning of Franklin D. Roosevelt's immortal words: "The only thing we have to fear is fear itself." I was so moved by the work that I told the author how much it meant to me. The book had gone into twenty-three printings when the publisher, Prentice-Hall, asked me to write an introduction for a Special Liberace Edition. I felt it was the least I could do in gratitude for having been given the one thing I needed—belief in myself.

I was happy when this special edition made Mr. Bristol's book a best seller all over again. I gave copies to all my friends, among them Phyllis Diller. She was just starting out on her career. Every time we meet she thanks me for *The Magic of Believing* and credits it with showing her the way to have faith in herself.

I write this as preface to a statement I wrote thirty years ago. After fifteen years of hard work I was "discovered" and called "an overnight success."

I hope the following will explain why I had the courage to write about myself. I hope it will prove an inspiration, as it outlines clearly and candidly how I live by this credo:

Life has taught me so may lessons, it's hard to decide which one is of the greatest value, but one of the most important is this: Nobody will believe in you unless you believe in yourself.

It's been proved to me more times than I can count. Not only in the beginning of my career in show business but all along the way. I've had first to prove to others that I could do what I was attempting. If I hadn't believed in myself, nobody would have!

There is something contagious about fear. If one person in a crowd panics, there can be a stampede. In much the same way, if one person feels uncertain, everybody else becomes insecure. Nothing thrives like fear and uncertainty.

So if a person doubts his own ability, how can he convince anyone else of his worth? If he approaches a problem timidly, with an "I guess I can" kind of tentativeness, he has usually lost his chance to prove or disprove.

When I started in show business, my kind of act, which consisted entirely of me, alone at a piano, had never before attained any success. The scoffers said it couldn't be done. After I proved them wrong, the same people said, it couldn't last. I had to show them, and I guess I did.

The entertainment world, more than any other, is a place where you have to sell yourself by having faith in yourself, but in all walks of life, the same holds true, essentially. When a young man or woman graduates from school and sets out to make his or her way in the world, that all important first chance comes only with self-confidence. And if you're middle-aged and find yourself out of a job, a positive approach, with calm self-confidence is your best and only passport back into the busy workaday world. Nobody wants to hire a loser.

So never let yourself lose your belief in yourself. With that you can be the greatest salesman in the world, selling the most important product in the world . . .YOU!

Foreword

Most people really have a very limited knowledge of me as a human being. They know only that I play the piano, wear flamboyant clothes, am nice to my mother, have a brother named George . . . and a candelabra. But there's more under this show biz exterior than most people know about, and for the first time in my life, I have a chance to tell about it. I intend to do so in depth.

I just didn't decide to "tell about it" for plain ordinary egotistical reasons, although I have some of those, too. The decision to tell more about myself came in part from the people who rush up to me after each show I do . . . no matter whether it's in London, England, or Baton Rouge, Louisiana, and ask me the most amazing and personal questions.

They say they want to know more about me than they've seen. Wouldn't you think that the clothes I wear would give them enough to see? They certainly give people enough to *talk* about.

A London *Daily Mirror* columnist named William Neil Connor, who hid behind the pseudonym Cassandra, "talked" about me so loud in print and said such insulting things that the English courts awarded me $22,400 in damages (plus apologies and court costs) as proof that the insinuations he made about me had no basis in fact. You'll read about that when you get into the book.

I really am amazed that my clothes attract so much attention, fascinate people so. Of course that's what they were designed to do. But people don't make fun of them or ask who designed them. They want to know where I *got* them, as if they wanted to buy some for themselves and thought I just walked into a store and bought the merchandise off the racks. It's very foolish to think that—I'm too difficult to fit.

As far as I'm concerned I don't think my stage clothes are any fancier than those some other groups of men wear on their jobs. Nobody rushes up to a matador as he's leaving the bull ring with two ears and a tail to ask him where he got his suit. And you know bull fighters rarely work in denims or mousy tweed jackets.

Have you ever studied the outfits cowboys wear? The dreamy hats, the scarves, the furry pants, the high-heeled boots! Wow! And the ones I see in the Rose Bowl Parade in Pasadena or the Santa Claus Lane Parade in Hollywood, or the Mummers' Parade in Philadelphia or the Macy's Parade in New York! Those old cowhands spend fortunes on their silver gear. And their horses are even better dressed than they are. But I've never seen a horse nuzzle another horse and ask where he got his fancy tack.

Generals and admirals don't dress too conservatively, either, with all their brass buttons and gold braid and medals and sashes, but that's *their* show. So why is there so much talk all the time—thank goodness—about what I wear in *my* show?

But that's enough about clothes. If I really wanted only to attract attention, I'd go without clothes. That would do it. On second thought, would it? Nudity is getting to be less and less interesting, and I wouldn't want to get in on a losing trend.

That's what I think the girls who seem to be wearing fewer and fewer clothes are heading for. Their scheme doesn't seem to be working. The law of diminishing returns has set in. The more they show the less attention they get. The net result is that the men are dressing more elaborately to counteract the fact that women are dressing less attractively.

But now let me tell you the second reason I wanted to write this book. I'm always honest with my audiences, and I'm going to be honest with you. I wrote it for the same reason I wear the clothes I wear. To be entertaining and to make money. I think those are the reasons a lot of people write books. What's more, I want to thank you for helping me to fulfill my purpose. I hope, when you've read the book through, you find I've told you everything you want to know about me.

And to show my appreciation, when you write a book that tells all about *you*, I'll buy it and read it with great interest. Because don't think I wouldn't like to know a lot more about you; you're a matter of very great interest to me.

The more I know about you, the more I know how to please you. The more I'm able to do that, the more you'll come to see my shows. And the more you come to see my shows and buy my records, the more. . . . Oh, well, you get the idea.

Oh, yes, there are two things more I think I should straighten out for you before you start reading the shocking details of my life. This is something I've been denying ever since the Presidential campaign of 1972.

I did *not* give vocal lessons to Senator George McGovern, nor did I give piano lessons to President Richard M. Nixon. Actually neither of them asked me to.

Just one thing more. If you like the book will you please write and tell me so? It would make me very happy.

To Answer
a Few
Questions

I think it would be easier for all of us if I took a page or two to give you a few of the statistics of my life, the dull details that are constantly being asked on questionnaires from insurance companies, banks, credit organizations and the United States Government. You see, if I do that, then as we go along I won't have to interrupt any interesting stories to fill you in on some unimportant matter of fact. Not that my stories aren't facts. But some facts are more interesting than others.

I was born on May 16, 1920, in West Allis, Wisconsin. (Actually it was 1919, but an even number is so much easier to remember.) West Allis is just outside of Milwaukee where my father, Salvatore L. Liberace, played the French horn in orchestras, including the Milwaukee Symphony. For those who can't remember which horn is French, it's the round one that the player holds against his belly with his fist stuffed into the bell of the horn. I think that it's the way he handles his fist that has something to do with the tone of the horn.

It seems a little obvious to add that my father was Italian. And I never did find out why his friends called him Sam.

I was christened Wladziu Valentino Liberace, but my name now is legally just the one word, Liberace. My friends call me Lee. That's one of my nicer nicknames. I have others, you know. I think I was lucky they didn't go for Libby, which is what the British call me.

When I was a little boy, and even when I was a young man,

people called me Wallie because Wladziu is Polish for Walter. The name reflects the fact that my mother, Frances Zuchowski, who also came from a musical family, was Polish. It also reflects that she was an ardent fan of the famous silent screen star, Rudolph Valentino. She actually christened my younger brother Rudolph Valentino Liberace. Rudy died some years ago.

As many of you know, I have an older brother, George, who is a violinist. He lives with his family in central California. And my sister, Angelina, took a lot of dictation for this book.

I have three beautiful houses and I'll tell you why I have so many and where they are and what they look like, inside and out, when the proper time and place presents itself. And I have a lot of dogs. The number changes all the time. So if I ever happen to mention a dog's name and it is not the same name I mentioned the last time I mentioned a dog's name, it's not a mistake. It's another dog.

I started studying music when I was four years old and won a scholarship to the Wisconsin College of Music when I was seven and one-half. The scholarship lasted seventeen years—the longest the college ever awarded.

My piano teacher was Florence Bettray-Kelly who worked with me and trained me for the concert circuit. She liked me, although my career didn't turn out exactly the way she had in mind.

I have a lot of hobbies. I collect things for their artistic value and historic interest, for the pleasure I can get out of them and sometimes just to keep them from being destroyed. I collect antiques of all kinds for their beauty and unique automobiles for the fun of it. I happen to agree with the man who said, "The only difference between men and boys is in the price of their toys."

Sparse as they are, I think those should be enough bare facts about my life to make it easier for you to understand what follows about my work and my play, my friends and my adventures and some of the tragedies that have brushed my life as they do the lives of everyone.

1

"**W**hen asked," wrote James Green of the London *Evening News*, "why he chose to wear a white mink coat at the Command Performance for their majesties the Queen and the Queen Mother, at The Palladium on October 31, 1972, Liberace said, 'I didn't come here to go unnoticed.' "

That was not just a silly remark on my part. I knew what I was saying. I knew it would be quoted. It's part of the showmanship that I rely on. The clothes attract attention. They get me newspaper headlines and interviews. They get me audiences.

"I've had to withstand ridicule," Mr. Green quotes me as saying, "and a storm of criticism, jokes and ribbing. I'm glad I persevered."

As I write this I'm sitting at a piano-shaped desk in my home overlooking the Hollywood Hills. A huge scrap book lies open in front of me. I am copying from it. Mr. Green says that he said to me, "Lee, this Beau Brummell bit has got to be a send-up. Surely you don't dress like that by choice?"

I tried to tell him how the wardrobe, the props and the showmanship changed the course of my career. I wish I'd had a story that appeared in the *New Musical Express* a few weeks later to help me. The anonymous article opens with a description and a picture of a cocktail pianist who was playing in the Chelsea Room of The Carlton Towers Hotel where I was living. It says this picture makes this young artist—and I know what it means to read things like this about yourself—look a loser, "the hair is straggly, the tuxedo looks pure rent-a-tux and though he's trying hard to smile it comes out more like a squirm. He's the epitome of the kid whose mother forced him to take piano lessons." (With me it was just the reverse. I forced my parents to get them for me.)

The article continues, "He makes his living pumping out delicate variations of Musak, Gershwin, some film themes, fragments of the classics." (There but for the fortunes of show biz go I.)

"What he and other cohorts of the keyboard lack, whether they be playing in bars, brothels or sleazy supper club joints, is real style. Panache, if you like, a taste for calculated outrage . . . the sequin suits and candelabra of, who else, but one Wladziu Valentino Liberace."

In these few paragraphs some nameless journalist has given good advice to all struggling young piano players. The secret of showmanship. Panache!

The James Green piece included a picture of me seated at a very plain, conventional piano. I'm wearing a simple, Edwardian style business suit which was considered very conservative for London in 1972. Nothing elegant. Nothing showy. I've always stuck to the theory that if people want to see my elegant outfits, they should buy tickets. The wardrobe, like the candelabra, is part of the show.

There's also a business reason why I only wear my elaborate things on stage. There are two reasons, really. The first is that if I wore them on the street I'd be arrested. You'll have to be patient until I am ready to tell you about the second. It involves the IRS.

Under the *Evening New*'s picture of me is the simple caption, "Liberace Is Back in Town." I remember when I read that line for the first time. It gave me a nice warm feeling as if it said, "a friend has come home." I took it to mean that they understood some of the love I have for London.

I always feel wonderful when I come back. It's been that way ever since the autumn of 1956, when I stepped off the train at Waterloo Station the first time I came to town to do a Command Performance.

It's always been fantastic to me, when I think about it, that the very first time I went to England it was to do, of all things, a Command Performance. It seemed to me to be a little like learning how to dive by going over Niagara Falls in a barrel. What do you do for an encore?

Well, I've been lucky. For an encore I've done two more Commands. But who counts?

I may even have done another one since 1972, because who

knows how long it will take this book to get from my desk to your library? I write slowly. And I wouldn't want to set any limit on the number of times I'll perform as Her Majesty commands.

It's always such fun.

I guess any place where you've had a good time you like to return to.

That's why I love London. Just thinking of those big clumsy red monsters that clog the streets gives me pleasure. Dick Cavett once said he liked London because you could go back, after being away a year, and find some of the same buildings still standing. I wish I'd said that. It's how I feel. I admire the Londoner's air of quiet reserve. That's how I am. Of course, I keep it well hidden. If I didn't I wouldn't be where I am today.

Some say that wherever I am, I shouldn't be there. But this group disagrees on whether my place is really at the piano in the cocktail lounge of a Midwestern hotel, or on the concert stage. The first I tried. The second I abandoned. Being a concert pianist is too lonely for a person like me. Maybe I'll get further into that idea as we go along.

But I'm wandering from London, and I don't want to do that. The moment I saw it, it was love at first sight. And, as far as the Londoners were concerned, that love was reciprocated. How else could I interpret that crowd, back in 1956 . . . 10,000 cheering men, women and children literally hanging from the girders of Waterloo Station? I did not have one relative living in England. Of course, they'd seen some of my TV shows. But if they hadn't liked me they'd have stayed home. So some of them must have come out of love. They couldn't all have been critics. They surely didn't act like critics. But I mustn't get started on them.

So in 1972, back in London for the tenth or twelfth time, three times for Command Performances, I felt very much loved. You don't get invited any place three times unless someone feels that way about you. And, having been successful on my native ground—Wisconsin, Minnesota, Michigan—I felt safe in saying they not only loved me in Sheboygan, but they also loved me in Great Britain. It started as a cordial friendship in 1956, blossomed into puppy love by 1958, became a burning, all-consuming passion in 1959, when I won my libel suit, and has remained since then that wonderful kind of mutual respect and understanding that is so strong you know it's going to last forever.

To bear me out in this, Michael Billington, reviewing the Royal

Variety (Command) Performance of 1972 for the prestigious Manchester *Guardian*, wrote. "Perhaps the biggest treat was the outrageous Liberace." In England the word "outrageous" is used differently from in the USA. For example, they might say, with admiration, "Sir Noel said the most outrageous things."

Billington told his readers, and again I'm copying from the scrapbook,

> Sitting cosily on a mink covered proofe [that's British for the French word "pouffe" meaning pillow or hassock, but what I was sitting on was a piano bench] sporting a sequinned coat that made him look like a fleshy Bela Lugosi [see what I mean by ridicule and ribbing?], exposing his diamond buttons spelling out his name on his blinding suit, Liberace shrewdly sent himself up before anyone else could do the job. He is the arch, self-promoting showman who says, "Just go right ahead and applaud. It doesn't bother me." And his highbrow, camp act works because it's founded on solid, ivory tinkling technique.

Now, you know, no Yankee visitor to "that tight little isle" who has *that* written about him can be all bad. In case you disagree, or just think I picked out an isolated item, I'll go back to James Green in the London *Evening News*. His review was headlined, "Liberace Lights Up The Whole Show." Then he went on to say, "Liberace's a rhinestone Rubinstein" (I like that) "with a suit of lights to rival the South End illumination, he gave a display of showmanship which was the highlight of the bill. He played, he sang, he tap danced, he sparkled like the Milky Way and why he closed the first half instead of closing the show is one of life's little mysteries." I don't know about you, but I like to read that sort of thing.

But I think I'd better explain to whoever might get the idea that Green was comparing me to a dog and pony act that this wasn't what he meant to do . . . .I think. While in the United States the closing act on a vaudeville bill was generally an animal act, it's not that way at all in Britain. The great honor, in England, is to close the Royal Variety Performance.

But I'm glad that the closing spot was given to Carol Channing. She was wonderful. She even tried to out-razzle-dazzle me by tossing diamonds at the Royal Family. I'll bet the Queen Mother and her daughters were sorry the gems weren't real, I mean the way things were, economically, in London in 1972.

I would have liked it if the newspapers had given more space to

Carol than to me. Well, I might not exactly have *liked* it, but it would have been the more gentlemanly thing for them to do. It would have been more gracious. One of the London dailies called her the only woman in the world with legs that start at her shoulders. I don't know whether that's good or bad. But it's a funny—and by that I mean strange—way to review such a great performer.

I like the word "performer" a lot better than a stuck-up word like "artist." I think that for a performer to call himself an artist is kind of putting it on. Of course, if someone else wants to call you an artist . . . okay! But it seems to me that the word artist suggests a self-oriented, inward directed person who creates only what he pleases, for himself, and the public can like it or leave it.

On the other hand a performer is frankly and honestly out to please other people. He's giving. And the success or failure of this giving is something he creates between himself and his audience. That's why each appearance before a different audience is in some respects a new performance. At least that's the way it is with me. There's always a different mix of people and a different chemistry of emotions. When the chemistry is right—both giving, both receiving—it's a joy.

Among the other Americans on the bill with Carol and me were Jack Jones and a rock group called The Jackson Five, which is a pretty conservative name for a rock group.

The rest of the acts were such famous and beloved British variety stars as Dickie Henderson, Ken Dodd, Elton John, Rod Hull, Mike Yarwood and Danny La Rue, the female impersonator who had just won the Entertainer of the Year Award. Not since the United States acclaimed Julian Eltinge has such a performer been so honored by his country.

But the big star of the show . . . the big surprise . . . he nearly stole all the headlines from me . . . was Warren Mitchell. Warren's the actor who created the role of Alf Garnett, the salty, blaspheming hero of the BBC-TV's show, *Till Death Do Us Part.* Warren's counterpart in the CBS version, *All in the Family,* is Carroll O'Connor.

Alf Garnett's language, his scolding against the government and his prejudices in general make anything that comes out of the mouth of Archie Bunker sound like honey and molasses. That Warren was invited to be on the show and given permission by the

Queen to say whatever Alf Garnett would naturally say is a beautiful example of the freedom of speech accorded to performers in England. I think it's just great.

The first time I met the Queen Mother was after a performance in Manchester in 1958. The second time was at the Command Performance in London in 1972. The first thing she said to me was, "It's so nice to see you again."

I said, "It's nice of you to remember, ma'am."

Then, after apologizing that Queen Elizabeth was prevented from attending the performance by affairs of state, she asked—apparently remembering that we'd sent Mother home ill during my libel suit in 1959—"How's your dear mother?"

I thought it was most considerate of her to remember.

So, in 1972, I apologized to the Queen Mother because my mother was not with me. "We just celebrated her eightieth birthday," I said, "and the trip seemed too much for her. But she sends her love to you." Then I added, "She loves anybody who is nice to me."

The Queen Mother laughed, "That's the way all us Mothers are."

Comparing the way the people acted at the performances in 1958 and with the one in 1960, when the Queen was present, I realized that everyone seemed more relaxed with the Queen "Mum" as they called her. She's more informal. More folksy. But I guess you can be that way once you've passed the job of being Queen along to one of your kids. You can relax a little.

Another thing the Queen Mother apologized for—I was overwhelmed at her apologizing to me—was being unable to see me in 1956 when I first went over to do a Command Performance. It was to have been an important "first" in my life and I can't tell you with what anticipation I looked forward to it.

We crossed on the *Queen Mary*. Planes weren't quite as spacious then as they became with the coming of the 747's. And I had a lot to take over with me—my glass-top piano, my Cadillac, my wardrobe, my cast, my candelabra, my brother George and his wife Jane, my mother and my manager, Seymour Heller. In return for carrying all this freight across, the Cunard people suggested that I do one ship's concert.

I had a secondary reason for wanting to cross by boat. I felt that because of the rising popularity of trans-oceanic air travel, the great liners, that took so much longer, were on their way to the dry docks or into the cruise trade. I wanted to ride on one while it was still everything it was built to be. And I sure got what I wanted; I had a ball all the way from New York harbor to Southampton.

I was invited to sit at the Captain's table, which is always good because that means the meals will be even better than they normally are. If the Captain doesn't like what he's served he can make the chef walk the plank. My mind always conjures up things like that, things that go back to legendary times. You wouldn't believe what my fantasies were about what the Command Performance would be like.

I thought of it in terms of gold and scarlet coaches drawn by six dappled gray horses and driven by men dressed as if they'd just stepped out of MGM's wardrobe department and were on their way to play courtiers in some Elizabethan drama starring Lawrence Olivier, Ralph Richardson, John Gielgud . . . and me.

I expected each act to be heralded by a sextet of musicians with long bugles. Then a man looking like the Lord High Chancellor in a Gilbert and Sullivan operetta would walk out and announce my name in stentorian tones. I have no idea what stentorian tones are, but I've read about them and they sound great. The audience—by this time all standing—would be dressed like friends of Henry VIII. And seated in the Royal Box would be the Queen wearing a crown on her head and looking exactly as if she'd just had her first taste of Imperial Margarine. No. I couldn't have thought that in 1956 because I'm sure that commerical had not yet been produced.

Anyway, to live up to my expectations of pomp and splendor, I figured I'd better plan my fanciest wardrobe. Not that I needed any added incentive to plan beautiful clothes, but it was a good excuse.

On the second day out one of the more experienced travelers aboard emerged from his cabin, and we met walking around the deck.

He put out his hand and said, "Liberace, I believe," and gave me a kind of smile that was both friendly and looked as if he were putting me on.

I knew who he was and I was amazed that he knew who I was.

"I've seen your act," he said.

"Thank you."

"You do what you do very well."

"Thank you."

"I'm Noel Coward."

"Yes, I know," I said. "I'm delighted to meet you."

"Leave that for time to decide. I hear you're giving one of those ship's concerts. Are you?"

"Yes."

"Don't!"

"Why?"

"Terribly stuffy lot. Don't do it."

"I've given my word that I would."

"Well, if you must! But not just for the first-class."

"They didn't tell me it would be just for one class."

"Insist they let everyone aboard attend."

I had always thought Sir Noel had very little interest in anyone but the brittle type of people he wrote about. I wondered if his concern in letting all the passengers attend my concert was because he was interested in people or simply that he thought the other folks in first class were such a bad audience they'd make me unhappy. I'll never know, but the seed he planted took root.

At the Captain's cocktail party I told him I'd like it very much if everyone on the ship were invited to my concert. He shook his head thoughtfully for a little while as he said, "Highly irregular. Highly irregular. But, if that's the way you feel it has to be, so be it." He said he'd look into the possibility of doing it my way. So the seed Noel Coward planted not only took root but flowered.

The word spread around the ship like wildfire, maybe Mr. Coward helped to start it, that I was going to give a concert and since, in 1956, television had made my name a household word, the people in second and third class knew me. They were my audience. So many of them came that they practically squeezed out the first class passengers. I played to standing room only and when it was over Mr. Coward said, "Glad you took my advice. Wish I'd thought of doing it myself. Marvelous audience."

They certainly were! Even the first class passengers were far from being "stuffy" or blasé because the enthusiasm of the rest rubbed off on them.

It was a wonderful voyage and when the *Queen* tied up at Southampton, instead of the red coach and six I'd dreamed about, there was a special train waiting for me. And instead of heraldic banners flying from its car-tops, it had only one simple decoration. It was a sign saying "Liberace Special." When I saw it I actually felt embarrassed inside. But I blushed too soon.

I should have saved my blushes for our arrival in London. When we pulled into Waterloo Station there were thousands waiting to get a look at the man they'd been seeing on their telly. When we tried to get off the train and out of the station they had to call out the police with horses and dogs. The following week *Time* magazine ran a picture of Seymour Heller, my manager, his wife, Billie, and me being crushed against the side of the train by screaming fans. It proved to us that television was just as powerful a medium in England as in the United States and, of course, all over the world. When I stopped to think about it, I couldn't help wondering what would happen if some power-mad despot gained control of the world's TV stations. It was the same story in London as it had been in Havana, which I'll tell you about later. Men, women and children all wanted to get a look at and, if possible, touch what one London newspaper called, "this strutting peacock who plays the piano."

The papers had made a big thing of the fact that I had not only come to London, but that I had brought with me my special piano and my Cadillac limousine.

Incidentally that car was a big headache. The minute the people saw it they crowded around and sometimes it was absolutely impossible to get where I wanted to go without the help of the London bobbies. Sometimes I couldn't get there at all. There were many London streets that the big Cadillac limousine couldn't negotiate. It couldn't make the tight little curvy ways. Many times the British chauffeur we hired to drive us would case the area and then say, "We can't make it, sir. You'll have to leave the car here and take a taxi the rest of the way."

But wherever the crowds came, I'm happy to say they came . . . at least the vast majority . . . in friendship. There were, naturally, the usual number of hecklers. Even among the crowds jamming every corner of Waterloo Station we saw a few nasties. There were signs saying "Go Home Yank" and "Stop chompin' Chopin" and things like that, not really bad. Just silly. The "Yank" one was just ungracious, I thought, to someone who'd been invited to perform for the Queen. The other was a critical opinion and everyone has a right to one of those. If someone doesn't like the way I play, well—as the kids in West Milwaukee used to say—"too bad for him."

But the bobbies got us through the crowds at the station without too much trouble and into the Daimler limousine that was waiting to take us to The Savoy Hotel. The Caddy hadn't arrived from Southampton as yet.

All along the route, and it isn't far from the station to the hotel, there were crowds surging around us and by the time the limo turned from the Strand into the motor court of The Savoy, the car had been stripped of everything that could be torn from it. When we got out they started to grab at our garments, hats, jackets, anything for a souvenir.

Later we learned that the insulting signs had been planted in the crowd at Waterloo Station just to make news and pictures—one paper actually admitted that they did it to create controversy—so we decided not to worry about the hecklers. Naturally we were all over the front pages with the pictures they'd asked us to pose for. When the headlines began to be a little cutting, we began to wonder. Do people who love you print such headlines as "Liberace Circus Has Arrived."

I mean, circuses are wonderful things, great entertainment. But when the word circus is applied to you as a term of opprobrium, it hurts. We weren't freaks or animals. We did no death-defying tricks. We were just there to play the piano and do our act for the Queen.

Noel Coward had warned me about the London press from his own encounters. Somehow he always emerged victorious which was a tribute to his genius. In fact he told me of some typical examples:

Journalist: "Mr. Coward, do you consider yourself a genius?"

Coward: "Absolutely!"

Journalist: "Don't you think it's a bit extravagant and egotistical to admit that?"

Coward: "My dear man, possessing genius is like having a hernia; no one knows you have it unless you show it!"

Or when he was put upon in Toronto, Canada, by a persistent woman reporter who constantly kept interrupting his press conference with "Mr. Coward, what do you have to say to the *Star*? To which he cleverly and finally replied, "Twinkle, Twinkle!"

Of course I was helped in my ability to absorb and slough off slurs about my piano playing, my singing, my clothes, my love for my mother, and in fact, my whole life style by the realization that only unsuccessful people go unnoticed and unattacked! Athletes use vinegar to harden the skin on their hands, padding to protect their bodies. Some sort of spiritual vinegar had hardened my skin to the things that were printed and whispered about me, some moral padding softened the shocks. I told myself it was publicity and, remembering that the great showman P. T. Barnum said, it doesn't matter what they say as long as they spell your name right, I quietly took my lumps. But there is always the final puff of breath that breaks the balloon.

On September 26, 1956, a columnist for the London *Daily Mirror* by the name of William Neil Connor (he's dead now) hiding behind the *nom de slur* of Cassandra, wrote something so scurrilous that it actually made my mother sick to read it. Connor got into some dirty, snide little sexual innuendos that really burned me up. The piece was written before I arrived in England. The man never interviewed me; we had no personal contact whatsoever; I had not yet done a show in London. The more I thought about it the more angry I became.

Finally I decided to talk to my lawyer who, at that time was also my business manager, the late John Jacobs. John was a wonderful, refined, soft-spoken Virginian, a member of the State Supreme Court, a man of great integrity and a fine lawyer. He was in New York. I telephoned him and we had a long and very serious talk. I asked his reaction and whether he thought I should sue Mr. Connor and the *Daily Mirror* or just forget the whole thing and let the matter drop, write it off to the breaks of the business. He said he couldn't tell until he read and studied the article.

"Can I read it to you on the phone, right now?" I asked.

He broke the tension by saying, "Do you think you can afford it?"

After I read him Cassandra's piece, and don't worry, you'll be able to read it before I'm finished with the matter, John, too, was very upset. He said, "This sort of thing has to be stopped. It can't be allowed to go on. It will get worse and worse. If this man gets away with this, he or someone else will come along seeking some circulation for his paper and write something even more scandalous. It's like a disease. It will spread like a malignant growth. Before you know it you, and a lot of other talented people, will be devoured by this cancerous journalism. It eventually could put you right out of show business. You'd be through—an outcast."

John was very eloquent but he didn't make an instant decision. He was too good an attorney. He asked me to airmail copies to him and give him a little time to look up legal precedents. He explained that the laws of libel and slander are very tricky and whether to sue or not to sue was always a slippery question.

Finally, John called me and said he'd decided that we had to do something and that we were going to sue William Neil (Cassandra) Connor and the London *Daily Mirror* for libel. Then he said why he chose libel. By definition libel means "To defame or expose to public hatred, contempt, or ridicule by a *writing, picture, sign,* etc." We felt that certainly covered Connor's action against me and should support our action against him.

We decided to bring our suit right after the Command Performance. In that way, my presence on the program could in no way embarrass the crown. Then a terrible thing happened.

When the United States refused Egypt the financing for the Aswan High Dam, Nasser expropriated the Suez Canal from the English and French Corporation that had built and was operating it in order to get money for his project. When he threatened to close the canal to Israeli shipping, England saw it as an act against the freedom of the seas, and the specter of war loomed menacingly over the British Government.

Totally oblivious of all this international intrigue, we went right on rehearsing our big show for the Queen. We had just finished a full dress rehearsal, a beautiful run-through of a great show even to the final playing of "God Save the Queen." When the anthem was over, the stage manager called the cast together, and we were told that because of what was going on in the Middle East and because the situation had developed to crisis proportions, it was thought best to cancel the Command Performance. The show was never seen by anyone.

While this was a great disappointment to all of us, most went on to other engagements. But it was a terrible blow to a chorus of sixty Welsh coal miners whom the Queen herself had invited to be on the show after she had heard them sing while in Wales.

They had been brought to London and given VIP treatment. They were taken to West End tailors and completely outfitted, and to the best barber shops where their hair was styled and their toil-blackened fingernails were manicured. And there they were, all dressed up and no place to go.

It was very sad. I turned around to see how they were taking it, and I think it was the first time I ever saw really hard, tough men crying—crying in anger and frustration. Here was something disappointing happening to them, and they knew they could do nothing about it. It was rage against events that had conspired to defeat them that brought tears to their eyes.

To make matters worse it was a holiday, Guy Fawkes Day. Guy Fawkes was mixed up in the Gunpowder Plot to blow up Parliament in protest against extreme penal laws against Catholics. And he got caught. It was sort of like our Boston Tea Party—the people against the administration.

We at the theater would have liked to pull off some sort of gunpowder plot against the Egyptians and their Suez Canal. Then one of the acts on the bill, a singer comedian named Harry Secombe, a jolly five-by-five type who combined a fine operatic voice with a lot of jokes, somewhat in the manner of Jim Nabors . . . well, Harry suggested that when everything goes dead wrong, there's only one thing left to do and that's to celebrate. It's like a woman buying herself a new dress when she's depressed or a man getting a new Cadillac when he loses his job. So we celebrated.

We all went to Winifred Atwell's house. She's a black honky-tonk piano player who was very popular in London at the time. She now lives and works mostly in Australia. I saw her the last time I was in Sydney. Winifred made a great big party for the whole unhappy cast. She and I played four-handed piano, and everyone cried in his beer and got over his disappointment.

Life must go on. And I had a number of other engagements planned for the British provinces, as well as London. I played the Palladium and gave concerts at Royal Festival and Albert halls.

Incidentally, at Albert Hall the London papers took pictures of me on stage and the next day, when the photograph appeared, it was almost identical with one taken almost thirty years before with a different pianist at the piano in the same hall. That different pianist was my idol, Paderewski.

Once again I had played in one of the famous places he'd played in during his magnificent career. Another was Madison Square

Garden in New York. Paderewski was the first pianist ever to give a concert there; I was the second and I think, the last, before the current rage of "rock" stars.

Also while in London I enjoyed a fantastic appearance at what was then the most famous nightclub in England—Cafe de Paris. My shipboard friend Noel Coward had played there and so had Marlene Dietrich. But they booked for talent not for star caliber or notoriety. Right after my appearance a young, unknown black singer named Shirley Bassey made her debut there.

She dedicated a number to me and my candelabra. The title of it was a line taken from an Edna St. Vincent Millay poem—"I Burn My Candle at Both Ends." It turned out to be one of her great numbers. She still does it.

The last time I was in London, I had the pleasure of being invited to participate in the English version of the famous Ralph Edwards show *This Is Your Life*. It was honoring Shirley and we recalled those early days at the Cafe de Paris. Believe me I'll never forget that opening night. Among other things I found out that there was a lot more to being the manager of a famous night spot than counting the cash at the end of the evening and ordering the groceries and sending out the laundry in the morning.

The manager of the Cafe de Paris was Major Neville Willing. He may have been an ex-army officer or perhaps they just called him Major for the same reason I called my musical director, Gordon Robinson, Doctor, because he looked like one. But whatever his background was, he sure knew his customers at the cafe, real British blue bloods, international and theatrical celebrities. Night after night they had the classiest crowd I've ever had for an audience—lords and their ladies, dukes and their duchesses and, sometimes, princes and their . . . friends.

Opening night I learned another show business lesson that I really knew but had never had the courage to put to the test. Major Willing was my teacher.

The Cafe de Paris was famous for a stairway that led from a sort of balcony down to the floor where we worked the show. Down these steps had come some of the greatest cafe performers of all times. It was quite a feeling coming down that flight of stairs, looking down—physically—on your audience. I said looking down "physically" because any performer who looks down mentally on his audience is on his way to obscurity. Well, I did forty-five minutes and then went up the stairs to make a fast costume change before finishing my show. When I got to the top of the stairs the Major was waiting for me.

"That's all," he said.

"But I haven't finished!"

"Just take a bow," he said.

"But I have a costume change."

"Forget it,'" he said. "Take a bow."

I went down the stairs and took a bow. When I came up he said, "Take another bow."

I did. "I must do an encore," I insisted.

"Just take another bow," he said. "Always leave them wanting more."

I took the next bow and when I got to the top of the stairs the Major said, "Go to your dressing room. That's all for tonight."

Long after I'd changed out of my show clothes and into my street clothes the people who had been applauding had come up the stairs and were still pounding on my dressing room door. It was kind of scary, even though I knew it wasn't a lynch mob. I knew they must like me. And a funny memory of an old radio show I'd heard when I was a child flashed through my mind. The line struck me so funny at the time I never forgot it.

The immortal Bert Lahr was telling of his triumphs in the theater and said, "The people loved me so, they unhitched the horses from my carriage and dragged *me* through the streets."

I didn't have to be afraid of anything. The Major was in full command. He opened the door of the dressing room a little bit to give them another glimpse of the man they were applauding. Then he asked them to step back and be patient. He came inside and told me what to do next. And I did it. I put on a white sheared beaver coat and walked out to my waiting Cadillac and drove off into Piccadilly Circus.

What a showman he was. Every evening after that I was instructed to arrive in my Cadillac and told to turn the lights on inside the moment the car hit Piccadilly Circus so the people could see who was inside. This caused crowds to form on the street outside the Cafe de Paris and got the club plenty of publicity. Sometimes they had to get the mounted police to get me from the car to the club.

Incidentally, I never did get to do the last half of my show. The

Major didn't care how many bows I took, but no encores. "Always leave them wanting," was his motto, and it sure worked. People kept coming back night after night so I sort of rotated my repertoire so they wouldn't hear the same show each time they came back.

I'm sorry to say the Cafe de Paris is there no more. Today it's a rock 'n' roll joint, and the elegance of the supper club is just a memory. But for me *what* a memory. It was the most exciting club date I ever played.

Then we toured the provinces and all through the north of England and Scotland, where we were generally well received. Only in the places where they'd read Cassandra's column about me did I have any trouble at all.

One of the things that gave British students reason to believe Cassandra's slurs was the way my syndicated TV show was handled in parts of Britain. It was so popular that the various stations tried to cram more commercials into each show than the producers had left space for. As a result, I was so shocked the first time I heard myself on British TV I couldn't believe my ears. I thought there was something wrong with the set. There wasn't.

In order to squeeze in those extra commercials they had speeded up the film. This caused me to be playing the piano at an impossible tempo, and it caused my voice, both speaking and singing, to be raised to a much higher pitch and be speeded up to sound a little like Donald Duck. Naturally I took immediate steps to correct this stupid blunder, but the damage had been done. There were a lot of cartoons and jokes that were unpleasant and criticism from music critics about the tempi that various numbers were being heard at.

I finally remedied this and enabled them to get in their extra commercial spots by cutting one full musical number. But to this day, whenever an English comic, especially in the provinces, does a Liberace imitation, it comes out sounding like Donald Duck.

The result of the student demonstrations was that I got nasty, insulting phone calls and in a lot of places the kids would make paper airplanes out of the programs and float them toward the stage to try to disturb and annoy me. I didn't let myself get upset.

I kept my cool, and whenever possible I laughed off what was happening. In one city where the air attack was a real blitz, one of the planes—it must have been made by some young man who is today a great aerodynamic engineer—floated gracefully around the piano for a moment before it landed on the floor.

While it was still in the air, gliding gently overhead, I stopped playing and watched it. Then I started to play Walter O'Keefe's famous song "Ohhhh, it floats through the air with the greatest of ease . . . " This broke the tension and stopped the overflights.

One thing all this nonsense in the provinces did was help to build up our case against Cassandra and the *Daily Mirror*. It served to substantiate any claims my lawyers might choose to make that his article exposed me "to public hatred, contempt and ridicule." Those occasional student demonstrations were all that kept my first trip to the north of England from being a very stimulating and gratifying experience.

I was to return again in 1958 for the libel suit, but they tried to schedule it in the middle of the theatrical season and it was hard to get all the principals and witnesses together. So it wasn't until 1959 that the case really got into court.

2

After a third Command Performance in London in 1972, I returned home to rest up for the Christmas holidays.

Then, early the following winter I began to rehearse for another season in the United States, Australia and finally England, again.

To sort of get myself in training, after a couple of months of rest, the way the ball teams go to training camp, I thought I should do something I considered challenging, something I'd never done before. I told my manager, Seymour Heller, about this, and with his usual efficiency everything was arranged.

So it happened that I found myself sitting in Johnny Carson's dressing room feeling the way I felt when I was a little boy and Mom took me to the dentist for the first time. It was another "first" in my life.

It wasn't nearly the most important. It couldn't even compete with being solo artist with the Chicago Symphony Orchestra. Or making my first movie. Or having my first television show. Or doing that first Command Performance. But like all firsts it created apprehensions. Every little cocoon of doubt that was ever spun into my consciousness developed into a great big butterfly and began fluttering around inside of me. But even that kind of "butterflies" can be beautiful. It makes you try harder. And that's important.

I'd played the *Tonight* show many times. This was a first because Johnny wasn't there. For one night, at least, it was about to be *my* show but a new kind of show for me. I wasn't teamed with a grand piano. I was doing a single.

A lot of people have sat in Johnny's chair. He's really the only absentee talk show host in the world. Now, they'd finally gotten around to me. I was glad. Hosting the *Tonight* show was something I'd always wanted to do. It could give me a clue as to what I might do when my fingers get tired.

On my own TV shows and on the stage I've never had any trouble doing all the ad-libbing I had to do. But I was curious to find out if I could sustain an ad-lib situation for an hour and a half with no piano to turn to. What if I suddenly dried up and couldn't think of anything to say? All I had to rely on was the knowledge that I couldn't think of any time in my whole life when that had happened.

As far as the piano was concerned, naturally, I was scheduled to play at the opening and closing of the show. One reviewer who doesn't seem to like me very much wrote that my opening piano solo was funnier than Johnny's opening monologues. Come to think of it, maybe he meant it the other way. Maybe he just doesn't like Johnny's monologues.

Anyway, there I sat in Johnny's dressing room facing a new kind of test. When you're doing that—like when you're drowning, which is generally something you've never tried before—your whole life flashes before your eyes. Except your failures.

I know this to be true, this life-flashing-before-your-eyes-business, when you're drowning. It happened to me when Aly Khan's yacht left me floating in the middle of the Mediterranean Sea. That was right after I'd finished my first starring picture and Jack Warner asked me to take a vacation with him in France. As his guest. I was so surprised I said, "You mean Europe?" I'll tell you all about that later. First, a word from one of our sponsors.

I just threw that last line in because it's the first thing you must learn to say when you host a Johnny Carson show. If you can manage to say it in such a way that it makes people wait for you to come back after a dose of deodorants, detergents and depilatories, you're a success.

At the beginning of the show I was talking to Johnny's boss, Ed McMahon. He must be the boss. He's always there seeing that things run smoothly. Johnny is always calling in sick . . . or something. That's why I was sitting in for him.

I didn't mind that it took him so long to get around to me. It was fun. And it was the best place in the world to plug the beginning of my 1973 season. That's the chic thing to do on Johnny's show. Plug something. Henny Youngman says the reason they always have dogs on the show is because there are so many plugs.

So when Ed asked me politely where I was going, I told him. I actually had to read the list because I couldn't remember all the places . . . Baton Rouge, Louisiana; Knoxville, Memphis and Nashville, Tennessee; Charleston, South Carolina, and Charleston, West Virginia; Savannah, George; Jacksonville and St. Petersburg, Florida; and then ten days in Miami Beach; then Phoenix, Arizona; Dallas and Fort Worth, Texas; and Tucson, Arizona. And that was just in January and February. Notice how I play the warm places in winter.

Ed's immediate reaction was, "What are you doing the week *after* that?" He looked at the diamond I brought home from Johannesburg in 1971 and then had the camera take a close-up of it for the TV audience. "See that," he said. "A family of three could live on that." I don't know whether he meant because it was so big or because of the money it represented.

My first guest was my good friend Bob Hope, and I surprised him by recalling the first time we met. It was in Window Rock, Arizona. Bob has been in so many places he claims he can't even remember which one is home. But he was in Window Rock all right. Who could forget a place with a name like that? It got the name from a rock that had a hole in it. It was in such a barren strip of desert, in such nothing land, the government gave it to the Indians.

But the Indians had the last laugh. One day somebody woke up and noticed that one of the rocks was kind of oily. So, you guessed it—it became one of the most lucrative oil fields in the country. And all the poor Indians there became very, very rich.

One of the first things they did, like everybody else who suddenly gets rich, was try to make friends with show business people. To do this they built a fabulous auditorium and began bringing famous people in there to perform. The night before I came in they had Mahalia Jackson. The next day after my show I went to the airport and I ran into Bob Hope. He said, "What are you doing in a God-forsaken place like this?"

I said, "I just played Window Rock." He said, "I'm playing there tonight."

Bob's immediate reaction when I told him this on the show was,

"You're kidding! Window Rock, Arizona! It must come under another name!"

The more I insisted that he played Window Rock, the more he insisted that he didn't. Finally I had to give in. After all, I was the host that night. So I said, "Well, I guess it's the kind of place you'd want to forget!"

Bob, like any good performer, doesn't want to offend anyone so he denied denying he was there by saying, "I wouldn't forget the money! Specially if there was oil. I'd be around. Licking or something. I remember meeting you in Texas. Window Rock, Texas, you have Texas mixed up with Arizona."

But I wouldn't let him talk me out of it. So Bob changed the subject by saying, "I see they wouldn't let Doc Severensen on the same show with you." He was talking about the great trumpet player and character who leads the *Tonight* show orchestra. He's a great musician and he, too, wears imaginative clothes. But I think there's a basic difference between what I wear and what Doc wears. But it's hard to say exactly what that difference is. Maybe it's that if you know the right places to look, you can buy clothes like Doc's.

I don't think you can say the same thing for what I wear. One thing I'm sure of. We don't fade into the background. And I'm certain as many people come to Doc's concerts to see how he will be dressed as come to hear him make beautiful noises come out of a horn.

But to get back to what Bob was getting at. He said he was sure NBC didn't dare have Doc and his wardrobe and me and my wardrobe on the same show because they were afraid "the friction would start a fire."

However, I was wearing one of my more conservative outfits, a perfectly conventional white dinner jacket like anybody else would wear. The only difference was that the lapels were black and the coat was completely studded with diamonds that really sparkled under the lights. Which was what they were there for. The shirt with the ruffled front and cuffs would have been considered far out a few years ago but had become something your average, conservative businessman wears when he attends the closing dinner of a national sales meeting in Akron, Ohio. Times certainly change.

If you can feel them changing and change with them, you'll survive as a performer. That's what Bob Hope, Jack Benny and men like that have done. If you try to stick in a groove, your groove could become your professional grave.

Bob plays golf at a course directly across from my home in Palm Springs, California. So when we talked about that Bob told the audience, "Sometimes I slice off that second tee and drive right into Lee's yard." Then he said to me, "Do you find many of my balls down there?"

I waited for a minute to think of something and said, "Now that you mention it, I'll start looking."

There was a short silence and then a roar of laughter. When it died down I added, "I wanted them to digest that for a minute." This got another huge laugh, the kind that overwhelms you, a wave that gives you the feeling a surfer must get as he comes zooming in on the crest of a big one. It makes you understand what a thrill it must be to be a comedian and get that kind of reaction. Over this laugh I said, "I waited to let that sink in."

Those late night audiences really look for double meanings. "I never saw an audience like this!" Bob said. "After all, I said hello to Oral Roberts this afternoon, and I'm not going to stand for this."

Just for the record, Oral Roberts is the famous evangelist who has parlayed that old time religion and the laying-on of hands to heal the sick and the halt, into the Oral Roberts University, a top basketball college.

To cool down the audience and change the subject completely, Bob started talking about my candelabra and wound up saying, "This guy burns more candles than Danny Thomas during Lent." I like that. But I think I top Danny because I, too, burn a lot of candles during Lent.

Then Bob came back to my wardrobe. That's what's great about it for talk shows. When there's a lull, or a change of subject is needed quickly, it gives the host or, in this case, the guest, something to talk about. What fascinated Bob was my jewelry. So I told him why I wear so much.

Like almost everybody I know, I've been robbed. Everything I wasn't wearing was taken from my hotel room. So now I wear everything. It's a little showy but it's safer.

Bob was on the show to plug his last Bob Hope Christmas Special. One of his guests on that farewell trip to entertain our armed forces was Red Foxx who had just that season become a smash hit on TV. As Hope was telling what a sensation Red was with the airmen in Bangkok, I interrupted him to ask if it was really his last offshore show for the military. He promised it was.

But the joke was that following right on the heels of Bob's statement came an NBC plug for a show that was called "Jack Benny's *First* Farewell Show."

I don't plan to start making farewell tours for a long time. I don't know whether the idea was invented by Harry Lauder, Sarah Bernhardt, Georgie Jessel or The Beatles, but it always works. Of course you have to be careful. There are acts who said they were going to start a farewell tour in six months and people asked, "Why wait so *long?*"

Getting back to Red Foxx in Bangkok, Hope said Red was robbed of $4,000. I guess it was my robbery that started the talk about Foxx. I said I thought that was a lot of money to carry around with you, even in Bangkok. Hope said, "I'd like to have seen the faces of those robbers when they looked at all those twenty-dollar bills with Flip Wilson's picture on them." It was the first I'd heard that Flip was printing his own money.

We got to talking about Adolph Zukor's 100th birthday party. What a grand old age! Almost everybody from the early days of pictures was there to honor him. Hope said Benny only went because he wanted to meet someone who was younger than he is. Zukor greeted everybody he saw with, "Are *you* still alive?"

One of the things that came out in the exchange of Adolph Zukor stories was the fantastic contract he was forced to make with Mary Pickford. "America's Sweetheart," as she was known, was a pretty good little businesswoman if what they say is true.

The contract said that Zukor had to build a studio just for her and that it would then belong to her. Her mother became *all* the vice-presidents of Mary's corporation that owned it. Maybe there's something smart about long curly hair.

When I first started it was great if a performer got 10 percent of the gate. Now the producer thinks he's lucky if *he* gets ten percent of the gate. The trouble is that when you read about rock shows, you vaguely get the idea most of the money is made by pushers before the evening goes all to pot. That's just a little joke I heard.

But mentioning Mary Pickford reminds me of some excellent advice she gave me after my first concert in the Hollywood Bowl.

I met Miss Pickford for the first time at a party given by that famous party-thrower Cobina Wright. And the first thing Miss Pickford said to me was, "I understand you had a very, very successful evening at the Hollywood Bowl." She said it was being discussed all over Hollywood and she wished me continued success.

I thanked her and said I was pleased, generally, with the bowl appearance. (It sounds like a sports event. Headline: LIBBY BATTLES BALDWIN IN MOVIE BOWL.)

But, I said that I was a little saddened by one review. I didn't know it, but later I was to receive much worse attacks, and I would learn to disregard them, at least partially due to what Miss Pickford said to me. She told me that in her entire career she had never read one review of her motion pictures. She said she thought if the reviews were good they might go to her head and if they were bad they might discourage her. So her rule of thumb was, whether or not the public liked it. I asked her how she could determine that? She said the box office told her whether she was doing well, not the reviewers.

So now I let the audience tell me through their attendance, their response, their applause, their reactions, their spoken comments after the show and the expressions on their faces, whether I've pleased them.

I guess I'd have gone crazy if I hadn't paid heed to Miss Pickford's advice. Many times when I'm on tour, playing in a different city every night, I don't have time to wait for reviews. They may not catch up with me till three or four towns later. I'd go mad waiting if I read and relied on them.

I think the people around me are more apt to become elated about good reviews (or depressed by bad ones) than I am. If they're good I just tell them, "Don't let my success go to your head." When the reviews are bad I tell my staff that they can join me as I cry all the way to the bank.

All this crying "all the way to the bank" is not intended to give the idea that I'm just in this business to make a living. Naturally, that's part of it. A man has to make a living in any way he knows how and I happen to know how to play the piano. Also, I have no aversion to money. I'm sure being rich is better than being poor. I've been both, so take my word.

But the time for just making a living is long past. Show business has provided me with many of the finer things in life and has given me the opportunity to indulge myself in certain luxuries. Now my interest and my work go far beyond making a living.

I'm more concerned about what I have accomplished for the people of this world. I'm convinced that a performer who has the loyal following I enjoy can do a lot of good for humanity and my attitude toward my work has become almost a religion.

I have met and talked to many high members of the Church. Cardinal Cushing of Boston was a very good friend. I had an audience with Pope Pius XII, and both of these holy men made me aware that as a performer I owed a debt to society . . . and to the people who believed in me . . . to set an example of good clean entertainment, of a good way of life, a love of family, respect for one's parents and . . . well, Cardinal Cushing said to me, "You do for the stage what I try to do in the pulpit."

This was a great compliment, I thought, from a great religious leader. I know I always feel better when I leave church than when I went in. In my little way, I try to perform so that people will feel better when they leave my show than they did when they came in.

But I find I've strayed from Bob Hope talking about Mr. Zukor's 100th birthday party. Bob said there were so many old timers there, "It looked like a live wax museum."

Then the way Hope jumps around (I do all right, too, don't I?) all of a sudden we were back to Red Foxx and Bob was saying that Red wanted to take over his Christmas tour next year. "I've heard of a lot things," Bob said, "but I never heard of a war-jacker. But I think it's a good idea. With those blue monologues of Red's he might close the war in one appearance." To prove what he meant, he had them play a piece of film that was shot at an all soldier show in Vietnam. They had to bleep out so much of what Red said for the TV audience that you could hardly tell what he was talking about. But those soldiers knew, and he had them doubled up. That's a good way to increase the size of the army, isn't it? I wish I'd thought to say that on the show.

Someone once said that "departee" is something clever you think of on the way home. When you host one of the talk shows you understand that. I should have told Hope, who has probably entertained more servicemen than anyone in the world ever did, that I, too, have a record. I think I'm the only performer around today who did shows for Civil War veterans. I'll tell you about that later.

Bob brought with him a Polish girl he had on the tour. He did it as kind of a joke because I'm half Polish. That means I only misunderstand half of the Polish jokes. When Mom started speaking Polish to me, I misunderstood all of it. I had to confess that because my Dad was Italian and my Mom Polish I didn't learn to speak either language. I *did* finally learn to understand a little Polish, though.

When my Mother got very angry at something I did wrong, or that she considered undisciplined, she used to throw a lot of Polish words at me. I got to know *them* pretty well. But, as I said to Bob, "I don't think you can say them on television."

"Were they bad words?" Bob asked.

"Not bad in Polish," I explained. "And they weren't even bad in our language. They were just words that the TV audiences have been told were bad. They've been used on the BBC in England. But we speak a different language than the English."

I learned that when I went over there for the first time to do a Command Performance. Like sitting in Johnny Carson's dressing room waiting for another first in my life, the trip to England was a first although I had been in France the year before as a guest of Jack Warner. We made the trip right after the completion of my second movie, a picture called *Sincerely Yours*. I still see it playing on the Late Late Show and wish I still looked the way I looked in 1955.

I touched on the beginning of my movie career with Shelley Winters, who was one of the guests I had on the Carson show. It was a picture called *South Sea Sinner*, finally released in 1950, and in it Shelley played a sexpot. When I mentioned that to Shelley, who had to put on a lot of weight for the part she played in *The Poseidon Adventure*, which had just been released, she said, "Now I look more like a sex-oven."

Maybe that's why her career has been continually so successful. She's been able to make fun of herself. Another long and successful career based on that same formula is Jack Benny's. Why do you think I make fun of myself so much? Anything good enough for Jack Benny is good enough for me.

Shelley and I got to reminiscing about a publicity tour she and I and my brother George made. We traveled all over the country plugging *South Sea Sinner*. Shelley recalled that when we were in Kansas City, "We had a party and the police arrived." She laughed. "I was the star," she said, "and I should have been treated with more respect. But after I had a talk with the police, they didn't arrest us. They thought we were drunk because we were making so much noise. I just told them it was our high spirits and gave them each a shot of it."

I tried to change the subject by saying, "How about remembering the nicer things?"

Shelley said, "I thought that was nice."

The nice thing that I had in mind was that the studio paid for everything. Because Shelley was, as she said "the star" (although secretly I thought I was), we let her do all the ordering. When the maitre d' told us at luncheon that the specialty of the house was Chateaubriand and that one of them served four people, Shelley said, "Bring one for each of us."

That turned out to be a lot of delicious steak but more than even a troupe of hungry actors could eat, no matter how much they appreciated fine food. Even a gourmand like Orson Welles sooner or later comes to the point where a light flashes on somewhere inside of him and says, "Tilt!"

So I asked the waiter for a doggy bag. This embarrassed everybody because we were supposed to be high-priced, high-living movie stars who didn't have to care about money. The maitre d' was embarrassed for us, and showed it, but he brought the doggy bag.

Shelley, too, had embarrassed him by asking to toss the salad herself. She was magnificent. That luncheon she qualified for the Olympic long distance salad toss.

After our last show we got on a train for our long ride back to Los Angeles. When we went to look for the diner, to have a late dinner, we were told there was none on the train. Some trains used to switch off the dining car after meal time and leave it to be re-stocked over night and picked up by another train in the morning. Only on the fastest, most expensive extra-fare trains did the diner go all the way through. Those weren't the kind of trains the studio had us riding on.

Believe me, I was very popular with my doggy bag full of delicious, cold, sliced Chateaubriand. Nobody objected to eating the same thing for dinner that they'd had for lunch.

Shelley said we visited about twenty cities on that tour and that she felt sorry for young performers nowadays because studios seldom do that sort of promotional work on pictures anymore. She said that's why young people in show business today think that Los Angeles and New York are all there is to America. Travel, as I do, and you'll find out that's not true.

There's a whole big, wonderful country between LA and NYC. It's full of lots of smart people with opinions and tastes of their own. You have to be prepared to please that whole country. You have to be prepared to entertain everyone. If you have something for everybody, they'll have something for you . . . their love and appreciation.

Of course, those public relations trips were different than from what they are now. We didn't just show up somewhere and say hello in a sort of condescending way or say a few words on some local radio and TV show. We did an act! Shelley sang, I played for her.

"And he kept me on key," Shelley threw in. She's a great gal, and she's come a long way from that first picture we made together. She wanted to be a real actress, and she made it. I thought I'd become an actor, but I guess I didn't go about it the right way. I practiced playing the piano instead of making faces. That's what I once heard the famous old actor, the late Harry Carey, say on a radio show. I was in my teens just starting out, and he was doing a guest shot with Bing Crosby. I don't know why that description of acting made such an impression on me.

Harry had learned his trade in silent pictures, and I guess that's what he really meant by "making faces." But it sure stuck with me. If it hadn't been for that promotion trip for *South Sea Sinner*, I probably never would have met Seymour Heller, who has been my manager now for nearly twenty-five years. Seymour had booked one of his clients, the Bobby True Trio, on the publicity tour with Shelley and me. And George and I got very friendly with Bobby.

Bobby kept raving about what a great guy his manager was, and I was worried because the one I had at the time had started to drink a little more than was good for him and a lot more than was good for me. I couldn't reach him when I needed him and often when I did reach him it was a waste of time to talk to him. I was very unhappy.

"Why don't you call Seymour?" Bobby asked. "I'll set it up for you." And I mean he certainly did. Right then and there he put through a call and raved for about ten minutes straight about how George and I were breaking it up at every show. Then he put George on the phone and after a few minutes George said, "I wonder if you'd be interested in handling my brother and me?"

When George hung up he told me Seymour'd like to talk to me and see our act. So when we got back to Hollywood, we had a meeting and it was decided that he should come down to see me work at the Hotel Del Coronado where we were booked for a month. He did. And it was the beginning of what must be one of the most beautiful business relationships in the world. One of the funny things was that while he was impressed with my piano playing he seemed more pleased with the way I sang "September Song," one of the few songs I sang at that time.

As you'll learn later, some other exciting things happened during that Hotel del Coronado engagement as a result of my new association with Seymour. And his love for the way I did "September Song" also bore fruit.

Yes, that year I did that tour with Shelley Winters and Bobby True was "a very good year." I was glad Shelley was on the Carson show with me. And I was glad I did the show. It assured me that if I ever get gout in my fingers, I may be able to find some producer who will pay me for just sitting and talking to people, which is something I've been doing for years for nothing.

3

When I was a little boy in the twenties the telephone had not yet become one of the necessities in everyone's life. Only the very rich could afford to use it socially. The only reason we had one was because we needed it in the grocery store.

Nowadays, people who live near enough to their place of business to walk to work like to say that they "live right over the store." That's what we did. Well, not *over* the store. We lived in *back* of it. When you walked through a door in the rear of our store, you were in our living room.

We got business calls on our telephone, orders that my sister Angie or George might have to deliver. I was too young for that kind of work. The only other time the phone was used was in an emergency, to call a doctor or the police.

Motion pictures were still silent in those days and my Mom was a fan of such stars as Francis X. Bushman, Milton Sills, Thomas Meighan, Wallace Reid, Douglas Fairbanks and, above all, Rudolph Valentino, whose last name she gave me as a middle name.

Radio was a very rare thing. It had not yet captured the imagination of the nation. It didn't start to become a source of information and entertainment until I was around eight or nine years old. And, at that time, like most people, we didn't have one. There was, of course, no such thing as television except to a few visionary scientists and technicians. So the medium that made me successful did not exist when I was a child.

The piano was the entertainment center of most homes. In ours it was more than a big piece of furniture to gather around for a little casual singing. To the Liberaces the piano was a way of life.

My dad's love and respect for music created in him a deep determination to give as his legacy to the world, a family of musicians dedicated to the advancement of the art. He almost succeeded.

Out of four kids, he got two. I think you could call George and me musicians. At least we both make a living at it. But I'm sure, because he let me know it, we're not exactly the kind Dad had in mind.

He's very old as I write this and has finally come around to admitting that he's proud of the fact that George and I have made the name Liberace internationally famous. He feels that only in America could such a thing happen to the children of a young French horn player who came to this country from Formia—a little village just outside of Naples. Dad brought nothing with him but his hopes and his talent.

"Talent" is to me such an important thing that every time I write the word I like to spell it with a capital letter . . . like, God. Certainly it is a gift He gives for reasons we may never know. Some people waste it. Others make it the key that opens many doors for them and their dear ones, and brings happiness to millions.

Music is one of the few fields of show business in which language is relatively unimportant because it is, itself, a kind of language understood by all.

It makes no difference whether people can understand what you say, if they dig what you play. If you can make those little dots on a sheet of music paper sound the way the composer heard them in his mind when he first scratched them out, you can get along. If you can add a little something of your own to the composer's original inspiration, you have Talent and you'll get along very well.

Dad must have felt this intuitively when he decided to pull up stakes and come to America. And he must have been considerably better than most men on his instrument, because he managed to get and hold jobs that were in short supply. Dad's problem was this: Although a lot of musicians worked in orchestras in those preradio, pretelevision days, when even phonograph records were a luxury, there wasn't a great demand for French horn players.

Trumpet men, cornetists, trombonists, tuba players, violinists, reedmen, drummers, pianists, yes. But the French horn, at that time, was just for brass bands and symphony orchestras. Most of the work for instrumentalists was in the pit orchestras of theaters, where plays or musical comedies were being performed. Or on the stage in the large motion picture palaces that were just coming into existence, where they featured singers and dancers in elaborate live shows to bolster up the sagging interest in silent pictures.

Dance halls had live talent, of course. And there were always orchestras in what were called cabarets. Many hotels had dance bands in their supper clubs and dinner music in their main dining rooms. But very few of these pop orchestras had any use for a French horn player. It severely limited the number of jobs available. I don't think the French horn was ever used in popular music until Mitch Miller rose to the top of his field and used it in some of his most distinctive arrangements. But that was far too late to do my Dad any good.

Recognizing that his life was dedicated to playing what has yet to become much of a "popular" instrument, he resolved that if he had any children—and what Italian doesn't speculate on that all the time?—he'd see that they learned to play something a little more in demand. In the meantime, he put his Talent to work where it was needed and won one of the French horn chairs in John Philip Sousa's Concert Band.

Some people have already forgotten—or never knew—how big John Philip Sousa, The March King, was. I looked into his biography and found out, among other things, that in 1906 he was offered $20,000 to play a gig in an amusement park on the South Side of Chicago. It was called White City. Sousa turned down the job because he said he wouldn't play anywhere that only charged ten cents admission. That's class! And remember, back in those days before income tax and inflation, $20,000 was easily worth $100,000 of today's money.

Five years later, however, Sousa did accept $70,000 for nine weeks at the Pan Pacific Exposition on the West Coast where they charged *no* admission.

Playing with Sousa was about as good as a French horn man could do in those days. But it kept Dad on the road a lot. That wasn't so bad when he was single, but after he married and then became a father he started to look for work nearer home. That's

49]

how he happened to hold down one of the French horn chairs in the Milwaukee Symphony Orchestra.

And right there you have the answer to a question I'm often asked by interested or just nosey people. How did I happen to be born in West Allis, Wisconsin? And where is West Allis, Wisconsin? It's a suburb of Milwaukee.

I suppose I could brush off the question of how I happened to be born in Wisconsin with the old joke, "I wanted to be near my mother." I guess the question *really* was, what was your *mother* doing in Wisconsin? It perplexed people because it's not a state generally associated with a large Italian population. But, as I've said, my mother was Polish. And Menasha, Wisconsin, was where she was born and was living when she and my father met.

It seems there were a lot of Polish people in Wisconsin. As so many immigrants from the old country did, the Polish found a climate and surroundings congenial to them. They knew how to farm the sort of land, and under the climatic conditions, they found in Wisconsin.

My grandparents had a farm near the mill towns of Menasha and Neenah. They were, like Minneapolis and St. Paul, right across the river from one another. But of course they were much smaller. Besides the farmers who came to the area, a lot of young Polish men might have been attracted there (or imported as greenhorns) because the mills always needed cheap labor. It seems strange, but there is every reason to believe that the Polish people liked Wisconsin because it had the same sort of severe winter weather they had been used to for generations. (I don't suppose an Eskimo would like Miami Beach.)

Mother used to tell us a silly story that she said her mother told her about the old days in Poland in a tiny town that was right on the Russian border. During the almost endless wars between the Russians and the Poles this little village sometimes changed nationalities two or three times a year as the armies fought back and forth before they became allies.

Once while the town was in Polish hands there was a fierce battle. But even when it was over the peasants didn't know which flag to fly, who or what to salute. They didn't know if they remained Polish or had become Russian.

Finally a dim-witted old farmer asked the chief of police which country had won the war. Not that it made much difference. Then, as now, the people always had trouble no matter which government was victorious. The police chief said the Russians had been triumphant, that the town was now in the hands of Mother Russia and that the old man was a subject of the Czar. "Thank God!" said the man. "I couldn't have lived through another one of those Polish winters."

I wasn't too crazy about the Wisconsin winters. But the summers were wonderful. Mom used to drive us kids to what we called Grandmother's Farm every chance she got because she wanted us to get some fresh air out in the country. Not that suburban Milwaukee was so metropolitan. But to Mother anyplace that wasn't a farm was "too crowded."

We made the trip in the family Ford, a vehicle you just wouldn't believe. How or where Dad got it, I have no idea. And that it survived the roads of rural Wisconsin should stand as testimony to the greatness of American automotive engineering. I wish I had it today. It would make a sensational addition to my collection of interesting automobiles.

Mother drove. And to this day whenever I smell new mown hay, my mind rushes back to those early morning automobile rides. Another thing always made me remember those motor trips to Grandma's. It is a song, one of the first great rock 'n' roll hits. You still hear it occasionally, "Shake, Rattle and Roll."

Grandmother was a sweet, white haired, tiny woman with a heavy Polish-German accent, and we adored her. It's not unusual of course. And like all grandmothers the world over, she idolized us children. There were no restrictions on what we could or could not do or where we might go on the farm and we got into all kinds of scrapes, falling out of hay mows, being kicked by cows, learning about life—and that every action brings a reaction.

It was all an adventure then. I didn't, at the time, realize what a tough rugged life my grandparents lived. The farm had no electricity. There was no indoor plumbing. There was a water pump in the kitchen. No running water. And all the cooking and baking was done on a wood stove. All this was part of the fascination, the glamour of the place. We loved the scent of oil lamps and the aroma that came from the stove, a combination of burning wood and baking biscuits, cake, bread—all the wonderful things that Grandma's magic brought forth from that huge black iron monster.

There was a large cistern outside the house to catch fresh rainwater which, I remember, my Mother used to wash her hair in because soft, fresh rainwater was the best thing in the world for washing hair. But the most favorite place of all, and where we kids tended to play most was the barn.

Grandmother raised chickens and cared for a marvelous kitchen garden. Grandfather took care of the pigs, a couple of cows and an old horse that was in about the same class as our Ford. There were fragrant fruit trees everywhere. From these and the harvest from her garden, Grandmother used to put up "goodies" for the winter. But, looking back, I can't imagine how she had any left by the time winter arrived.

I was a very skinny little kid, and Mom found that our visits to Grandmother's house were not only fun for me but healthful as well. In this Grandmother concurred and collaborated. I always managed to gain a few important pounds at her urging. Her favorite expression, at least the one I heard her use most, was "Yitz, yitz, liebchen." In a combination of Polish and German, I learned, that meant "Eat, eat, dear child." And eat I did! I loved my grandmother and I couldn't refuse her anything.

It must have been a very hard life for those two. Besides running the little farm, both of them worked part time in the paper mills of Menasha and Neenah. But it must have agreed with them because they raised a family of seven kids and both of them lived to a fine, rugged old age.

The winters on that farm must have been fierce. It was hard for us to get to, but when we did it was a wonderful world of white that only children who live deep in the country ever know. It was then that Grandmother and Grandfather relied and lived on the canned goods they put up in the summer. And there was always enough to see them through to spring in spite of the fact that everytime we all piled into the Ford and headed for home the car was loaded down with jellies and preserves that also helped us through the winter months.

In addition to their work on the farm and in the mills, Mom's parents had a strong feeling for and interest in music. Menasha is not now, nor was it ever, a very big place. So it was perfectly natural that a family living near there and interested in music, would attend the concert when the great March King, John Philip Sousa, came to town. And it was also perfectly natural that a young

French horn player, when he wasn't blowing his horn, should look out over the audience in search of a pretty girl. And so it follows that it was perfectly natural for Salvatore Liberace to spot Frances Zuchowski. "Liberace-Zuchowski." It sounds like a rhyme in a comedy song by Cole Porter or Noel Coward.

Meeting the girl he spotted in the audience was no great problem for Salvatore. Menasha was not such a big town, and when a concert was over, people interested in music would have no trouble finding one another. So it was quite natural that Salvatore met Frances. The Zuchowskis were a family of amateur musicians who gave lessons and were very popular in concerts on the local church and charity circuit.

The meeting of Salvatore and Frances kindled the spark of love at first sight. Their marriage quickly followed because the young people, anxious to do, as Irving Berlin wrote, "what comes naturally," saw no good reason for waiting.

Dad was twenty-five at the time. Mom was eighteen. After the honeymoon the newlyweds moved to Philadelphia for two reasons. Dad wanted to be near his older brother, my Uncle Benjamin, and Philly, with its many theaters and its great symphony orchestra, offered more opportunity to a man who played the French horn. But Mom was a small town girl. The City of Brotherly Love didn't instill any sisterly love in her heart. She didn't like the metropolitan pace. Imagine Philadelphia being too fast for anyone! She longed for the simple life in a small friendly community where everyone knew and loved his neighbors.

I was too young ever to know much about my Uncle Ben but he must have been a personality. He was the father of a whole bunch of very talented men, my cousins, who all went into medicine or dentistry. I can understand that. I think if I hadn't been so strongly pulled toward music I would have become a doctor. I liked that because it meant helping people. (Perhaps that's the reason I once thought I ought to become a priest.)

The star of Uncle Ben's family became the head of surgery at the Fitzgerald Hospital in Derby, Pennsylvania. It was funny. In order to make it easier for his patients to remember and pronounce his name he called himself Liber-ace (to rhyme with place). And when he was on Morton Downey's Coca-Cola program, *The Star of the Family*, Dr. Liber-ace introduced his cousin, Liberace. It must have been confusing because we both spelled it the same way.

53]

A few months after George was born in Philadelphia, Mom got Dad to move back to Wisconsin, even though she knew it would reduce his opportunities for finding work. She thought the country was a better place to bring up kids. So, although Dad did get jobs in local Milwaukee theaters, they were not as lucrative as those in Philadelphia or on the road. Before long, Mom was running a little mom and pop grocery store to augment the family income. As I said, we lived behind it.

I guess running a grocery store is a little like running a farm. You may not make a lot of money, but you can always find something to eat. I can remember running from our little kitchen out into the store to get a couple of potatoes, or something, for dinner. I was very proud, in those toddler days, of being able to distinguish between a potato and an apple. But I was never really very involved in the grocery business.

But George and Angie, although they didn't like it much, either, would help in the store after school—after they did their practicing on the piano. Sometimes the piano practice doubled as baby sitting with me. While Mom was taking care of the store, waiting on customers, she used to listen to make sure that Angie was practicing. And when the practicing got too tedious for Angie, because it was such a hardship, she'd skip out to play baseball or something with the kids and I'd carry on with her practicing. It worked out well for both of us. It improved my fingering and Angie learned to go to her left. She was always a tomboy. This, I guess, was a subconscious effort to keep up with three brothers and be one of them. As far as I was concerned she was better than all of us.

I didn't care very much for the games the other kids played. It wasn't that I had anything against the games. It was just that you got dirty playing them. I didn't like that. This, too, helped to draw me closer to my piano playing. You didn't get dirty playing Mozart.

But I'm getting way ahead of my story. About three years after Mom and Dad moved back to Wisconsin, Angelina was born and six years after that along came little Wladziu. I was followed a few years later by my brother Rudy—Rudolph Valentino Liberace. Mother finally got up enough courage to give one of her sons the full name of her early idol. That was our family, George, Angie, Walter and Rudy and just as soon as the sun rose in the east every morning each of us began taking piano lessons at the age of four.

That was Dad's plan. Get them early and keep them at it. He followed this routine just as carefully and as perfectly as he followed the beat of whatever conductor he was playing under.

Angie, who is sort of the family historian, insists that I didn't wait for Dad to start my piano lessons. I started to play without them. I guess it must be true because I can remember that I could play anything I heard long before I had any idea how to read music. The classics, pop hits, sacred music . . . if I heard it, I played it.

It's really embarrassing for me, when Angie starts to reminisce about the days when she "mother-henned" me as my big sister when I was still in diapers. But I don't mind it when she says that as soon as I could reach the keyboard, I played whatever I heard her practice . . . and accurately!

Mom backs Angie up in this business about me starting to play when I was still in diapers. But what neither of them ever tells is that I designed the diapers myself. They were the only gold lamé diapers in town. (I'm only fooling. We couldn't afford lamé.)

Angie had a rough time not only with the piano lessons but also with me. It wasn't that she didn't like music or that she didn't like me. It was that Dad was such a hard taskmaster. He turned her off to music and I guess I made her self-conscious because music that was a problem for her came easily to me. She should have done what George did. He hated piano lessons, too. So he switched to the violin.

Poor Angie. I should have helped her, but instead I showed off and acted like all little brothers the world over. The more she put her mind to her practicing the worse it turned out, because her heart wasn't in it. Finally I'd really try to help her, but that didn't thrill her very much either. What girl wants her little brother showing her how to play a piece correctly?

We all took lessons from the same local piano teacher whose name was Mrs. Martin. And every so often, like all piano teachers, she'd hold a recital on Sunday afternoon to show off what her kids could do. And what they did to the simple tunes they were given to play, was plenty. Mom and Dad and George would all go to enjoy the recital. I had an awful time.

Angie would get so nervous and emotional that I thought I could feel the whole room shake. It was not only that she was afraid she wouldn't play well; she was terrified of being up there in front

55]

of all those people. I'm fortunate that I've never suffered from that. I wouldn't ever want to go through what Angie went through.

When it was all over I'd do my little brother act and rush up to her and say, "Angie! Did you play that *bad!* You hit a clinker. It was awful! Let me show you how it should go." Then I'd play it right there in front of all the people. Angie would cry and Mom would get angry at me. I couldn't help it. Like my Dad I'm a perfectionist. I want to see that everything is done properly.

But Angie never quite got over "big-sistering" me. Sometimes she'd come along on the road to "take care of me." What I think she really meant by "taking care of" was "saving money."

For instance when I was in Miami Beach years later playing at the swank Fontainebleau Hotel, one of the terms of the contract was that I have a suite for the duration of my engagement. The management lived up to the agreement very handsomely. They could have gotten $250 a day for that suite. Since I had the extra room, Angie decided to come along and "take care of me." She didn't want one room to go to waste. And I was delighted to have her there. We were all happy.

One day I went out shopping for some new clothes, and I guess I spent two or three hundred dollars on some shirts and jackets. When I came upstairs with the boxes and walked into the suite, it looked as if a cyclone had struck it. Sox were hanging from the crystal chandelier, underwear was draped over the top of the furniture . . . you never saw such a mess. "My God! What happened?" I yelled. As Angie came out of her bedroom to greet me I rushed toward her and said in alarm, "Are you all right?"

"Sure!" Angie said and she seemed surprised. "I just washed your clothes and they're hanging here to dry. I'm trying to save to save you some money."

Years later, in a Pittsburgh hotel I did some similar home laundry—much to my regret.

Sometimes life got so involved at home and at the store that Angie wasn't available and my father had to be the baby sitter. And when a man who has a job is a baby sitter, the baby has to sit where the sitter is.

At the time I remember—and it is one of my earliest recollections—Dad was working in the pit at the Alhambra Theater in Milwaukee. The house played vaudeville and silent pictures, and

I remember being there so often that it almost became a second home to me.

I spent many hours each day sitting in the first row engrossed in the happenings on the stage, while Dad watched me out of the corner of his eye from the pit, which he called "the hole." Between shows he'd come and get me and take me with him to the orchestra room where his fellow musicians, who were not involved in the continual card game that is always going on in an orchestra room, would take a little time to play with "Boo-Loo." That was Dad's nickname for me. Why he called me that even he couldn't remember.

But there were times when conditions were such that Dad couldn't take "Boo-Loo" with him. Then the full time job of baby sitting fell to Angie. And, like Dad, Angie did her baby sitting by taking me with her. On one of these occasions she got so engrossed in a game she was playing with the other kids that I got bored and wandered off to explore the world all by myself.

The Wisconsin State Fair Grounds was only about twenty blocks from where Angie had plunked me down with instructions to be quiet and not move. I couldn't understand the game—and what does a little boy know about being quiet? So I wandered off. Twenty blocks isn't far for sturdy little legs. (If you've ever seen me in my hot-pants outfit you'll know my legs are still pretty sturdy.) Anyway, I made it to the Fair Grounds, although I'm sure I didn't know where I was heading. Possibly, as I approached it, the music and happy noises that rise from any fair attracted me.

For a little while I lived in the beautiful world of sights, sounds and smells that make a wonderful place of any fair or amusement park. I don't know how long it was before one of the fair policemen spotted me and got the idea that there was something strange about a little boy wandering around all by himself. He talked to me for a few minutes, and before I knew it, at the age of two, I was busted—the charge must have been vagrancy.

The police were very nice and very thoughtful, and I can't remember having any fear of them at all. For that matter, it never occurred to me to be afraid that I was all alone in the world. They asked me questions and I gave them typical two-year-old answers.

"What's your name, sonny?"

"Boo-Loo."

"What's your Daddy's name?"

"I don't know."

"What does your Momma call you?"

"My Mama calls me kid."

"What does your Daddy do?"

"He plays a toot-toot."

"Where does he play the toot-toot?"

"In the hole."

Armed with nothing more than that for what the cops call "a make" on me, it's a wonder the fair police ever succeeded in locating my parents.

Of course Mom was frantic and called the local city police. There is no record of what she must have called Angie for letting me wander off. Finally the fair police, unable to get me back to my parents, reported a missing child to the city police, and in this way I was reunited with my anxious parents.

The reunion was preceded by one of the happiest times of my life. What two-year-old kid wouldn't find sheer, unadulterated joy, riding through the streets of his home town sitting in the sidecar of a police motorcycle? I'd get fun out of doing that today.

Of course I couldn't understand what all the fuss was. I'd had a grand time. But from that point on, Mom and Dad took great pains to teach their wandering third born the vital statistics of his life. Little things like his father's name and occupation, where he lived, his mother's name and all the other statistics everybody has that enable his parents, his teachers, his government and his creditors to keep better track of him all through his life.

It was not long after my unscheduled visit to the Wisconsin State Fair that I discovered the upright piano in our living quarters behind the grocery store. And shortly after that Angie discovered that I could pick out by ear the pieces her piano teacher, Mrs. Martin, had her practicing. Then came the great deception that I've already told you about. I didn't know there was any deception of course. I was enjoying myself playing Angie's pieces on the piano, while Angie was out playing with the kids.

It was only after the big fraud was discovered that Dad decided I needed formal music lessons and Mrs. Martin was called in for me. Practice sessions were then regulated so that Angie and I had equal time. But that created the usual competitive situation between siblings. The idea of her little brother catching up with her on the piano didn't sit too well with my big sister so she'd refuse to relinquish the piano when it was my turn and the fight was on.

Mother would have to make some excuse to the customers in the store and come back into our living quarters and break up the rumpus. She'd excuse herself by saying, "Imagine those children fighting with each other over who can practice on the piano."

This was surely a problem no mother who happened to be in the store at the time had ever been forced to face. Mom would go on to gain sympathy from the customers by adding, "Those two practicing the piano and George taking violin lessons—all that money being spent on music lessons—while I have to slave here in the grocery store. But their father insists they're all going to be professional musicians like he is. Personally, I think they'd be better off learning the grocery business, but I have nothing to say. He's the boss."

I remember hearing many arguments and loud words when things didn't go just the way he wanted them to go. His Italian temper was something we grew to fear and Mother had only to say, "Wait till your Dad comes home," to turn rebellious hellions into little angels.

My brother George, on the other hand, was always a force for good in the musical feuds over the piano. He was a model student and didn't have to share his violin with anybody. His music lessons always met Dad's approval and, what's more, he pleased Mom by pretending to be interested in the grocery business.

I say "pretending to be interested" because if he really had been he'd have gone into it instead of becoming a musician. But in those early days I remember my brother George as the great arbitrator, the great keeper of the peace among us children.

4

I am constantly being surprised at the things I remember even though sometimes I only recall a segment of a whole incident. One day a lady with a little boy in tow stopped me in the lobby of a hotel. I have no idea anymore what hotel it was. Hotel lobbies in the main are all so much alike that, I suppose, it made no impression on me. If I remembered what hotel it was, I would, of course, know what city we were in. But when you spend over half your life traveling from city to city, they, too, like the hotels, sort of blend together into one big Holiday Inn, Hilton, Palmer House, Sheraton, Howard Johnson or Waldorf-Astoria. At the end of every tour your mind is full of little bits, like the glass fragments in a kaleidoscope, and the more you try to sort them out, the more you find yourself getting a pleasant pattern but no clear picture.

Well, enough of this, back to the woman with the little boy. She used the usual gambit that every performer has heard ever since he made enough of an impression on the public to make them want to have his autograph. Like all performers I, too, wonder what becomes of the thousands of little scraps of paper and programs and books that we all autograph. And, like most adults who are a little embarrassed to ask a person to sign his name on a little piece of paper, my fan in the hotel lobby said, "Could you please autograph this for my little grandson?" Maybe one of the reasons I remember the incident is that what she asked me to sign was the back of a check.

I was taught by my manager, very soon after I began getting

61]

requests for autographs, always to look at everything I signed. And I must say I was surprised to find a blank check in my hand.

"I'm sorry, dear," I said, "but I can't sign this."

"It's the only piece of paper I have," she explained with an embarrassed little laugh. "Just sign it on the back."

Well, I didn't really think the woman looked like one of your typical hotel confidence hustlers, so I just tore off the corner of the check where the signature should be and wrote on the back, "This check null and void. Liberace."

Then, because it was really for the little boy that I was supposed to be signing, I leaned over and asked the kid his name. I guess he must have told me what it was. I don't remember. But I do remember his answer when I asked him where he lived. He said, "We moved!"

Immediately these simple, childlike words made me relate to him. Because they made me remember what an overwhelming experience it was to me when we moved into a new house in West Milwaukee.

It's a traumatic experience to a child, the first time he has to say good-bye to everything he's learned to associate with his security. But while it is difficult saying farewell to old friends and familiar things it's full of the adventure of finding new friends and exploring new surroundings. All this is an example of how deeply I was affected by our first move.

I guess the most wonderful thing about our new home was that you didn't have to walk through a grocery store to get into it. It was, as my friends in England would say, "a proper house" even though, architecturally, it wasn't much different from all the other little houses around it.

We moved into it not long before the great stock market crash in 1929, although what happened on Wall Street made very little difference to us. We had bought the new house with the money Dad had saved from his work in various bands and orchestras plus the money we got when we sold the grocery store. The transaction left us broke but with a roof over our heads and a mortgage over the roof.

Visitors to any one of the various homes I now have sometimes comment on how neat the place is. They make some reference to the fact that a bachelor's home isn't generally so tidy. Well, I have people who help me keep it the way I like it. And the way I like it is the way Mom used to keep our new house in West Milwaukee. It really sparkled inside and out. Mom had a flare for interior decoration, which I think I inherited from her, and Dad was an expert gardener as so many Italians seem to be. I don't want anybody to think that we didn't have nice neighbors, but our house stood out from all the others.

Mom made sure there were real lace curtains in the windows and kept old-fashioned lace antimaccassars on the arms and the backs of all the chairs, so that people's hands and the oil from their hair wouldn't soil the upholstery.

Sometimes people wonder why my home, any one of them, has two kitchens. It's because I think I should have it as nice, now that I can afford it, as I had it when we could hardly afford anything. You see, that little house in West Milwaukee had two kitchens. Both of them worked. One we used when we had company and one just for the family.

The company kitchen was on the first floor and boasted a gas stove and a real Frigidaire, although I don't know how we could afford what was then such a luxury. The family kitchen was a huge one in the basement where Mom cooked on a great big coal stove and kept things fresh in an old-fashioned icebox, which hadn't as yet become old-fashioned. It was just on the way out.

If I ever see one that looks exactly like the one we had, I'll buy it and fancy it up and use it for something. There's no way to use it, anymore, as an icebox. Time has contradicted Eugene O'Neill. The iceman no longer cometh. He does not even existeth.

Our dining room, which was off the modern upstairs kitchen, was used only for special occasions, as was the living room which was also our music room. Here we not only had our precious piano but a very special Orthophonic Victrola. Dad had to have the best possible record playing machine, because we had a marvelous collection of phonograph records, as they were then called. We had Caruso, of course, and Galli Curci, Giovanni Martinelli, Geraldine Farrar . . . all the great opera and concert stars of the early twentieth century. But my favorite of all was the great pianist (naturally) Paderewski. I'd spend hours listening to his recordings, playing them over and over again. Then I'd try to imitate his interpretations.

Those old acoustic recordings seemed wonderful at the time, but when you hear one today, played in comparison with the electronic recording devices we now have, you realize how imperfect the sound was on those records that seemed so miraculous. The first big improvement I can remember was when they practically cut the cost of a phonograph record in half by making them double faced. Lots of the ones Dad had were the old one-sided ones. The flip-side was blank. What a waste that was. When the double-faced discs came out everyone was delighted because they either gave you a longer piece or two pieces for the price of one. And even that wasn't so very much music because those old 78's only played about three-and-a-half minutes per twelve-inch record.

The classical Victor records were called Red Seal Records, and people took pride in owning a large collection of them. We did, too. But the difference between our collection of Red Seal records and most people's collections was that we really played ours . . . all the time.

I still have some of those old acoustic recordings and I'm glad I wasn't recording then. Not only were they of a rather poor quality but they didn't sell very well. When I look at the collection of recordings I have made—monaural, stereo, albums and singles—I have to believe those who tell me that I sell more recordings annually than were made in a year by all the recording artists combined in those years when I was a little boy.

Which reminds me what a hassle it was before I made it on records. I'd done just one for Signature label. It was a kind of specialty thing and either the market wasn't ready for it or it wasn't ready for me; whatever it was, the record bombed.

That was my whole record career until Dave Kapp, who had succeeded his brother Jack as head of Decca records, came to see me when I was playing at the Hotel Del Coronado in California. I'm going to tell you a lot more about that particular hotel engagement and what it meant in my life, a little later. Dave offered me a deal to cut a couple of sides for Decca, so when we got back to Hollywood we had a session.

It was in the studios on Melrose Avenue that were originally built by NBC for radio shows like the Rudy Vallee and Bing Crosby programs. When the session started Dave handed me some music, the pieces he wanted to record, and said, "I want you to play these exactly like Frankie Carle." Well, I was young and eager and said to myself, "The first thing to do is to get a foot in the door. I'll play what they want, the way they want it and then, when I'm all set I'll start doing what I think is really right for me."

So I made some mild objection about copying another pianist's style and allowed myself to be talked into trying. After a couple of hours Seymour Heller came out and said, "Lee, we're not going to make it." Dave Kapp followed Seymour and asked, "What's the matter?"

"It just doesn't sound right," said Seymour. "It's not Liberace, and who wants to hear a second rate imitation of Frankie Carle?"

Kapp said he thought it was pretty good.

"All right," Seymour said. "Who wants a first rate imitation of Frankie Carle when he can get the real thing for the same price? Lee just doesn't feel it, I can hear he hasn't got his heart in it. I suggest we call the whole thing off. It's better to make no records than to make bad ones."

Dave argued me into going on with the date, and we finally cut three sides. But Seymour stuck to his argument that I shouldn't be doing what I was doing, that it wasn't me, that asking me to perform like someone else was stupid and the results were no good. Finally he canceled the date. I was never happier.

But Seymour didn't give up on the record idea. We both knew I had a place in the recording field, and finally he got to Mitch Miller, who was then A & R (that means artist and repertoire) man for Columbia Records and offered him a deal he couldn't refuse. We agreed to pay for a date to record one side of our choice and the flip side his choice. The side we chose was "September Song" which turned out to be a big hit record. And that's how I got to be one of Columbia's top money-makers. I even made a concert album for them with Paul Weston, who in those days was one of our outstanding composer-arranger-conductors.

I didn't mean to stray into a long story about how I got to make records, so I think I'll just go back to my Dad and his fine record collection that introduced me to the great names of music . . . . and to my introduction to one of the greatest.

You can imagine what a thrill it was to all of us, but particularly to me, when Dad came home one day and announced that Paderewski was going to give a recital at the Pabst Theater in Milwaukee, and we were all going. I hope you'll forgive the pun I say it was with a very frothy anticipation that we filed into

Pabst Theater and for days after I was intoxicated by the joy I got from the great virtuoso's playing. My dreams were filled with fantasies of following his footsteps . . . or finger prints.

These dreams were encouraged by the fact that the great man had graciously received our family after his performance. He talked to us and gave sincere words of encouragement to my parents and to me when he heard that I could play some of the famous selections he played that evening, selections from Liszt, Bach, Mozart and Beethoven. The scope of this repertoire impressed him so that he put his hand on my head and said, "Someday this boy may take my place." I was eight years old.

Inspired and fired with ambition, I began to practice with a fervor that made my previous interest in the piano look like neglect. I put in so much time at the keyboard that it worried my parents.

"Stop!" Mom used to say. "Go out and get some sunshine. You look too pale. People will think you are sick."

"Go out and play with the other kids," Dad used to urge me. "You need the exercise. To be a great pianist you must have great physical stamina. Run around. Build yourself up physically."

I tried to obey my parents, but my heart really wasn't in it, and I don't think exercise that you don't enjoy really does you any good. So I continued to plug away at the old masters. This determination, and I guess, the skill I showed at handling this difficult music, finally led to the ultimate confrontation with Angie. She could no longer stand the competition and flatly refused to have anything more to do with the piano.

I don't think I was entirely responsible for this, however. As Angie grew up she turned from being a tomboy and suddenly became very feminine and concentrated on being and looking attractive. She was very successful at this. The result was that she discovered boys. And boys simultaneously discovered that there was a very pretty girl named Angie.

She still plays the piano once in a while . . . but not when anyone is listening. She laughingly says there's only room for one great pianist in the family. I wonder who she means. Certainly not George. He plays the fiddle.

My mind is so associative—always running from one thing to other instead of going in a straight and logical course. Just tioning George's violin playing in relationship to piano playing reminds me of one of my favorite musician stories. I guess it reminds me of the story because I understand so well and am so sympathetic to the truth behind it.

By this time, the story has probably been told using many different names. The way I heard it was that the famous violinist Fritz Kreisler was attending a recital by young violinist Jascha Heifetz who was just beginning to make the world realize the depth of his genius. With Mr. Kreisler was a pianist, the late Mischa Levitzki. Carnegie Hall was crowded and after Heifetz's first number, Kreisler took out his handkerchief and wiped his face, saying to Levitzki, "Isn't it awfully hot in here?"

"Not," said Levitzki, who had a puckish sense of humor, "for pianists."

It is a curious feeling for a pianist to hear another pianist interpret something as well or maybe better, than he knows he can do it. You love him for his Talent and for what he's shown you about the music he's playing. But you hate him for being so much better than you. Fortunately with me this envy of another's skill always serves to inspire me to try harder. Does that mean I'm only second?

It didn't take any great debating skill on the part of my teacher, Mrs. Martin, to convince my father that I required more advanced training than she was equipped to give me. After four years of lessons with her, there was no question that I knew more great music and could play it a great deal better than she could. So, tremendously pleased with my musical progress, Dad asked some of his musical colleagues what he should do next about my education. They reminded him of a fine pianist and teacher who, it turned out, he had performed with in concert. Her name was Florence Bettray-Kelly and she was on the faculty of the Wisconsin College of Music. She had been a protégé of the great pianist Moriz Rosenthal.

She heard me play and accepted me as a pupil. She even got me a scholarship which turned out to be the longest scholarship the school had ever awarded. It lasted seventeen years.

During this time I made my debut as a solo artist before the Society of Musical Arts in Chicago when I was sixteen. You would not believe the preparations that went on at our house as Mom and Dad got things ready for the great event. I don't know how I felt. But I remember the amount of cleaning and fixing up in a home that was always spotless. It was as if Mom expected everybody who attended the concert to come back to our house in Milwaukee for a cup of coffee after it was over. She would have loved it if they did.

About three years later, I was selected by Dr. Frederick Stock to be a soloist with the Chicago Symphony Orchestra. It was hard to get Mom and Dad down off the cloud they suddenly found themselves on. Their little Wladziu was about to make it in the big time music business. Of course, they had no idea the direction this "making it" would take. They only knew that the scrimping and scraping they'd done to continue my musical education was going to give them the respected performer they both prayed would bring honor to the family name. But I'm getting way ahead of my story.

There was plenty of scrimping and scraping around the Liberace home when the Great Depression of the thirties cut giant holes in the job market and unemployment forced millions to stop spending money for anything but the bare necessities. Radio, which supplied free entertainment to people without the means to go to theater, cut down box office grosses all across the nation. This combined with sound pictures, a great novelty, began to cut the heart out of vaudeville. Theaters didn't need musicians anymore. Live talent simply ceased to exist as far as cities like Milwaukee were concerned.

An occasional broadcast job didn't give Dad enough to support us, so he had to find other ways to make money. He managed to get himself some factory work. I really never knew what it was.

It was a terrible blow to his aesthetic sense. His once immaculate hands turned calloused and grimy from handling tools and machinery, and he rarely played his beautiful brass French horn. He did, however, get it out occasionally and polish it with loving care.

Mom, too, found work in Johnston's Cookie Company. There was one saving circumstance about her bakery job. When she came home her clothes were permeated with the scent of chocolate. Although it was maddening to be so close to the aroma of chocolate and not be able to taste it, I think just smelling it was better than not experiencing the joy of chocolate at all.

Don't let me give you the idea that the Liberaces didn't always eat well. It might not be rich, it might not be chocolate, but it was always plentiful and good. All of us kids, except Rudy who was younger than I am and so was still too young to contribute to the family coffers, chipped in whatever we were able to earn.

Both Mom and Dad were such good cooks that they made whatever our money would provide taste like a feast. Mom with her Polish-German dishes and Dad with Italian ones could turn low-budget foods like beans, pasta, tripe, dandelion greens and vegetables that grew in our garden into foods every bit as delicious as those I've since found on the menus of famous gourmet restaurants throughout the world.

George, by this time, was earning money giving violin lessons and working as a waiter in a restaurant. We took whatever we could get. Angie did secretarial work and acted as a nurse's helper in a doctor's office. I played the piano for dancing school classes and fashion shows. And sometimes when piano playing jobs were scarce, I worked as a busboy or dishwasher.

Fortunately, for my hands, my career as a dishwasher was short lived. One of the many freak accidents that it has been my misfortune to experience was when a faulty hot water tank spewed boiling water all over my hands scalding them severely. If I wasn't by nature what Oscar Hammerstein in one of his *South Pacific* songs called "a cockeyed optimist," I think perhaps I would have quit doing anything and retired to the relatively safe confines of a monastery.

But somebody quickly applied a lot of soft butter to my burns, which seems to have prevented them from blistering. But, of course, my hands were very sore and sensitive for weeks. People often ask me, nowadays, if my hands are insured. I tell them, "My whole body is insured." It's not just my hands that go into piano playing. There are physical and mental demands, as well.

The truth is that the accident with the boiling water was only the first of several accidents to my hands that I had when I was young. I must have had my full quota, because I don't seem to have accidents anymore. And I pay no more attention to my hands than I do to any other part of me I'd hate to have hurt. I guess that's all of me. I'm not crazy about pain and don't stand it very well. I don't even like to write about it.

I once had an infection in one of my fingers that became gangrenous and the finger would have been amputated had not my mother, conscious of what such an operation would do to my chances of becoming a concert pianist, defied the doctors. She applied an old-fashioned hot milk-and-mustard poultice. This old wives' remedy, like so many of them that are being rediscovered today, miraculously drew out the poison and saved the finger. There is a one-legged tap dancer, Peg Leg Bates, whom I used to see at the Alhambra in Milwaukee, but I don't think there's ever been a nine-fingered piano player.

Another of the strange, almost weird accidents I've had to my hands happened when I found my baby brother, Rudy, playing with one of the very sharp butcher knives that Dad used in his culinary activities. In trying to take the knife from the baby I accidentally cut three of the fingers of my right hand all the way to the bone. The doctors placed the hand in a cast with a splint to immobilize it until it healed. Of course, after the cast and the splint came off, I had to practice therapy exercises for months before I regained the full use of my fingers. All I have left of this experience is the scars. And to those who tell me that I'm accident-prone, I point out that I also seem to be recovery-prone. I guess I'm a born survivor.

And speaking of survivors, I'm probably the only performer alive today who entertained the veterans of the Civil War. We lived across the street from the National Veterans' Administration on National Avenue in Milwaukee. And as a child I was frequently asked to go across the street and play in what we called The Soldiers Home. At that time there were still four or five Civil War vets in the "Home." So, besides them, I've played for veterans of five other wars, Spanish-American, World War I, World War II, Korean War and Vietnam. I hope there will be no more wars to create more veterans. The world doesn't need any more.

As Hal David wrote in his lyric to Burt Bachrach's melody, "What the world needs now is love, true, love." I, too, am a strong believer that this is the greatest force known to mankind. It has meant mankind's survival. It shows itself in many ways.

One of my reasons for writing this book is to let everyone know that I care about people and know the importance of love and how it can help mankind today. It has many expressions beyond the touch of bodies, the caress of words. It can be conveyed through music, art, poetry; through something as simple and ordinary as a smile or a handshake. It has seen me through some very difficult periods in my life. From these I've learned that when you show you care, people reciprocate, people care about you.

I think I learned a little about caring very early at the National

Veterans' Administration. I can see it anytime I want to shut my eyes and think about it. I do that most often in the spring. To me, as a child, the place seemed absolutely surrounded by huge lilac bushes. And every May they burst into bloom to celebrate. my birthday on the sixteenth. We had lilacs all over the house around that time. They remain my favorite flower. In fact, one of the things I miss in California are the lilacs. They don't grow there as they do in the Midwest. But people who know that I like them always bring me lilacs, if possible, on an opening night or any sort of celebration.

I do a lot of work around the house, the garage and the kitchen, making things, hanging things. Sometimes I even do a little upholstery, which is one of the things I learned when I was young. While the boys I played with made model cars and model airplanes, I liked to make things out of fabrics I found lying around. For example, if a nice piece of cloth came to hand, I'd figure out how I could fit it to one of our chairs that needed recovering.

Once Mom had a piece of goods and I showed her how to make it into a hat. She got lots of compliments on it, but I wouldn't let her tell anyone I showed her how to make it.

As for my work in the kitchen, I get a lot of fun out of that. I not only inherited Dad's and Mom's recipes, I also inherited some of their skill in preparing food. Maybe you've run across the cookbook I wrote. It's called *Liberace Cooks*. Original title? I reconcile myself to the lack of originality with the fact that if the function of a book's title is to tell people what it's about, I think I came up with a perfect title. (I wanted to call it "Mother, I'd Rather Do It Myself!" But the publishers decided *Liberace Cooks* was more to the point.)

Any skill I may now have with English, either written or spoken, I owe at least in part, to a teacher I had in sixth and seventh grade. Later she was transferred to West Milwaukee High School, where she taught me English. Her name was Sylvia Becker, and I owe her a lot. I guess every kid in the world has one teacher he worshipped.

I ran into her not long after I started writing this book. I was playing an engagement in Miami Beach. I told her what I was doing and she asked, "Who are you going to get to correct the grammar?" I told her that's what publishers had editors for.

She told me she's happily married, has been for years, and her husband was retired. She must have found what Ponce de Leon missed down there in Florida because she's managed to make her seventy years look like a scant fifty. We had a wonderful reunion. One of the things she's proudest of is the way she taught me to speak proper English instead of talking with a Wisconsin Polish-Italian accent all my own.

You see, in the Polish language there's no *th* sound. So from my Polish Mother I picked up a hard *d* sound for words like "these" and "those." My Italian Dad had a tendency to put the accent on the wrong syllable. So between the two of them I had a very peculiar accent which was neither charming, continental nor pleasant. It was just bad English. Sylvia used to keep after me to correct it. She gave me a lot of lessons. These included sentences to say over and over to help me break my bad speech habits. One of those sentences I remember to this very day. She had me repeat it over and over again in rapid sequence. It was, "He was the talk of the town." Whenever I came across the *th* sound ahead of the *t* sound, I said it, "He was da talka da town."

When I got up to recite, it used to make all the other kids in the class laugh. (Come to think of it, I talked a little the way Lawrence Welk still talks.) Finally, at Sylvia Becker's suggestion I enrolled in a summer course to get rid of my dialect. That was back in 1934 and the course helped me a lot, as anyone who's heard me speak must know. I have no more "dese" and "dose." But it isn't because I don't occasionally have to stop and think.

At the end of the course we had to write a term paper on our favorite person or subject. I chose George Gershwin. Then we had to read the paper aloud using only the proper English construction and pronunciation. I got through it just great, but even today I still find myself going for double negatives and split infinitives and an occasional "dis" or "dat," words which cause English teachers intense anguish.

Sylvia Becker was not only interested in my language, she was also interested in my music and did a lot to encourage me. She was very active with Junior Hadassah and she frequently asked me to come to play at their luncheons and fund-raising drives even though I was hardly more than a child. I became very popular at the Hadassah, and I began to suspect very strongly that they thought I was Jewish. My feeling about this seemed completely confirmed when I noticed that the program for one of the luncheons had my name spelled Liberatsky.

5

As I continued to grow up, I played the piano better and better and became more and more of a show-off. The life of the party is what I actually became whenever Dad's musical and show biz friends gathered at the house to enjoy one of Mom's feasts. There was always entertainment after the meals, and I was always it.

I can remember one of Dad's friends, (a man I called uncle although he was no relation) Uncle Emilio, saying to my father, "Sam, that kid's going places."

Knowing some of the jobs I secretly played, I thought to myself, "You should just know the places I'm going." but, of course, I didn't interrupt, and he went right on saying, "You should let him work in some kind of child prodigy act and tour the country with it. He'd make big money."

Dad's answer was always, "No kid of mine's going to take over the responsibility for my family. Wallie's going to study music and finish his schooling in the proper manner. I won't let him prostitute his Talent." I didn't know what the word prostitute meant, but it somehow sounded like something I ought to find out about.

What Dad didn't know was I'd discovered that I was in demand for such widely different but sometimes sequential events as stag parties and Polish weddings. I don't really know why I join those two very different kinds of affairs. But they seemed to be the ones I got the most calls for. I used to lie and say I was visiting a friend to practice duets or going to rehearse a concerto with my teacher when actually I was off to play a club date or casual for fifteen or twenty bucks. The amount varied with the size of the tips I got.

I had a terrible time with Mom and Dad when they found out about my secret activities as a pianist. One of the club dates I worked happened to be a stag party that featured dirty movies. Now they're called porno films and people pay $5 a ticket to go into a theater to see them. Then the admission was a buck and it included dinner. They also had live singing and dancing girls who stripped down to nothing at all and mingled with the cheering men in the audience. In the midst of all this there I was, a kid of sixteen, playing up a storm, when the police came charging in. It was the second time I was busted.

I was turned over to the juvenile authorities who took the matter up with Mom and Dad and from then on my musical activities were more carefully supervised. I was only allowed to accept playing dates at genteel gatherings like afternoon tea dances and fashion shows. I never knew why these always wound up with a bridal gown. I guess at the time that was considered the culmination of any girl's ambition. And while the model was strutting around in her trailing train and bridal veil I, of course, had to honor the occasion with the Wedding March which I grew to hate with a considerable passion.

I grew awfully bored with playing the same monotonous music for the same dull occasions after I'd had a taste of a little faster type of life. At least the strippers showed a little imagination and a lot of themselves. And this fired *my* imagination. I mean musically I loved to punctuate their movements with special chords and riffs as I accompanied their weird gyrations.

Needless to say, before the joint I was playing in was hit by the police, I had ceased to be a virgin and found out exactly the meaning of the word "prostitute."

Dad should have been used to my getting involved in theatrical activities, if playing stag shows could be called a theatrical activity. Maybe it was. I met one of the prostitutes who used to work those stags, after I had already become an established performer. She came back stage to say hello and to recall the "good old days." When I asked her if she was working in town she said, "No! I've given up show business." She was married, had two kids and was as domestic as an old broom.

Actually, by the time I got busted at the stag party, I was a veteran performer. My first job, I'm proud to say, I got all by myself. I was ten years old. I didn't think I was so little at age ten, but everybody said I was. This may have been due to the fact that I'd had a severe case of pneumonia that it took me a long time to recover from when I was very young.

At the Alhambra Theater, where I'd gone with my father when he worked there, they were holding auditions for a promotional thing called "Milwaukee on Parade." I showed up and told them I played the piano. But a skinny little kid of ten doesn't get a lot of attention at an audition that was planned for adults and I got the brush.

I hung around anyway and finally the dancers in the Fanchon & Marco unit that was playing the house began talking to me. Chorus girls are a sentimental bunch, anyway, and I suppose I brought out all their latent motherly instincts. One of the girls finally got one of the people holding the auditions to let me play for him.

I don't think it's immodest to say that at the age of ten I really rocked him. I must have; he put me in the show. The girls in the chorus got the costume woman with the unit to work me up a costume. They had to build a special platform for me to play on and fix the piano stool so that I could reach the keys. Then they had to give me something to play because they couldn't see Liszt's "Hungarian Rhapsody" as the ideal number for a vaudeville show. It wasn't that I didn't play it well. It was way too long and I wasn't, as yet, enough of a musician to know how to cut it. So they had a man play a number for me and I learned how to play it from listening to him.

One of the girls came over to me after the show and told me it was wonderful. She said that the man who had played the number for me said to her when I was on, "Why can't I play like that?" He and I wondered the same thing. I, too, wondered how I played like that.

Instead of that appearance being a triumph for me at home, it was a disaster. Dad got awfully mad. I wasn't playing the kind of music he wanted me to learn or to perform, and he told me so with a lot of emphasis and muscle. But he didn't really stop me.

A little boy who could play the piano the way I could play it was not going to be denied some sort of an outlet and my Dad and Mrs. Kelly knew it. So I was delighted when I got a spot on a local radi show on station WTMJ in Milwaukee. Since Mrs. Kelly was a staff pianist on the station and my father played French horn in the station's symphony orchestra, I have a suspicion some strings were pulled to get me the job.

Naturally having a friend who was on the radio was a big status thing with my fellow students at school, so I became quite a big shot among them and all the adulation I was getting went straight to my head. I thought I could do no wrong. Well, I found out. Like Humpty Dumpty, I had a great fall.

I wanted to play a new number on the radio show, but Mrs. Kelly said I wasn't properly prepared to play it. She said I hadn't practiced it enough, that I just wasn't ready for it. I thought I was ready for anything and told her I was going to play the piece anyway. And I did.

It is possible that I played that tune (I'm sorry but I can't remember the name of it anymore, probably for psychological reasons.) worse than I have ever played anything in my life. I fluffed all the way through it and tried to fake my way out of it and every musician for miles around must have been holding his ears.

When the program was over I walked out of the studio into a sort of lounge area where other performers waited between rehearsals or to get into a studio to do a show. Mrs. Kelly was waiting for me with fire in her eyes. She had a terrible Kelly-type temper and she was so angry she grabbed my music from me and flung it in my face, sheet by sheet. She reminded me that she'd told me that I wasn't prepared to play that song and I'd proved it to the whole world. She really let me have it, and I was more embarrassed than I'd normally be because all the musicians sitting around in the lounge were friends of my father's. They taunted me with lines like, "Shame! Shame! Wally didn't do his lesson," or "You didn't practice! You didn't practice! Teacher's mad 'cause you didn't practice." It was a big joke with them. But no boy likes to be made fun of, particularly by adults. It was an awful experience.

When I got home the news had already reached my father and, of course, perfectionist that he was, he agreed totally with Mrs. Kelly. He decided that success on the radio was turning out to be just a little too much too soon, that it was giving me a swelled head. So he called the station and told them that he'd prefer it if his son didn't appear on the air anymore until he was more thoroughly prepared for it.

What a blow! I had to face the questions from the kids at school. "How come you're not on the radio anymore?" So I had to admit that I'd been fired because I'd played badly. I began, as a result of that setback, to practice harder and harder. I was resolved that nothing would ever come along that I couldn't play well. Finally, Mrs. Kelly decided I'd learned to take a little advice when given. So she called the station and had me reinstated on the show. I thought nothing more wonderful could ever happen to me, and I resolved not to let it go to my head again.

I did plenty of other piano playing, too. Being the only pianist in school, I spent more time playing the piano for various school events and functions than I spent in the classroom. But I was good at cramming. I have a fantastic memory when I want to make it work for me. So I got through each semester with reasonably good grades and graduated from West Milwaukee High School in 1937 second in my class.

Finally out of high school I began to get the itch to branch out. I felt I'd exhausted all the really great possibilities there were for a young piano player in Milwaukee. I felt, as it says in the song about Kansas City, that I'd "gone about as far as I could go."

I'd not only done all that solo work, played at various affairs and been on the radio, but while I was still in West Milwaukee High I joined a group of older, married musicians who did weekend engagements at various nightclubs and roadhouses around the Milwaukee area.

The group was called "The Mixers" and there were five of us. I still remember the names of some of them. There was Delbert Krausy on drums and Wallie Schaetski on trumpet. I've forgotten the name of the guy who played bass and doubled on guitar, But I could never forget that the sax man was my Latin teacher, Dr. James Archer, who is now a philosophy professor in Arizona. He was a pretty good saxophone player and an awfully good Latin teacher. If it hadn't been for him I never would have known how to make the great Caesar salad all my friends compliment me on. I, of course, played piano with the group, and you'll pardon the expression, I also sang.

Most of the spots we played didn't have anything as modern as a microphone. So I took a leaf out of Rudy Vallee's old book and had a megaphone beside the piano. Although I was only sixteen, I'm sure I looked much older in George's tuxedo. So no one ever questioned the fact that during intermissions I hung around the "26-Game" that almost all hatcheck girls in the kind of spots we played used to run to augment their meager income from tips.

I don't see many of these "26-Games" anymore. The idea was to get as high a score as you could rolling five dice, three times. If you were able to beat the hatcheck girl she'd give you a token. When you got enough of these you'd win various dolls and stuffed animals. Naturally it took an awful lot of tokens to get a prize.

I got a yen for a wonderful Charlie McCarthy doll the girl had in her showcase and after looking at it longingly for a while, I managed to con a slightly sozzled patron of the joint, into winning it for me. When the hatcheck girl found out that I'd been the incentive for this "high roller's" action, she had a little talk with me and we became business partners.

The setup was that I'd get customers to win dolls for me. Then at the end of the evening I'd turn them in and she'd give me a percentage of the evening's profit. It wasn't much, but it was a welcome addition to the small amount I earned on such dates. Usually this came to about $5.00 salary plus a share of the "kitty" we'd divide. This came to another $5.00 or sometimes as much as $10.00, which we took in as tips from patrons who asked us to play special numbers.

One night there was a grand Silver Wedding Anniversary Party in a place called Sam Pick's Club Madrid. I'll never forget the name of *that* place although there were lots just like it, the names of which I've forgotten. And I'll never forget that whole night. To start the evening off right, the wedding party presented the band with a bottle of what I knew only as "booze." Memory tells me it was probably gin. As we played, the bottle was passed around from one of us to the other. Naturally I wanted to be "one of the boys" (although I was the only boy among them). So I got a lot of satisfaction out of taking a good healthy swig—it almost choked me—everytime the bottle came to me.

The evening was only about half over when someone requested us to play "The Carioca" which was one of our showier pieces. I played the introduction and just as I was about to go into the full arrangement I fell right off the piano bench, dead drunk. The next thing I remember was being delivered to my outraged parents, very much the worse for wear in George's very messed-up tuxedo. Obviously I had become extremely sick on the way home. The incident not only taught me a lesson, it taught George a lesson. He never again let me borrow his dinner jacket. I had to buy one of my own.

I can honestly say I've never been drunk since. And I never will be. I have, in the years I've been in show business, learned how to handle alcohol in a sensible way. I instinctively know when I've had enough. Some kind of inner mechanism tells me and I obey.

Realizing that there was no sensational future with "The Mixers," I was able, with the help of Mrs. Bettray-Kelly to get a contract with a Chicago booking agency. And they got me a job playing a Community Concerts Course. This meant that I toured all over the Midwest playing large towns and small cities in Wisconsin, Minnesota, Illinois and Michigan as a concert pianist.

I got to be pretty well known in this limited field. But I yearned to make it in the big city and finally, after being recommended, and auditioning, I had the opportunity to give a concert at Kimball Hall in Chicago. That was in 1938 and it was the biggest city I'd ever played in. I guess it's still one of the biggest cities I've ever played in. And it's always been good to me. My very first fan club was started in Chicago.

One of the Chicago critics wrote that I had every quality a virtuoso should possess. So on the strength of the Kimball Hall recital and the reviews that followed it, Mrs. Kelly was able to get me an audition as a soloist with the Chicago Symphony Orchestra. And I was chosen to appear with them in 1939. But that was a year away, and I had to do something more than sit around and practice for those twelve months. I had to eat. I had to send money home.

So having created kind of a name for myself in the north central states, I was able to get booked for a concert in La Crosse, Wisconsin, where, as it turned out, I really shook 'em up and created a lot of critical tongue clicking among the cognescenti.

The local music critic was something of a musical snob. And it hurt his aesthetic sensibilities when I played, as an encore request, after an all classical program, a tune Kay Kyser had made popular that was then America's most popular song, The "Three Little Fishies."

I not only played it, but I showed I understood the humor behind the request and threw in a couple of winks and a big broad smile. I was trying to tell the people that you could have fun at a concert without sacrificing the greatness of the music. I was trying to show that music is not all heavy-handed culture, that it has its humorous side, just as great literature does.

Well, the news of my excursion into funny pop music—from the serious concert platform—made headlines in the local papers which trumpeted: THREE LITTLE FISHIES SWIM IN SEA OF CLASSICS. Then the news was picked up by the wire services because then, as now, there's little enough in the news to laugh at, so anything funny that comes along is given a break. This break, of course, did a lot for me.

It even made my Dad swallow his pride and allow me to contribute to the support of the family which was still very badly off financially. Dad also relented and let me follow my musical career in any direction it led me or that I chose to direct it.

The fact was that somebody just had to bring in some money, and I was already earning more than Dad did at the height of his musical career. I think that may be why an awful lot of French horn players who are ambitious find other kinds of work. (Milt Kamen who played French horn with the New York Philharmonic, is now one of our leading comics.)

At last I felt free to play and interpret any kind of music without fear of raising any parental wrath, restrictions and restraints. And I think that was when I began to develop the style of performing that in the not too distant future was to win me the sobriquet "Mr. Showmanship," which I am very proud of. It tells people who don't already know it that they are going to get more than just a piano recital when they come to see me.

I wanted to give the world *entertainment* that would be new and different to them, to introduce people, who had never been to a piano recital or a symphony concert because they thought it would bore them, to the wonderful works they'd been denying themselves.

Actually, as I've said, I felt being a concert pianist was a very lonely business. I felt as if I were up there playing alone and each of the people in the audience was alone in his own little world listening to me. The audience never came together as it did when I played the "Three Little Fishies." So I realized, after that incident, that my heart was not in concertizing but in entertaining.

I knew I had to find some way to get away from the formalities of the classical music field without sacrificing what talent I had, some way to combine the fun of the "Three Little Fishies" with Mozart,

Strauss, Liszt, and Tchaikovsky, as I now sometimes do in my act. But what I was setting out to do was a fairly unexplored field. To be successful in it, I knew, I had to get some audience reactions, find out how people took to what I proposed to do. I started by taking one giant step, as everyone thought, backwards: From concert pianist player in a cocktail lounge. But when you're young as I was then, you're ready to do anything that has to be done in order to do—as they say—"your own thing."

The first thing of my own that I did was to get myself a job in a spot called The Wunderbar in Warsaw, Wisconsin. The first problem I ran into in making the transition from Kimball Hall in Chicago to The Wunderbar in Warsaw was what name to use.

Walter Valentino Liberace sounded too high class. It even sounded a little like a put on. W. V. Liberace sounded like a sign on the desk of a vice-president of something. I couldn't use Walter Valentino because it sounded too Latin for that part of the world. All these things were what the management of The Wunderbar told me. Finally, in a burst of inspiration they came up with a name they hung on me.

As Phyllis Diller would say, "Are you ready for this?" I, myself, can't believe it. The new name was Walter Buster Keys. A lot of thinking went into that name. They used Walter so that if someone called me by my first name, I'd know who he was talking to. Buster was an acknowledgement of my youth and seemed to describe my *joi de vivre* as well as my piano playing technique. No manufacturing company about to market a new product could have given more thought to endowing that product with a name that had psychological impact. And, as so often happens, with the big companies, they came up with something that seemed sensible only to them . . . silly to everyone else.

Naturally, Walter Buster Keys only worked about six or seven months. He then disappeared forever into the more obscure pages in the history of entertainment business. I went back to my own name . . . and just my last one. Why complicate an already rather difficult looking name? I say, rather difficult *looking* because it isn't hard to say . . . just confusing to look at. And I didn't really care how people pronounced it, as long as they recognized it. With the greatest conceit in the world, I reasoned that if my idol, Paderewski, could become world famous using only his last name, Liberace couldn't be so bad. It didn't matter if people said

Padder-oo-ski or Padder-eff-ski, everybody recognized the name. I hoped someday that it would be the same with me Libber-ah-chee or Libber-ace. What difference did it make, as long as people remembered it and came to hear me? I knew if they did, they'd enjoy themselves.

But just as I do today, when I was Walter Buster Keys I did some singing in my act. One day the choir from the local church came in for a bite to eat after choir practice and encouraged me to join them in singing at the church. I said, "You must be awful short of singers." I thought they were putting me on or maybe that they wanted me to play the piano for them. But they made it clear that they wanted me to sing, so I said, "Well, I'm not exactly a hymn singer, but if I don't have to do any solos, it might be good experience for me."

After about three or four weeks of singing, the director of the choir asked me whether I'd do a solo during the offertory of one of the Masses.

"You mean play an organ solo?"

"No," he said, "I want you to sing."

I thought to myself, "Well . . . it's a challenge." I didn't know whether I meant it would be a challenge to my voice or to the ears of the worshippers, but anyway, I said I'd do it and asked, "What would you like me to sing?"

He responded by saying, "There are a whole group of songs that would be appropriate," and handed me a list of them.

Well, I picked out an "Ave Maria" by a less well known composer than Schubert, or the one Charles François Gounod, the composer of *Faust,* improvised from the music of Johann Sebastian Bach. I picked the obscure one, so that if I went too far wrong, nobody would notice it. And I began to rehearse it.

While I was working in Warsaw I lived with some lovely Irish people who had taken me in, and the only place I had to rehearse was their basement. You've heard of tenors and baritones who can break glasses. Well, I found out my voice was very rough on preserves. The reverberations from the noises I made singing "Ave Maria," bounced around from wall-to-wall-and-ceiling-to-floor of that basement, setting up vibrations that somehow started the homemade preserves and canned peaches "to work," as the saying goes.

While I was singing I kept hearing a kind of hissing sound. I

2

thought there was a snake somewhere in the cellar. But when I went looking for it, what I found was that my singing had caused the preserves to get ready to explode. It cheered me quite a lot to think that my voice was so powerful because that's the way it sounded to me in the basement. Maybe it wasn't really my voice that did it to the canned goods. Maybe they just wanted to blame it on me.

When I finally got to sing in the choir loft of the church, my voice sounded nothing like it did when I was singing to the canned goods. It was a very large church and I made a very small, unresonant sound. They never asked me to sing another solo. But I did play the organ occasionally during the offertory. I felt much more at home doing that than singing, you can believe me.

Finally the time came for me to appear as soloist with the Chicago Symphony, and when that was over I was again able to use my own name. When I went back to Warsaw for a return engagement, I was billed as Liberace. But under it, "The former Walter Buster Keys." Can you imagine that?

But the work of a cocktail lounge pianist can be just as lonely as that of a concert pianist. For different reasons. In the lounge you soon learn that your audience didn't really come in to hear you. They came in for a whole catalogue of personal reasons involving getting a drink. A salesman wants to relax a prospect. A guy wants to make a girl. A fellow's been jilted and he wants to forget. He may be the only one listening to you.

And, as the evening wears on, you find that you're not really entertaining them . . . they're trying to entertain you. A man wants you to hear his girl sing because "she's great." You play for her. The man's wrong. She's awful. Everybody has his favorite song which he hums for you. An impromptu quartet is formed to serenade you. And, suddenly, you wish you were someplace else.

So the cocktail parlor work was eliminated, and I went to what used to be called "intermission" playing. That meant that you went on while the regular night club band "took five." The "five" was generally about ten minutes. The net result was that people couldn't dance to your music, as they could to the star band you were subbing for, so they ate. Have you ever played "Tea For Two" while listening to celery and olives, cold consommé, tossed salad, beef Wellington with broccoli and Lynnaise potatoes, strawberry parfait and coffee for one hundred and thirty-two people? Th isn't very rewarding either. And those who are not eating are doing something inattentive. The girls are on their way to the powder room to touch up their makeup, and the guys are absorbed in speculating whether the cost of the evening has been worth it so far and whether it'll get any better. If the chances for the latter look good, it's likely that he'll call for his check and they'll leave . . . for his place or hers to be decided in the cab.

Although I played intermission piano in some of the finest rooms in the finest hotels in the country, including The Persian Room at the Plaza in New York, the work did nothing to disprove my feeling that I'd never get anywhere just subbing for the star. I had to get some attention on my own. That was me. It was the way I was when Dad had his musician friends in for coffee and I showed off for them. So little by little I got together an act that would hold an audience's attention, be more than mere background sound.

I'd seen vaudeville acts where men who couldn't sing a note, mouthed their impressions of Rudy Vallee, Bing Crosby, Morton Downey, Jimmy Durante and other big recording stars. It always got a big hand, although I was never sure whether the hand was for the mimic or the star whose recording he was using. But it set me to thinking about how the gimmick might be adapted to music.

Ever since I was a very little boy I'd been able to play, almost immediately, anything I heard. So with that for a starter I began to experiment on doing an act with me at the piano, "sitting in" as it were, with some of the big popular bands of the day or substituting for one of the great concert pianists playing with one of the big symphony orchestras. I figured if people with no voice at all could get big hands mouthing along with a singer, I, who really could play the piano, could make it big with the same basic idea. Very quickly I abandoned playing with pop bands. It wasn't impressive enough. So I decided to specialize in the better kind of music.

I spent many hours rehearsing with recordings of Arthur Rubinstein, Vladimir Horowitz, Paderewski, José Iturbi, playing as solo artists with the greatest symphony orchestras like the New York Philharmonic under Toscanini, the Philadelphia Symphony under Stokowski, the Boston Pops under Fiedler, the London Philharmonic under Sir John Barbirolli—all pretty good bands. I was brazenly placing myself in the same league with these great names of music. But I realized that in doing so I had to be very good.

I spent many, many hours rehearsing with my recordings so that no noise or distraction of any kind that might take place while I was performing could throw me off my synchronization with the great soloists. Finally I had it down note for note and nothing could confuse me. What emerged was the music of two pianos, mine and the great artist with whom I was playing. These blended into one as if I, alone, were being accompanied by a great concert orchestra.

Naturally to do this properly I had to have very fine reproducing equipment and I think what I actually had was the forerunner of what we now call stereo. I had it designed specially for me by some very fine sound engineers using several speakers placed around the room so that it actually had a live sound to it. The whole thing was great training for me in discipline and self-control. And that was the act that I finally brought into The Persian Room when I followed Hildegarde as the star attraction.

The reason for abandoning this unique act I created was the union. They said by doing what I was doing I was using records to take the place of live musicians and keeping them out of work. It was, of course, silly, because live musicians were working in the same places I worked and it was preposterous to think that I could afford to hire a hundred or so men to play with me even if there was space to put them in a supper club.

So my gimmick, like most gimmicks, was short-lived, and as I say, I am now glad because it forced me to come up with my own individuality in playing rather than bask in the glory of other performers by imitating them.

My regular act began with me playing the piano on my own, without the recording gimmick. Then for the big finale I'd use the records. When the unions made me cut it out, I used the live musicians wherever I was playing. The musicians weren't as fine as those on the records and there weren't nearly as many of them, so to me the sound was thin and unsatisfactory. But I soon discovered that the audiences preferred the live music to the gimmick with the records, so I was grateful to the unions.

And I'm even more grateful today than I was then, because if I hadn't been forced to abandon the trick, the crutch that I was relying on, I might never have developed myself as an individual in the entertainment world, which I can honestly say I believe I am. I can honestly say I know of no one who does the same thing I do, good or bad, in the same way I do it, which puts me in a class all by myself. Getting into that class is what show business is all about.

In spite of all this hindsight, I seemed to be doing all right with my recording and my stereo system back on July 11, 1945, when the following notice appeared in the great show business journal, *Variety*. Incidentally, the signature *Abel* at the end of the review stands for the late Abel Green who was the editor of *Variety*. (Abel died suddenly in May, 1973, aged seventy-two, shortly after writing an obituary for the comedian Jack E. Leonard.)

LIBERACE
MUSIC
12 MINUTES
PERSIAN ROOM, N.Y.

Following Hildegarde into The Plaza's svelte room, Liberace brings a nice style to the big league nitery circuit with his legit and synchronized piano recital. It runs the gamut from synchronizing with the Boston Pops recording of Gershwin's "Rhapsody in Blue" (playing the Jesus Sanroma part) to a legit Chopin recital of the "Polonaise," Greig, "12th Street Rag," boogie-woogie, Beethoven and a novelty piano duet with a femme customer (who gets a token gift for her collaboration).

Liberace looks like a cross between Cary Grant and Robert Alda (who plays Gershwin in the Warner Picture). He has an effective manner, attractive hands which he spotlights properly and, withal, rings the bell in a dramatically lighted, well-presented, showmanly routine. He should snowball into box office, which at the moment he's not, but he's definitely a boff cafe act. *Abel.*

Reading that over I'm amazed. I certainly got a lot of stuff in twelve minutes, didn't I? Mr. Green's stop watch must have been slow, I'm sure I was on longer than twelve minutes. But that review certainly shows why he became the leading show biz journalist. He knew how to criticize, evaluate, predict and present the news of show business. And that's the job of a paper like *Variety*. I think Mr. Green did all those things in that review and his death was a great loss to the show biz he loved.

I'm getting tired of the reviews that pay more attention to my smile and my teeth than to the fact that I do certain things with my fingers to produce beautiful sounds. Obviously, though, Abel wrote that review before he got his glasses. Saying that I looked like Cary Grant, even in combination with Robert Alda, is the kind of inaccurate but flattering comment I like to hear.

Which reminds me, years after that review appeared I was playing in Las Vegas at Caesar's Palace and Cary—this was before I knew him well enough to call him by his first name—was in the audience. After the show he came to my dressing room and introduced himself. Isn't that silly? "Introduced himself." I knew who he was the moment he walked in. Anyway, we shook hands and talked a few minutes about me and when he left he said, "I've only seen you on television up to tonight. This is the first time I've ever seen you work on the stage. And after seeing you work and meeting you, I regret dreadfully that we haven't been friends long before this. And I hope we can be friends in the future."

I've always found that truly great people are always the easiest people to know and the most accessible, although I hate those who go around "ringing doorbells" and getting themselves invited to places. So what Cary did was really appreciated because I honestly am in awe of the giants of my profession. So I love it when they come to me because I'm really too timid—would you believe that to watch me on the stage?—to go back to see them after a show or to stop them on the street to introduce myself and tell them how much I admire them. I'm always convinced they'd rather be left alone, although I have no idea why I think that . . . I wouldn't.

You've read the reviews of my first big New York break at The Persian Room. But naturally you don't get into a room like that until you've proved yourself, till you've shown that you're able to attract an audience. I did this in two very interesting Manhattan night spots. One was the once famous Ruban Bleu, a great place for new young talent, the other was Spivy's Roof . . . which was a favorite hangout of very sophisticated East Side clientele. One of our favorite customers was an elegant gentleman who used to invite us to his swank Park Avenue town house after hours to entertain his friends and guests until the wee hours. He never failed to slip a folded bill (usually a $100) into my palm when he shook hands as I left the party. Or the time he slipped something into my handkerchief pocket of my tux when I wasn't aware of it. I later discovered accidentally when I pulled out the handkerchief to mop my brow that the something was five $100 bills which came in very handy during those low-salaried days ($175 a week salary was the going rate in those "chic" East Side places if you were lucky). Thanks to this generous benefactor I was able to afford a few extras in my budget and I never refused his invitation. Oh, by the way, his name was Paul Getty and I saw him in London last year and he remembered me from those soirees during those early forties.

For several months at the Ruban Bleu I appeared on the bill with a young comet in the singing field—a jazz singer who really rocked the hip crowd that first got acquainted with her type of singing when she worked the spots on 52nd Street in New York. She then made it big with everyone in the world with her great recording of "A Tisket, A Tasket." Ella Fitzgerald!

Spivy's Roof was a penthouse on top of an office building at 57th Street and Lexington Avenue in New York. It featured the risqué songs of its owner and manager, Spivy, who was not only a helluva performer but a great discoverer of talent. When I played at Spivy's, on the bill with me was a quartet called The Revuers. They sang original comedy songs and did sketches which they made up themselves. It was one of the most talented groups ever to hit show business. And because it was so talented it broke up very soon. The four people in The Revuers were Judy Holliday, one of Broadway's and Hollywood's finest comediennes; Betty Comden and Adolph Green, who have written some of our greatest musical shows for both the stage and pictures; and Imogene Coca, who also went on from The Revuers to enormous success as a comedienne.

I often used to go with my boss and fellow performer, Spivy, to Reuben's, a restaurant that started out as a delicatessen and became one of the great after-midnight hangouts of the show biz gentry. It was one of the spots that Walter Winchell made regularly every night looking for gossip when he was a force to be reckoned with in the night life of New York. One night when we were lingering over Reuben's famous cheesecake, a fascinating lady stopped at our table and invited us to stop by her apartment for a nightcap. There were never any introductions when you were with Spivy. She assumed you knew everybody and if you were anybody they knew you. And if this wasn't true, in either case, it was your loss.

Spivy's friend spoke in a very basso voice with a heavy Russian accent and sounded a little like Tallulah Bankhead playing Catherine the Great. I knew she was a celebrity and I was dying to ask who, but I was afraid to expose my ignorance. I kept hoping someone would drop the hint that would give the clue I needed to identify her.

As we sat over our drinks in her apartment she and Spivy

reminisced about old friends they knew, people I'd heard of and worshipped from afar, while I sat quietly on the sidelines listening. There was hardly a big name she hadn't known. So when she asked me if I'd like to see her guest book, I could hardly wait to leaf through it. There was one famous name after another whom she'd entertained from time to time. And I can't tell you how flattered I felt when she asked if I'd like to add my name to her illustrious list.

What I wrote in the book was, "My dear Polly Adler, my sincere thanks for one of the most wonderful evenings I've ever spent in my life." It wasn't until later that I found out that Polly Adler was the most famous madam in New York and the guest book I had signed was a list of her preferred clients.

I was still young enough then to think Polly Adler's business was against the law so Spivy explained to me that Polly's place was periodically raided by the New York police and she was forced to spend a few days in jail. This wasn't too bad when you consider that she was allowed to have her food catered by a nearby Schrafft's Restaurant and was visited daily by her personal maid and hairdresser. It was just a formality she was forced to go through three or four times a year. Evidently her business flourished because of it.

I met Polly again after she retired, came to Hollywood and was living a very domestic life in a little house in San Fernando Valley. She invited me to come out for a home cooked dinner and we had great fun reminiscing about the years before when we'd met, years about which she knew so much and I, at that time, knew so little.

But don't imagine that our conversation was entirely one-sided. I told her how, when I was "between engagements," I used to manage to see the best shows on Broadway—and there were some great ones during that era. The trouble was, by my method, I only saw half the show . . . the last half. What I did was put on my dinner jacket and mingle with the crowds in the lobby during intermission. Then I'd casually walk back into the theater when the time came and see the second act. If they gave out door passes, as some houses did, I just fumbled in my pockets for so long that I held up everyone else who wanted to get in and the doorman figured I was some stew who dropped or misplaced his pass and let me in.

Usually the second half of the show was better than the first half, which I could hear about from friends who could afford to buy tickets to see the whole show. This system worked equally well at the Metropolitan Opera, and I must say that half an opera is better than no opera at all.

I understand from some of my young friends that the "Liberace System" of seeing one half of all the shows on Broadway is still being used. Only now you don't have to wear a tuxedo. You can dress in Levis or kookie as you wish and everyone will think you're a visiting millionaire from Chillicothe, Ohio.

Polly's reaction to my story of show crashing was typical. She said, "But my dear, all you have to do to get into any theater is just call up the manager and tell him who you are and there are two marvelous seats waiting for you at the box office." I wouldn't even dare to do that now, when it might really work.

But to get back to The Persian Room at The Plaza, that's exactly what I did. It was about seven years later that I returned and this time with my candelabra. I also had my own specially made $150,000 oversized grand piano. I still have it. I tell my audiences that there is only one other piano like it in the world . . . "and I own that one, too." That's the one I keep in London.

In 1945 I saw Paul Muni, Merle Oberon and Cornel Wilde in a movie about the life of Frédéric Chopin. It's possible that I was the only one of all the people in the audience who went to see that film who was not interested in the three stars, only the man whose life they were depicting . . . the man and his music. I love to listen to Chopin, and I love to play Chopin.

It interested me to see that in the film, whenever the great composer played, he had a candelabra on the piano. I guess the lighting was very bad in those days and he needed those extra candles to see the keyboard. But I didn't think of that at the time. I said to myself, "If candles make Chopin play that well, I'll have candles on my piano." So I went out to a little antique shop and bought a brass candelabra for $15 and a quarter's worth of candles and put it up on the piano that evening when I did my act. After that whenever I opened somewhere, reviewers commented on the candelabra. So that's how that happened. People started to send me interesting candelabras. It's wonderful. People everywhere like to give me things.

I don't try to stop them. I encourage them. If giving gives *them* pleasure, it gives *me* pleasure, too. So with the candelabras that were given to me and the ones I found and admired and bought, I now have a handsome collection.

And my show starts as the lights go down and the flickering little electric bulbs in my candelabra light up to say to the audience, "And here's the star of our show—Liberace. "

6

Once upon a time you had to take a little ferry across San Diego Harbor to get to the resort town of Coronado. In the winter tourists came from the Midwest and the East to enjoy the warmth of Coronado's Silver Strand, a semicircular sweep of wide, flat beach where refugees from less friendly winter climates came to swim in the sea or sneak down to Tijuana, only about seventeen miles south, to see the Jai Lai games and haggle with the local storekeepers over all sorts of Mexican goodies at bargain prices.

The ride on the little ferry across San Diego Harbor, filled with the pride of the United States Navy, used to be sort of an introduction, a slowing down, to prepare you for the enormous but quaint (if that's possible) old Hotel del Coronado which looked as if it were built by an architect who hoped that Queen Victoria would come and stay in it some day. I don't think she ever did. But the hotel still stands there hoping. And it's such a grand old museum piece I wanted to buy it.

It's most impressive with its enormous public rooms and guest rooms that have bathrooms larger than some New York apartments; its tennis courts, its swimming pools, its stretch of ocean beach and its long, handsome bar that used to have little bowls of parsley sprigs, whole cloves and coffee beans on it. They were the breath decontaminators that served the dandies of Queen Victoria's time. The huge dining room planned to serve the 1,000 guests the hotel could accommodate, is one of the most interesting rooms I've ever been in. And the food, you could eat all you wanted when I was there in 1950, could only be described as fabulous.

Those who remember *Some Like It Hot,* that marvelous pictrure with Marilyn Monroe, Jack Lemmon and Tony Curtis—the one in which Jack and Tony both played girls and the girl they both were playing was Marilyn—well, if you remember that film, you'll remember the massive old hotel in the picture. That was Hotel del Coronado.

Needless to say, it was patronized by other refugees from Eastern winters. When the weather was fine, people from all over California drove down the coast and took the ferry across the Harbor to Coronado. But they take the ferry there no more; that's because the ferry is there no more. You now drive across a bridge. Some think it's an improvement. Not I.

But you still get a wonderful old world feeling as you enter the hotel's sweeping driveway and draw up to its welcoming verandah. As you step from the car you feel you're in the presence of a queen from another era, graciously dominating her modern California environment.

If I seem a little lyrical about Hotel del Coronado, it's because (as I've hinted earlier) this grand old lady of hostelries represents for me the start of an entirely new phase of my career as a performer. Not long after I played a curious show in Coronado everything took such a turn for the better it made my head swim. And the marvelous thing about it was, it all happened because I did what I thought was right. I guess someone up there was watching and gave me a little reward.

This is the story. While I was appearing there at The Circus Room, we had one weekend of thick fog and rain. It must have been bad all over the country. The planes from the East were delayed, and of course, nobody drove south along the California coast for a weekend on the Silver Strand because the fog was so bad you could hardly see the coast. Even the peaked turrets of the hotel disappeared into the heavy overcast. I didn't mind. I just stayed in my room. It was a great time to catch up on my resting and reading. Naturally I knew nothing about the hotel's lack of business.

When the evening came, I went down to my dressing room to get ready to do my show, and as I was starting to make up the manager came in and said, "It's one of those nights. Check-ins have been very light on account of the weather and . . . well . . . what can I tell you! There are only seventeen people in the room."

I thought to myself, "If it's that bad, how wonderful that seventeen showed up!" But I didn't *say* anything. The manager stood silent for a minute as if trying to think of something to say that would make the fact that almost no one came to see me easier on my ego. Finally, he came up with, "If you don't want to do the show, you don't have to. I'll have the orchestra leader make an announcement that the show is canceled. However, it's up to you. Entirely up to you."

I have since wondered, although I didn't think about it at the time, if that manager wanted me to cancel the show so that he wouldn't have to pay me. That could have been why he said it was entirely up to me. If *I* had decided then, I guess, he could get out of our contract. So, you live and learn. But I'm glad I don't think about things like that. All I thought of were those seventeen souls in "The Circus Room" hoping to get, at the very least, a show for their trip to Coronado. So I decided to go on.

I said, "Well, seventeen people are better than no people. And if those seventeen are expecting a show—a show they will *get*." It was the smartest decision I ever made. And I never worked harder in my life. That evening I learned that an audience that is disappointing in number—and I think you can safely call seventeen disappointing—makes greater demands on a performer psychologically than a capacity house.

In the past several years I've been lucky to be one of the acts that continually does well at the box office. My people who keep track of such things tell me that in most engagements I consistently average ninety percent of capacity. I wish they hadn't told me. Now I wonder what I did to offend the other ten percent. And you can believe me that those capacity houses are much easier to work to than the seventeen people in "The Circus Room."

When the house is full a certain amount of excitement rubs off on the audience before you even get on the stage. Everyone in a packed theater says to himself, "If all these other people came, I must have been right to come, too. I was lucky to get in."

Empty seats, on the other hand, put doubts in the minds of the people who came. They begin to feel sorry they spent the money for the ticket and this makes them more selective about what they see on the stage and harder to please. The fact that more people didn't come makes them feel that maybe the performer is slipping. The result is that you have a house full of critics. But those wonderful seventeen that night in Coronado certainly didn't fit into that mold; they were glad they got to see a show at all.

After the show was over a very distinguished-looking gentleman, one of the seventeen people I'd played for, came back to see me. With him was a friend he introduced as Jack Hellman who, I found out later, wrote about radio and TV for the *Daily Variety* in Hollywood. The distinguished-looking gentleman was Don Fedderson, a television producer. He and Hellman had been up the coast a little way at Del Mar, a race track started by Bing Crosby and Pat O'Brien and some of their friends. Don had had a good day and wanted to celebrate. Since there was nothing to do in Del Mar, in spite of the weather they drove to Coronado to have something to do and because, Jack Hellman told me much later when I got to know him, "Don said, 'there's a piano player at Coronado Seymour Heller asked me to take a look at.' " Seymour hadn't bothered to tell me.

Wouldn't it have been terrible if I'd decided *not* to go on?

After the introductions I asked them if they'd have a drink, and then Mr. Fedderson said, "You know, Mr. Liberace . . ."

"Just call me Lee," I said, as I must have said a million times.

"You know, Lee," he continued, "if you can entertain a handful of people . . . how many were there?"

"Seventeen."

"If you can grab the attention of seventeen people and hold them the way you held us tonight, Seymour Heller is right, you should be on television."

"I should? Surely television has more then seventeen viewers," I said, sounding stupid. "I mean, I just don't understand."

"Contrary to what everyone believes," Don said, "when you're on television you're not playing to tens of millions of people. Your audience is really small groups; families sitting around in their living rooms, or play rooms or people in beds in hospitals. Maybe it's not a group at all. Your audience may be just one lonely person.

"So you see, television is not one huge audience. It is a huge number of small audiences. These are people you are playing to, personally. You are alone with them in their homes. While you are entertaining them, you are their guest. It's a very personal kind of thing, and it's that personal sort of entertainment that you gave us this evening. If you can produce this kind of show on television," Don concluded, "you'll be holding lightning in a bottle."

And that's how my career in television got started. Most of the TV stars were people who had made it big in radio and moved on, when the time came, to the visual form of the medium. I'd never been in radio, except when I was a boy. And I was anxious to try what Fedderson suggested, transferring the way I work a theater audience to television.

We didn't do much negotiating. Within a few weeks, I did my first television show on KLAC, a local station in Los Angeles. But well before we were ready to do that show, Don said to me, "Come on Lee, I want to take you for a little drive around this area."

We went through the various neighborhoods and little communities that have been put together to make Los Angeles, which a man named Wilson Mizner once called "six suburbs in search of a city." We drove through the slums, the trailer parks, the San Fernando valley, the middle-class areas in the hills and the wealthy city of Beverly Hills. All the time Don kept talking and pointing out various homes as attractive or run down or unusual . . . anything to keep me looking at the houses.

Finally, I asked, "Why are we taking this ride?"

He said, "As we were driving through Beverly Hills, how many TV aerials did you notice?" Remember this was in 1950.

I told him I remembered seeing very few. Then I realized why he'd been directing my attention to houses everywhere we went.

"But I remember seeing lots of them in the middle-class residential areas of Hollywood and in the trailer courts on the outskirts of town and in the tract houses in the valley."

"Draw any conclusion from that?" Don asked.

There was only one conclusion to draw. While the affluent people in Beverly Hills were waiting for television to be perfected or waiting for it to disappear as a passing fad, the working classes, the middle income people, had seized on it as entertainment the like of which they'd never expected to *see*. It was the seeing that got them, and they were entranced.

That little automobile ride reminded me of what Don said down in Coronado about little groups of people, possibly lonely people, watching TV. The audience was not the sophisticated, intellectual element that had a kind of snobbish attitude about all popular entertainment anyway, and so had nothing but sneers for TV. It was the solid backbone people of America. The ones who did the work, kept things going and were ready to be friendly to anyone who was friendly to them.

Playing to an audience intimately, of course, wasn't hard for me to learn. It's what I did all the time. I tried to set up a one-to-one relationship between me and every individual in the room. This is what Don saw. The only job I had was how to make it work when I could not get the "feel of bodies in a room," and the audience could not, if it felt like it, reach out and touch me.

After thinking about it for quite a long time, I decided that what I had to do was to pretend that the camera was a person and work to it, talk to it as if it were alive and responding to me. This was just the opposite of what motion picture directors told you. In the one picture I'd worked in up to the time I started on TV, I'd been told never to look at, or into, the camera.

That's just exactly what I did when I got on TV. I looked it right in its one big eye just the way I'd look you in the eye if you were sitting talking to me. That's why, when I winked, everyone in the whole television audience could see for themselves that I was winking right at them.

To this day I have people who come up to me and say, "You used to wink at me on television, and I used to wink right back." Then they laugh a kind of embarrassed laugh.

I try to put them at their ease by saying, "I know. I saw you." For some reason that makes a big hit. We have something going between us that nobody else knows anything about.

What was funny is this. When I was treating the camera as a person, I began to believe it myself. If, during rehearsal, I happened to bump into it, I'd say, "Excuse me." Really. Of course, if I bumped into it during a show I also said the same thing. And if I bumped into it, that was that. TV was all live . . . no tape . . . in those days. We couldn't go back and shoot it over. We made a lot of mistakes and all those people watching (who knew that they too made a lot of mistakes) loved us for the fact that we were human.

To this day when I do any work in television I have to be constantly careful not to allow myself to be "over-produced." On the stage, my shows are simple. Just me and a piano and a few hundred thousand dollars worth of clothes. No scenery. No dancing girls. And that's the idea I always want to keep in my TV appearances. I don't want to wind up looking like a speck way down there on the stage somewhere, because some director wanted to get arty.

Naturally there was more to the intimate relationship I created than just winking and treating the camera like a person. I talked to the viewers as if they were my friends, my next door neighbors. We had a kind of over-the-back-fence relationship. I showed them my pets. I talked about my mother and my sister and my brother. My family became everyone's family, sort of.

I modestly say that the first TV appearances were nothing short of sensationally successful. The first year I was on television I won two Emmys. Those are television's awards similar to the motion picture's Oscars. Gee, I'd like to win one of *those*. I have an empty space at home just waiting for Oscar. It looks awful, empty.

One of the Emmys was for the best variety show on TV and the other was for the best new talent on TV. As a result of those first few live television shows we were emboldened to go into film and syndicate the show. I did a series of one hundred seventeen (there's that seventeen again) programs that played in over two hundred areas throughout the United States and Canada and in twenty countries around the world, to an audience of over 45,000,000 people. Believe me it takes some strong eye muscles to wink at 45,000,000 people every week.

There were two interesting things about that syndicated TV show. One was that in spite of the fact that it was on film, it was actually a "live" show, not a carefully edited show. We made no retakes, we filmed the mistakes just as we would have done using electronic cameras with no opportunity to stop and go back and shoot it over. We had to use film. There was, as yet, no video tape. Actually we did use electronic cameras and a live audience, as well as the film cameras. But if I perspired I just mopped away the perspiration with a handkerchief as I do on the stage. Or if I made some kind of a language slip . . . mispronounced a word or committed a grammatical error . . . I just excused myself and corrected what I'd said. It was just the way anything would happen in a family situation. And I came across as a human being, not some sort of a facsimile person, the way some performers do in shows that are filmed and refilmed, and edited and cut and fixed up until they have about as much humanity as a plastic puppet.

The personal, intimate touch of early TV has been replaced by elaborate, synthetic glamor, but a little of that goes a long way.

You have to know how to use it, carefully, like oregano in cooking. And while, in terms of grand dining, a lot of television today is comparable to Chateaubriand, that glorious and supreme form of steak, there are still a lot of folks who prefer good homey hamburgers, hot dogs or spaghetti and meat balls.

So I made sure that all my shows, although they were on film, were very "live." They were so "live," they ran for almost eight years. By then I was so overexposed that audiences almost knew every word I said and every piece I played.

But my desire for simple production techniques did one very important thing. It left the shows "timeless." There was no scenery and stuff that might date them. Certainly my costumes wouldn't. And another thing good about my simple life on TV is that it made it possible to produce the shows at an unbelievably low cost. Week after week we brought them in at ten or twelve thousand dollars. Once I think we went as high as sixteen thousand. I guess we got a little more elaborate than we should have. But, simple as they were, those shows today would cost ten times what they cost us then.

There are lots of reasons for this. One big one is that everything has gone up . . . even my salary. Besides that, there's so much stress on what they call "production values" that soon the scenery becomes more important than the performer. One thing I'll never need is scenery that's fancier than what I'm wearing.

There's an old show business saying, "Nobody ever walks out of a theater whistling the scenery." I'll go along with that.

Every once in a while someone says to me, "Wouldn't it be wonderful if you could bring back those old TV shows you did?"

Well, it would be wonderful, I think, when the right moment rolls around. It's still a little too early for nostalgia on television. First radio has to finish its turn.

It would not only be wonderful, but to bring back my old shows would be entirely possible. Being on film, they're all there, ready to go. We could run them just as they are or we could do a little reshooting to update some of the pop tunes and take out references that are possibly dated and wouldn't mean anything anymore. But there aren't very many of those, if any. So be patient. They're ready when the time comes, and I think it will.

The old *I Love Lucy* shows are still running, timeless and wonderful examples of Lucille Ball's comedy magic and Desi Arnaz's charm, which were what made *I Love Lucy* not only the most popular, but also the most highly honored show of those early television years.

I feel the same way about Jackie Gleason's great *Honeymooner* sketches. I think a lot of people will agree that they'll never grow old. They are basic expressions of human nature, and I can enjoy seeing them again and again. And speaking of Jackie Gleason, in a book about early television, *How Sweet It Was*, which takes its name from Jackie's famous catch phrase, Jackie said, "How sweet it *is.*" The book has a picture of me, wearing a very conservative dinner jacket, and half of George's head, the half that leans on the fiddle. What the book says about my show follows. The italics are mine.

LIBERACE
(Full Name Wladziu Valentino Liberace) had a mouthful of luminescent teeth... [*That's not true. My teeth have never lit up! Yet!!!*]... a scalp full of wavy blonde hair, a silky voice, sequin-festooned costumes and a flamboyant piano style which placed as much emphasis on how the pianist looked as on how he sounded. He also had, through the fifties, an idolatrous audience consisting mostly of older women who, apparently, felt the urge to mother him... [*More likely they admired me because I admired my mother and they liked that. . . .*]
He started with a Los Angeles television show in 1951, went national in 1952 ... [*that's when I replaced Dinah Shore for the summer*]...and began filming a syndicated series in 1953 ... [*That's what I've just been telling you about. The piece goes on to describe my candelabra and my brother and then says*]... All celebrities are subject to ridicule but none more vicious than that which was directed at Liberace. He accepted most of it with good grace (though he did sue a British columnist, Cassandra, for libel) [*That whole story comes later*]...His favorite answer to his critics was "I cried all the way to the bank."

It was, incidentally, in San Francisco that I coined that phrase and to this very moment it shows up in almost everything that's written about me. I almost used it as the title for this book. But I think a title should tell what the book is about and this book is about me not my money.

If writers have to fall back on some line about me, I'd rather have them remember one that was in a review of a show in Philadelphia. A man named Brookhauser said, in the Philadelphia *Inquirer*, "He was television's first matinee idol in the old sense of the word . . . Frances X. Bushman, Wallace Reid, John Barrymore . . . and he remains, perhaps, the only such idol in its expanding history."

Another line I like is, "Liberace is no Rubinstein, but then, neither is Rubinstein any Liberace." I'll bet Rubinstein is glad. Personally, I'd like to be both of us.

I think it's all very nice, and just because I played one night for seventeen people in an empty hotel room on an island across the harbor from San Diego.

That ought to be the finish of that chapter. But I'd like to do what I do in my shows. After it's all over I give an encore that could be called a whole new show in itself. It's a come-on, of course. But they don't call me "Mr. Showmanship" for nothing.

I guess I'm the only performer who ever graduated from television to radio. Most of them came into TV from being on the air when pictures had to be painted in words that made you "see" the most wonderful things in your imagination. Whenever anything is a success in one medium someone wants to put it into another. Books become plays and movies. Nowadays, plays and movies also become books. Everything becomes a television show. And, finally, a packaged game.

Well, the success of my TV shows made my producers want to make them into of all things, radio shows, and that's what I did. Everything the same but no pictures. In some countries these shows are still being broadcast. It's funny, occasionally when I'm traveling abroad, to turn on radio and hear a show I recorded back in the 1950's. But I never had a network radio show.

Want to know why? Everything was all set. My managers and my agent were very happy. Even I was very happy, because radio is a lot easier to do than TV. Just a couple of days ago I heard a commentator on the radio saying that the reason President Nixon is using radio more and more—much more than recent Presidents—is because it takes less of his valuable time to prepare for. "And besides," the commentator said, "he can wear his reading glasses."

Everything was ready to tape my network radio show. "We will do the show straight through," the director said, "and then we'll put in the commercials later." When "later" came they handed me the copy I had to read to lead into the advertising spot that a regular announcer was to read. I looked at the line in amazement. I just didn't believe it. I handed it back to the producer saying, "Very funny. Now give me the right copy."

"That's it," he said.

"I won't read this. I don't have to say things like that."

"Yes you do. Read your contract. That's your sponsor."

"I won't do it."

There was a big crisis meeting, and I was told that if I didn't read the line I'd lose the show.

"I'd rather lose the show than lose the respect of half the people who listen to me and come to see my shows," I said. "If they want to cancel me, let them." They did!

The line was—and I still wouldn't read it on the air because to me it's the depth of bad taste—"Girls, do you have briar patch legs?"

I've never felt that it was right to call upon a performer, an artist of any kind, to sell a product or a service that he doesn't believe in; or to try to sell something he really believes in, in some way that is contrary to his style and personality. I think it damages artistic integrity. I know I would have suffered audience resentment if I had said those awful words about "briar patch legs." I realize that advertisers do that sort of thing for its shock value and to get themselves talked about. But it's the kind of bad-taste hard sell that just isn't my cup of tea.

It's not that I'm against commercials. I've done hundreds of them, but it has always been very soft sell done with sincerity and believability, reflecting my true feelings about the product. I get the commercials to sound like me in the same way that Arthur Godfrey did on his long running radio show. I never read the script some advertising writer wrote. How could he or she know how I would talk? So I'd have them give me a rough outline of the points they'd like to have me make, and then I'd make them in my own words, in my own phrases, in short, in my own way.

On my syndicated TV shows I had over 200 sponsors ranging all the way from cookies and crackers to funeral parlors. And I never ran into any problems with any of them doing commercials my way. After what happened once with a Drano commercial, which I'll tell about later, I even insist on supervising the placing of every commercial on any show I may do.

While I was always very careful about the content of each show, there was one thing that none of us really knew about in those early, exciting days of television. Nobody had yet learned the danger of overexposure. And that's what I suffered from during the great years of my syndicated show. People literally got tired of seeing my face on the screen no matter what I did.

For example WJZ in New York City—it's now WABC-TV and a much different type of station than it was then—ran the show twice a day five days a week. Naturally, with our one hundred seventeen shows, we didn't have enough product to support that kind of programming so some of our shows were seen fourteen, sixteen, eighteen times a year. Take it from one who found out the hard way, that's too often.

The result was a monster slump in my popularity and the show's disappearance from the air. Then came another slump that I'm surprised I ever recovered from.

I made some mistakes. I took some bad advice. My lawyer, the late John R. Jacobs, Jr., reasoned that because this overexposure was making great holes in my box-office draw on the road, it would be better to lay off for awhile. Following this line of argument he said that since I wasn't traveling, booking concerts, what did I need a manager for? He said he could do everything a manager did, and at his urging I severed my connection with Seymour.

MCA, my agents at that time, were the hottest in the entertainment field, for everyone but me. So when Don Fedderson came to Jacobs with the suggestion that I do a daytime television show, just to keep me busy while I was recovering from my attack of overexposure, Jacobs talked it over with the people at MCA, and they thought it was a great idea.

In view of what had happened to my popularity, my new "brain trust" decided I should have an entirely new image for this proposed daytime series.

It was finally produced by Don Fedderson and an MCA executive named Gil Rodin. Gil had been Bob Crosby's manager. It was while a sax man with Ben Pollak's Dixieland group, that Rodin convinced the rest of the band, (when Ben decided to quit) to get Bob Crosby to front their outfit. And that's how Bob Crosby's Bobcats were born.

Because of his wide background in the pop music field, and because he had been co-producer of the Bob Crosby successful daytime show, Rodin was selected as producer. The image he and

Don dreamed up for me was the direct opposite from what I'd had. They cut my hair very short, put me in Brooks Brothers suits and shirts with button-down collars. I was hardly able to play the piano because my hands were always so full of detergent boxes which I was obliged to hold up and try to sell. This show almost put me entirely out of show business. When it failed, which was quickly but not soon enough, I not only couldn't get any concert bookings, I couldn't get any TV bookings either.

Finally I saw the light. I'd been doing well when I was with Seymour. When I left him I began to go from bad to worse until I found myself playing in a second-rate club in Indianapolis where only a few years before I'd made $15,000 in one night. I only mention this money because I doubt if that club made that much profit in a whole year.

Finally I called Seymour at home. Billie, his wife, answered and said he was playing bridge but that she was sure he'd want to talk to me. I was immediately glad to hear he wasn't angry.

After a few short friendly greetings, "How've you been?" "What are you doing," I got down to telling him that I hadn't been doing well at all. He knew this because that sort of thing is never a secret in show business. And I asked him if he'd meet with John Jacobs, the lawyer who had talked me into getting rid of him, and work out a new management deal.

A few days passed and the next time we talked Seymour told me that the deal Jacobs had offered him was unacceptable. "I don't think he really wants me around," Seymour said. So I, personally, took over the arrangements, and Seymour's been with me ever since.

Almost immediately he turned my career around, got it on the right track, got me back in Vegas where I hadn't played for several years, and at this writing I am doing as well as I've ever done in my life. I could be doing even better if I wanted to work harder and steadier.

That's one of the reasons I'm not doing a TV show. I make enough guest appearances on TV to promote my concerts and that's really all I need. It's confining and exhausting to do a regular, big new television show week after week. And often you spend more in time and energy than you can possibly make back in hard cash.

Fortunately, the "cash" is the last thing I have to think of now.

But for the businessmen who may be reading this and like to know a little about the financial side of any business, here are some figures. When I did my first local TV shows in Los Angeles, I got $1,000 a show, which represented a week's work. Within two years after the one hundred and seventeen syndicated programs were released, I'd cleared $7,000,000. That comes to about $60,000 a show and that was over ten years ago when $60,000 was worth a lot more than it is today. Any CPA will tell you that's not bad appreciation on my original investment. And what I'm now getting in Las Vegas, and in concerts all over the world, makes even that $60,000 pale by comparison.

I hasten to add that all that television money does not include the TV shows I've done abroad, not only in England, where I was honored to be on the first Command Performance ever televised, but also in Australia and the Republic of South Africa. I even did a series of ten shows in England for the ATV British Network. They've been played all over the British Commonwealth and finally in America. They were all in color, of course, although some of the Commonwealth countries didn't as yet have color TV. I thought they were pretty good shows, but the thing that I like most about making them was that while I was over there doing it I became acquainted with Mr. and Mrs. Richard Burton. You must know the name, he's the actor who married Francis Taylor's daughter Elizabeth.

I was staying at the Dorchester Hotel and had just come home from a shopping trip. (Have you ever been to the silver vaults in London? They're marvelous!) I stepped into the waiting elevator at the Dorchester, and as I turned around I saw the elevator man close the door right in the faces of two approaching guests. I said to him, "Do you realize you just slammed the door on Elizabeth Taylor and Richard Burton! Would you please go right down and pick them up."

He said, "That's all right, sir. I'll be going right down to get them as soon's I drop you, sir."

I said, "No! Please pick them up immediately. I don't want them to think that I might have told you to close the door on them. I don't want them to think that I don't want anyone to ride in an elevator with me." I know some performers who *are* that way. They're afraid of getting trapped. I'm not. In fact, I kind of like talking to people.

Grudgingly he reversed the car and returned to where he'd

picked me up. When he opened the door, just as I'd said, there stood the Burtons and in they walked.

I quickly apologized for the operator's actions. You'd think I was the manager of the hotel. I said I hoped they didn't think that going up alone was my idea.

Inwardly I was so excited I was afraid they'd hear my heart beating. The only reason I don't actually carry a little autograph book with me and ask stars like the Burtons for their autographs is because I know they'd think I was putting them on.

Elizabeth was immediately very sweet and charming and recalled that we'd met a few years earlier at a Hollywood party. I remembered, but I was flattered that she did too, because there were so many people at that party I didn't think she could possibly remember anything about it or anyone there, particularly me. Then she introduced me to Richard and by this time we'd stopped at their floor. We kept the elevator waiting for quite a little time while we chatted and finally Richard said, "Let's not hold up the whole hotel any longer. Would you like a drink? Please say yes."

I knew he probably wanted a drink, too, and who am I to refuse Richard Burton? So I said, "That's very kind of you. I'd love one."

With my arms still full of packages, I got off and went with them to their suite. She immediately excused herself. When she came back in a few minutes she was wearing a beautiful kaftan. Then we lifted our drinks and began to get acquainted. I knew Richard would be interested and maybe a little unhappy to hear about the chorus of Welsh miners who got all fixed up to do a Command Performance and then had it called off on them. I told him how these men cried and he said, "We're a sentimental lot."

"That's right," Elizabeth agreed.

"Hard but sentimental," Richard added.

"That's right," said Elizabeth. Then they both laughed at some private joke they had. They were great. Good host. Lovely hostess. And I listened like a college freshman as they told me story after funny story of the things that had happened to them in their two sensational show business careers.

Time passed so quickly I was afraid I'd overstayed my welcome and was possibly interfering with their plans for the evening so I tried to excuse myself but they insisted I stay and have dinner with them. Well. This was just too good to be true and after getting a lot of assurance that I wasn't intruding, I finally accepted.

We went to a marvelous London restaurant—very elegant, very

107]

private (I wouldn't dare mention the name of it) it's so exclusive, so chic . . . and so expensive. Honestly. I've been to some very fine restaurants all over the world. But this place impressed me so I could feel my mouth hanging open in awe and admiration.

Every dish that was served to us was surrounded and garnished with fresh flowers. Everything that came to the table looked like a gorgeous corsage. Imagine a corsage of saddle of lamb. Whenever I'm in London I go back there. It's my favorite restaurant because I not only love flowers . . . I love good food, and they have it and know how to cook it. But even more than that, I like it because it holds a happy memory of my first exciting meeting with two of my favorite people, Elizabeth and Richard Burton. If I ever do a talk show of my own, they'll be my first guests if I can possibly get them.

7

Whenever I happen to meet Shelley Winters we eventually get to talking about what I laughingly call my career in motion pictures. I have to admit that no one is now, nor have they ever been, battering down my door to overwhelm me with a fabulous contract to star in a $10,000,000 film epic. I think there are several reasons for this.

First, I have passed the age where I could be cast as a handsome leading man, and even when I was *at* that age the idea never occurred to anyone.

Second, although I think that if someone came up with the right character, I could make a very different kind of villain, the idea has yet to enter anyone's mind. Come to think of it, I did play a villian in a two-part *Batman* episode. The kids loved it.

So all that's really left for me, and all I ever did in films, except when I played the prissy coffin salesman in *The Loved Ones,* is some kind of guy who plays the piano. As far as I know the only piano players who ever got anywhere in pictures are the late Oscar Levant and José Iturbi.

I can't exactly see myself slipping comfortably into one of those Oscar Levant roles. I'm too healthy and too happy. I think I'm more the Iturbi type even to the extent that we both use a Baldwin piano. So if MGM ever decides to remake any of the films José starred in, I'm ready.

I'll even give some film maker an idea. Rewrite *The Maltese Falcon* with a girl playing the part Humphrey Bogart played, maybe

Ann-Margret or Raquel Welch, and let me have the Sydney Greenstreet part as a man who collects pianos. He is trying to locate the fabulous all jade instrument that disappeared from the palace of a famous maharajah. When the guests enter the room for coffee and brandy the piano is missing.

I think that ought to be enough to give any writer a start.

Because our family was always in need of money the thought of ways to get it has always been one of my motivating forces. While I prefer to work at what I like to do, after I've determined what *that* is, the next step is working out ways of making money at it.

I thought I was doing fairly well for a kid of my age from West Milwaukee, when I got a job as intermission pianist at Ciro's, a night club on The Strip in Hollywood. Now I could practically drop a piano straight down from my home in the Hollywood Hills and have it land right on the spot where Ciro's used to be.

Although I don't think any performer who works in the Hollywood area is ever quite without the idea that maybe some day some smart casting director will discover him, I must say *that* idea hadn't yet entered *my* head. I was still so wrapped up in being a good piano player that nothing else was on my mind except getting as much money as a good piano player could possibly earn.

Then one day my agent, at that time it was a fellow named Bill White, phoned me and said, "Play just as good as you can tonight."

"I always play as good as I can," I told him.

"Then tonight, play better."

That's the way agents talk. "What's so special about tonight?"

"A producer is coming over to hear you play."

"So what? Every night the room is full of producers. If you want to thrill me, tell me a musician is coming to hear me play."

So, about ten o'clock, Bill leads me over to a table and introduces me to Michel Kraike and his wife, Jane.

"Mike's interested in you for a part in a picture out at Universal-International," Bill said.

"I didn't say that, Bill," Mike laughed. "I said I'd like to hear Mister Liberace . . ."

"Just call me Lee," I said.

"I'm just interested in hearing him play and seeing how he looks at the piano."

To break the tension, I said, "I look different at different kinds of pianos."

"What do you mean?" Mike asked.

"Well, put me at a big concert grand, and I look much grander than I look sitting in front of an apartment-sized upright."

Everyone laughed politely. We talked for a little while and I was crazy to find out what sort of part Mike had in mind. But he wouldn't say anything and pretty soon I had to go back to the piano. I'm sure I tried to play much mellower, much flashier, and much more brilliantly than I'd ever played before. Wouldn't anyone?

When I finished the set, I went back to the table and Bill was alone. "The Kraikes said to say good night and thank you."

"Thank me? For what?"

"For the drinks you bought them."

"Oh. I didn't know I'd bought them any but they're welcome."

The whole incident was so casual that I really didn't give it another thought. Then, about a week later, Bill called to tell me to meet him out at Universal in Mike Kraike's office. Mike wanted Louis Lipstone, who was in charge of music, to hear me play.

"What kind of music do they want to hear?"

"Mike said to play anything you thought would show you off to advantage."

I figured if they wanted me to play the piano they must want me for the part of a pianist. That wasn't too hard to figure out. Besides, why in the world would they want me for any other kind of part? I didn't know whether I should play some pop stuff or something classical.

I said to myself, there are a million very flashy jazz and boogie woogie pianists playing the lounges and clubs around town. If they wanted something like that the chances are they'd have picked one of them. So I cut and made a six-minute arrangement of a Liszt concerto and played that.

"Forget it," said Bill. "Why'd you have to play that long-hair thing anyway! It went on forever!"

"You didn't tell me . . . and I figured. . . ."

"What do they know from that stuff" he interrupted. " 'Stormy Weather,' maybe, or even some 'Rhapsody in Blue' might have done it." He then clammed up, and we drove back to Hollywood in silence.

The next thing I knew there was another call from Kraike to come in and read some lines for him. It turned out that I'd been lucky in selecting what I played for the audition. The part, to quote Mike, "Is not a very challenging one. It will make no heavy demands on your acting ability."

When I read it, I realized he was right. I was supposed to be a concert pianist who, for some reason I've now forgotten, (probably because his girl jilted him or something—that's the way all those B-pictures went) was on the beach in the South Seas.

Although, I understand, there was some front-office questioning about what I should play in the picture, Kraike and Lipstone finally agreed that since I'd made the special arrangement I auditioned, I should be allowed to play that.

A long time later I found out from Mike what finally went on behind the scenes before the film was released. First, William Goetz, who was one of the executive producers at Universal, thought my number was too long. "Who's going to sit still for that much Carnegie Hall stuff?" he asked Mike. "Cut it."

Mike explained that the number had already been cut down from a much longer work and that it would be impossible to cut it anymore without ruining it. "As it is, it'll ruin the picture," Mr. Goetz said.

Finally, Mike, who was on my side all the way, got Goetz to compromise, saying, "Let's leave it in until we sneak preview the picture, and we'll see how it goes." So that's what they did.

"It was the strangest thing at the preview," Mike told me a long time later. "Bill Goetz and I were sitting together, making notes on audience reactions. And when your number was followed by heavy applause, Goetz, who hadn't been looking at the screen because he was writing something, turned to me and asked, 'What happened?' "

"What happened!" I said, "They *liked* it!"

"Yeah. I can hear that. But *what* did they like? What did I miss?"

"You didn't miss anything. They liked the *music*." Of course it stayed in!

Apparently, Mr. Goetz had been so busy making notes on how to cut the music he was hearing, he never did see my acting. About that, I got a lot of help from Shelley.

A good accompanist can usually make a singer sound a lot better than he may be. In the same way, a good actress, if she wants to, can help the person she's acting with. And that's what Shelley did for me. She must have. The picture got decent reviews. Nobody raved. But nobody knocked it.

If you want to form your own opinion, it's on the late, late show all the time. You'll be amazed when you see me. I, who wear such fancy clothes in my act, play a beachcomber-bum in tattered pants and shirt.

Shortly after the picture was released I got a chance to show Mike my appreciation for getting me my first movie job. The employees of Universal-International Studios had a club that put on a little show every Christmas, and they asked me to be in it.

When I came to my closing number I said, "I now want you to hear a little piece I composed in honor of Mike Kraike, whose wife Jane is now in the hospital where she had a little girl. The baby hasn't been named yet but the name of the piece is 'Lullaby.' " It took Mike completely by surprise.

I remember the first time I met Seymour Heller's wife. I was still working at Ciro's and she wasn't his wife as yet. He'd proposed to her, several times, I think. She hadn't given him her answer. But in romance as in business Seymour hangs right in there till he gets what he wants.

Well, this evening, it was shortly after Seymour and I had gotten together and I think just before *South Sea Sinner* was released, he had arranged a birthday party at Ciro's for this girl, Billie. She had been his secretary but had graduated to being the president of the Frankie Laine Fan Club. At that time Seymour also handled Frankie Laine.

Well, to make a long story short, it must have been a very successful party because after I'd done my show and they'd brought in the cake and cut it, Billie told Seymour that if he asked her to marry him one more time she'd say yes. He did and she did and they're still living happily ever after.

The reason I'm telling you all this is because Seymour told me later that it was the way I sang "September Song" that convinced Billie she shouldn't make Seymour wait any longer. I guess she came to the conclusion that although they were both young it was wrong to wait till neither "had time for the waiting game."

I was so touched by the fact that I had sort of played Cupid to this marriage that when we were doing our syndicated TV show I included the party sequence at Ciro's, starring both Seymour and Billie. But there was one thing different. The table we used was a very high one. It had to be, because by that time Billie was pregnant with their daughter Elizabeth, who, with Bruce and David makes up their lovely family.

Carried on the wave of enthusiasm that followed the release of *South Sea Sinner*, I didn't make another picture for seven years. The motion picture industry, always anxious to cash in on anybody's success, figured that the excellent reception I was getting from the television audience indicated a popularity that would draw people into theaters. I thought this was funny. Even before my TV show started I had been drawing people into theaters to see me in person. But, I thought, now that I could be seen on television for free, why should people buy tickets to see pictures of me?

The film Warner Brothers finally came up with was another winner like *South Sea Sinner*. It was called *Sincerely Yours* and it, too, gets regular late night airing on the telly.

Sincerely Yours was sort of a birthday present. We started shooting it on my birthday and Dorothy Malone and Joanne Dru, who were my costars in the picture, and everybody on the set, gave me a great big party with a cake and everything. I loved it, but the Warner Brothers hated it, because it held up shooting for a whole day.

Again I was cast as a concert pianist. It's funny that in the first two pictures I made, the character I played was what I started out to be in real life, the kind of musician Dad wanted me to be but which I never became, because I had convinced myself that the life of a concert artist is a very lonely one. There are hours and hours of practice. When you do play for people, you play for comparatively few.

The character I played in *Sincerely Yours* was even more lonely than most concert pianists, because he was threatened with deafness. I'm sure the guy who wrote the script was influenced quite a lot by the life of Beethoven.

I'd always been interested in reading stories about how this or that star didn't use a double in the shooting of some scenes. Or how somebody learned how to play the violin or the banjo or something in order to give a realistic performance. Well, I didn't have to learn how to play the piano in order to depict this pseudo-Beethoven character I was playing, but I did do one thing that—now that I think of it—perplexes me. I learned how to read lips, as any deaf person would naturally do. But why?

There is no way in the world that you can show the difference between a person really reading lips and one who has just learned a part, which I had done.

But I'm glad I learned how. Now when I'm on stage working, I can look around the audience and if someone is talking, I know what that person's saying. Sometimes I want to stop playing and answer her. It would be fun to do that sometime, just to see what would happen. And it would certainly keep my audience quiet for the rest of the show.

I often think, when there's a noisy audience, how wonderful it would be not to hear them and to go on not being bothered by the extraneous sounds. And then I realize how awful it would be. Silence is only golden when it can be broken at will. Those who suffer endless silence, as the deaf do, seem to me to be locked in a prison, denied the one thing I can't imagine living without, music.

Yet I know, because they've told me, that many deaf people are able to enjoy music through feeling the vibrations. I experienced one of the greatest revelations of this one week when I co-hosted the Mike Douglas television show. Among our guests was Anne Bancroft who had played Helen Keller's teacher in both the Broadway production and the motion picture of *The Miracle Worker*. Anne brought with her some students from a school for the deaf, dumb and blind. Can you imagine what it must be like deprived of those three senses, isolated in a dark, silent world, unable to say what you think, ask for what you want? The thought makes me shudder.

But because of Helen Keller and her great work, these young people could understand and communicate, to a remarkable degree, with those around them, and they were living what to me seemed courageous lives that had become, to them, just normal routine.

When Anne Bancroft introduced me to one of these students, a young lady, the moment she "heard" my name, she was able to say quite plainly, "I am one of your greatest fans. I never miss your TV shows." Well . . . I didn't know how to react to such a remark from a person so handicapped. I guess I was speechless. It wasn't until much later, when the show was over, that I was able to ask Anne how that young lady who could neither see nor hear, could get anything at all from a television show.

She explained that these people's senses had been developed to such a degree that they were able to experience a great deal of what is heard on television and radio through wave vibrations. Later I conversed with the young lady by having her touch my lips as I spoke.

When people can overcome such devastating handicaps, those of us who have all our faculties and senses intact should not take for granted the beauty that's available to us.

We should consciously and actively appreciate, become aware of the world of music, the magnificence of nature, the fine art that generations of artists and craftsmen have bequeathed us.

In almost every city of the world, so many things of beauty are free; works of architecture, museums of art, promenades and esplanades, woodland areas and beaches, that it is almost sacrilegious not to enjoy them to the fullest. No one in the world has any right, ever, to be bored, because it's true that the best things in life *are* free: Sight, sound and everything those senses open to us.

It's nice to have money and fame. It beats poverty and obscurity all to hell. But one thing I never want to become is an unhappy millionaire, nor do I want to be the richest piano player in the best cemetery in town. And so I don't work as much as I could. This gives me time to enjoy the wonderful life I see around me, to hear the beautiful sounds there are and to replenish myself at the bountiful fountain of beauty this world provides all who will look and listen.

One thing I almost forgot about *Sincerely Yours* is the practical joke Mario Lanza played on the producer, Henry Blanke, while we were shooting the film. You will always find practical jokers where clever, talented (and maybe jealous) people find themselves with too much time on their hands. The Hollywood scene is full of actors, musicians, writers and directors who occasionally have to work off their aggressions (and their anger at not working) and do so by playing jokes on, of all people, their friends.

Henry had produced a film called *Serenade* starring Lanza, that remarkable singing star who lit up the movie horizon for a little while before, I think, he literally ate himself to death.

While Lanza was not working and Blanke was busy with me on *Sincerely Yours* he'd come on the set and sit around being "helpful." I was willing for anyone to help me. It was only my second picture, I had a percentage of it, so naturally I was doubly anxious for it to be good. I wasn't making trouble for anyone. I never do. Except myself.

But I'd notice that every morning when the company met on the set Henry would look at me in a funny way and ask me questions that he could easily see I didn't understand. There grew up a strained atmosphere between us that neither could explain until the picture was nearly over. Then it all came out.

Every night Mario Lanza, who could imitate anybody's voice, inflection and tone perfectly, would call Blanke and, using my voice, call him all kinds of names and bawl him out, telling him what he did wrong and what he should have done.

Of course when the truth came out we all had a good laugh but only Mario thought it was funny. And only Mario knew that the joke wasn't over. Henry had his house up for sale and finally sold it to an order of nuns. Periodically, Mario would call the house and say things that shocked the good Sisters right out of their quiet habits.

On the last day of shooting, Jack Warner came on stage to say good-bye to Dorothy Malone, Joanne Dru, Bill Demarest, Henry and the other members of the cast and me. There was the usual exchange of gifts that always takes place when they wrap up a film. We were all standing around talking, and Jack asked me how I liked being a movie star. I said I thought it beat starving to death.

Then he asked, "What are you doing now that the picture's finished?"

I said, "Well, I think I'll take a little rest and then go back to playing the piano and doing my act. Unless you have some other ideas for me?" I threw in that last little hint as an afterthought.

The hints didn't work . . . very well. I've only been in one picture since then, Tony Richardson's wonderful film of Evelyn Waugh's satire on the undertaking business as it's operated in Southern California and, I suspect, every place else in the world. I played a cameo role of a coffin salesman and while I didn't get an Oscar, I didn't get panned.

Tony Richardson had enjoyed tremendous success with a previous picture, *Tom Jones,* based on Fielding's eighteenth-century novel, one of England's first, *The History of Tom Jones, a Foundling.* It was a rather ribald story and Tom was probably the first antihero in literature. Some of the scenes in this film were highly suggestive, but Tony did them in such a subtle way that no one was really offended. Actually they could not even be compared with some of the things quite commonly seen on the screen in the 1970's.

Since *Tom Jones* had been so successful, it was only natural that Tony employ some of the same techniques when he came to shoot *The Loved One.* What he didn't realize was that the Fielding novel was accepted by everyone as an old classic while the Waugh novel was a modern satire in what some thought to be dubious taste. People in their snobbish way accepted the former simply because it had been around a long time while rejecting the latter because it hadn't been around long enough to assure them of its worth.

The result was that many of the scenes in *The Loved One* were cut out because they were considered pornographic (at that time), and this watered down the picture disastrously when it was finally released to the public.

Just as it's impossible to slice important movements from a musical work without in some way injuring it, so you can't do it with a novel, a play or a motion picture. You have to let the artist's concept stand or fall on its own. If it falls because it's been cut and rearranged, as it is liable to do, the fault is not that of the artist who created it. I think Tony made a good picture that suffered from mutilation.

My part as a casket salesman only lasted a few minutes, but it made its point and I got very good notices from critics who, as usual, were surprised that I did it well.

I guess *The Loved One* was just about five years ahead of its time. It was frankly satirical and, as conceived, a little raunchy. But by today's standards it was not the pornographic work some thought it to be when it was made. I think if it were put back together in its original form and reissued it might be more of a success than it was when it was originally released.

Personally, as I look at it now, I doubt, if the film had been a really big success, whether it would have increased my following since the people who came to see the movie because I was in it were largely the type who would have been turned off by anything they thought off-color. For instance, Jayne Mansfield had one scene that was completely cut, but as I said, by today's standards the film is about as racy as *The Sound of Music.*

One of the reasons, I guess, that I haven't made any films since *The Loved One* is the nature of the films being made. The need seems to be for nudity, pornographic explicitness and violence. None of these are really my bag. Even some of the so-called "family movies" today sneak in some of the sex stuff and blood letting that passes as "box-office." So I guess I'll wait. I'm no Burt Reynolds. I have to reconcile myself to the fact that I may never do a centerfold for *Cosmopolitan.* Some people are famous for taking off their clothes. I've become famous for wearing them. And I think I'll stick to that.

But the funny part of it is, I truly hate to dress. When I'm relaxing in the privacy of my home in Hollywood or Palm Springs, I just go around in swimming trunks because I love to swim and I love the sun. I truly hate to dress up when I'm not appearing before the public. When I *am,* I want to look like their image of me. Of course, I can't wear my stage clothes on the street, but I will never appear inb public when I'm not well groomed. I wouldn't if I were totally unknown, because I think looking well is part of keeping your self-respect. Anyone who loses that loses everything.

My little hint to Jack Warner about doing another picture didn't get to him. But I was taken aback when he said to me, "Now that you have a little time off, why don't you come to France?"

He actually surprised me so with this, as it turned out, invitation, that I said one of the dumbest things I've ever said in my life. "France? You mean in Europe?"

"Certainly," said Jack. "There's only one France. I have a lovely home down near Cannes. There's room for plenty of guests and I'd like to have you be one of them. I'll show you the time of your life."

"There's nothing I'd like to do better," I said "But I'm not prepared to go. I haven't had the shots I need. I haven't even got a passport."

"That's no problem," Jack said. He made a couple of calls from a phone right there on the stage. One of the still photographers on the set took my passport picture—in white tie and tails which I wore in the last scene. The studio doctor gave me the shots I needed and Jack's office handled all the paper work necessary. The next morning I was on an Air France plane, together with Kirk Douglas and his wife, on my way to Paris.

It's the only way to travel. I was very impressed. Now I have people who handle all my travel details. But then the whole business of having people do most of the routine things for me was a complete novelty. I don't think I'll ever get used to it. I really like to do things for myself and do things for other people. I think a man has to be involved in his own life. That sounds funny but I mean, when you let others do a lot of things for you, that you should do personally, you're really *not* involved in your own life.

Of course our arrival in Paris was no secret. Warner Brothers had arranged for transportation and for us to be met by the press. There was a big cocktail party for the newspaper people and friends, for the Douglases and me. Warner Brothers was killing two birds with one stone. They were plugging the release of *Sincerely Yours* and its impending release in France and the start of the filming of Irving Stone's book *Lust for Life* starring Kirk as the mad painter Vincent van Gogh.

One of the nicest things about this Parisian interlude was that the studio furnished me with one of the prettiest interpreters you ever want to see. Her name was Lynn Renaud. She sang at the Dunes in Las Vegas for years, but at the time she was serving as my interpreter, she was sort of the Marilyn Monroe of France. She went everywhere I went to tell people what I said and tell me what *they* said. And when she wasn't interpreting for me, she was acting as a tour guide. She was wonderful to have around. So, I say again, it's the only way to travel.

When I got to Jack's house I found it was New Year's Eve twenty-four hours of every day. He really lived up to his word and carried on with parties that you just wouldn't believe. I met people whose names I'd been reading in the papers for a long time but didn't really believe existed. I secretly thought Grace Kelly was a myth, even though I'd seen her in pictures with Cary Grant and Bing Crosby. And, of course, I found out that there actually is a Monaco, that it isn't just a pretty little country that someone made up to write a musical comedy about. Naturally I met Princess Grace and Prince Rainier, and I wish I could remember all the other guests who attended the string of parties that were hostessed by Elsa Maxwell, the most famous party giver in the world at that time.

I remember meeting Peter Ustinov for the first time at one of the parties. And Ann Miller. I wandered through the whole thing like Alice in Wonderland at the Mad Hatter's Tea Party.

I was thrilled when Princess Grace asked me to play at a gala she was having for the benefit of the Red Cross. When I wasn't playing, Danny Kaye was singing, dancing and doing all the things he does so well. What a show!

Of course any party has a lot of class if it is held where you can look out over the blue Mediterranean and the harbor and see literally hundreds of expensive yachts with their lights all twinkling. You wonder what's doing on board them. I even found that out.

Jack's daughter, Barbara Warner, was my date for all this partying and she and I were invited on a little trip to St. Tropez for some bouillabaisse aboard Aly Khan's yacht. I had always heard that headquarters for bouillabaisse was Marseilles, but these beautiful people to whom the South of France was as familiar as Hollywood Boulevard was to me, said there was no better bouillabaisse in the world than at this spot in St. Tropez.

So off we went aboard that fabulous yacht. Yacht! It was a liner! You could sail anywhere in the world on her. Young Wladziu was impressed. There was nothing like it in West Milwaukee. Her name was the *Princess Yasmin* after Aly Khan's daughter, whose mother's maiden name was Rita Hayworth.

What a wonderful host. Anything a guest wanted, he got immediately. But mostly, anything you might want had been anticipated. I also got a lot of activity I didn't anticipate on that junket.

8

I f I had remembered what I'd been told, instead of being so impressed, I never would have gone on Aly Khan's boat ride to St. Tropez.

Several years before I started in television, George and I were playing The Empire Room in the Palmer House in Chicago. It was a twelve-week booking. Featured with me on the bill was a young male vocalist who used to sing with Kay Kyser's orchestra, whose name has become an institution on daytime television, Mike Douglas, and the Merrill Abbott Dancers a refreshing group of well-trained and disciplined young and talented girls. Because of the long booking, they designed a rather homelike apartment or suite for me; it even had a "kitchen", which was really a converted bathroom. The tub was covered over with a counter and a refrigerator. To hide the toilet, I placed a card table with a long tablecloth which concealed the plumbing. Knowing how I liked to cook, the publicity department set up a picture story with the women's editor of the Chicago *Tribune* of me preparing a complete dinner for the Abbott Dancers and Mike as my guests. All went fine and the lady editor was very impressed with my culinary talents until she asked me to step behind the card table for a better picture angle, and because of the awkward position I accidentally flushed the toilet! Boy, was I embarrassed, but the very proper lady who was writing the story was amused and even wound up staying for dinner. Even though I was cooking in the rooms (it was cheaper than room service), we were making good money and had high hopes for the future.

One of the things that encouraged these high hopes was that we'd see the same faces night after night. People were coming back to see us again. This makes you feel good. It makes you work harder.

Among our returnees was a man named Ed Hall. Numerology was big in those days and Ed was a famous numerologist. He'd written several books on the subject and I'm told he'd made some prophesies that had come to pass. He had evidence that he'd prevented some people from committing suicide.

His record was very impressive but like the records of all men and women who deal in vague, mystical, occult and esoteric pseudosciences, they're open to question. Just the fact that I automatically wrote "pseudosciences" is an indication of my doubt although I've been given reason to believe.

Ed Hall's regular source of income was the department store business. He was on the staff of Marshall Field & Company, one of the world's greatest stores. And the fact that he was working for them proved that somebody believed in his ability to foresee coming events. His job was to cast numerological charts to determine the best time to hold sales, to figure out on what days certain hard moving items should be heavily plugged in the advertising.

I remember talking about it with George. We agreed that he must have something or hardheaded businessmen wouldn't pay him hard dollars. And there were no doubts in our minds that the managers of Marshall Field were hardheaded businessmen. Anytime you walked into that store, the crowded aisles let you know that the guys who were running it were doing something right.

I tell you all this about Ed because, possibly, if I had remembered what Ed told me one evening during an intermission in the Empire Room, I wouldn't have joined the bouillabaisse expedition to St. Tropez. I'd have stayed as far away from Aly Khan's yacht as I could. Because in a numerology chart Ed had cast for me, he'd predicted a lot of trouble on a yachting trip. After everything was over I remembered he specifically said a yachting trip, not just a boat trip.

Here's what happened.

We were steaming along in the Mediterranean. Champagne was flowing like water and there were buckets full of Iranian caviar. All of a sudden someone had the bright idea that we all should go swimming. Naturally the yacht was supplied with all the swimsuits needed so she was immediately hove to—or whatever you do to stop a yacht—and people began going over the side into the water.

I was never crazy about the idea of jumping off a boat in the middle of the ocean, and I got to thinking about sharks and sting rays and all the other ugly things that inhabit the sea and give so much pleasure to Jacques Cousteau. I'm willing to let him have my share of them. But I didn't want to be a party pooper so I went along with the rest. Pretty soon, there I was climbing down the ladder into the warm, sun-flecked blue water.

Many years ago I discovered that while I might not be any Johnny Weissmuller—he was the Mark Spitz of the day when I made the discovery—I was a terrific floater. I'm very buoyant. It's fantastic! I can float for hours. So whenever I find myself in the water and my feet won't touch the ground, I float.

I found it very relaxing floating out there, looking up at the cloudless sky and listening to everyone around me laughing and splashing like a bunch of kids in a wading pool. Then I must have closed my eyes and dozed off for a little while. Can you imagine that? Asleep in the deep!

Anyway, all of a sudden I realized that I no longer heard any laughing and splashing. I opened my eyes, looked around and there, like an insect on the horizon, was the good yacht *Princess Yasmin*, steaming away from me . . . a long way away from me.

If you stop to think about that situation for a minute and take a moment to think how you'd feel, floating out there all by yourself in the middle of the Mediterranean Sea, you'll only get about half an idea of how I felt. I'd heard that when you're in danger of drowning, your whole life flashes before your eyes. That's how I knew I was in danger of drowning. It does.

"My God," I thought to myself, "as good a floater as I am I can't just go on floating out here all alone—where no one even knows where I am—forever." Then I'd reassure myself that they'd come back for me. Then I'd ask myself, "even if they miss me on board and come back for me, how will they ever be able to find me in this vast expanse of water?" It was very scary.

What had happened was that I'd quietly floated around from the port to the starboard side of the ship (or vice versa) which put me on the opposite side from where everyone was swimming.

When they all came aboard, they naturally thought I did, too. Who counts? Then they all went to their cabins to change clothes and it wasn't until they came back on deck that someone asked, "Where's Lee?" They checked the cabins and then, finally, it dawned on someone that they must have left me in the water.

Naturally the *Princess Yasmin*'s Captain had made a note in the ship's log exactly where we'd stopped for the swim, so he turned around and steamed back to that spot and there I was. You can imagine what a relief it was to me when I saw that ship turning around and coming back. The whole incident only took about an hour. But sixty minutes in the ocean all by yourself . . . nothing around you but a speck in the distance . . . .Believe me, don't try it.

They threw me a life preserver and I came up the boarding ladder feeling a little sheepish and self-conscious, as if it were my fault that they'd forgotten me, my fault that I'd created such a scene.

I tried to laugh it off, saying it was nothing, and went below to change. But when I came back on deck, all dressed, the shock of the whole thing suddenly hit me, I began to tremble all over. They didn't know what to do for me. I guess I had a chill from being in the water so long and the shock and everything. They wrapped me in blankets and when we finally arrived at St. Tropez they carried me ashore to this bouillabaisse place because they said I needed something warm inside me.

I just wish I had some home movies of me all wrapped up in those blankets looking like an enormous papoose with Aly Khan spoon feeding me hot bouillabaisse. Suddenly I started to perspire. It was summer, the blankets, the hot soup and all, and then the shaking stopped and I began to calm down. Just writing about it could start me shaking again. But if you think that was the end of an imperfect day. Wait.

When I was finally calmed down we all decided that I'd had enough fun for one day and instead of taking the long slow trip back to Cannes by boat, they'd send Barbara Warner and me back in the fast motor launch under the command of Aly Khan's son who was about eighteen or nineteen. This was just as well, we figured, because Barbara and I had a dinner engagement at one of Elsa Maxwell's fabulous parties.

As the young Khan began to start the engine of the launch, Barbara and I headed for the boarding ladder, but we didn't get very far. Something went wrong, gasoline fumes or something had formed, and when the motor sparked, the launch literally blew up.

Luckily we weren't aboard it or we would have wound up in the water, which was ablaze with burning gasoline. The young Khan was severely burned, and we were thrown to the deck of the yacht. Clearly it wasn't my day for boating.

Shaken up for the second time in a few hours, I decided I'd had enough of the seagoing life and we found that Barbara and I could get a taxi to take us from St. Tropez around the coast, back to Cannes . . . by land. It was a long trip in an uncomfortable car, but it was better than any boat ride I could think of at that moment.

By the time we arrived at the party in the Carlton Hotel in Cannes the news about everything that had happened had been on the radio. Anytime Aly Khan went anywhere the press followed him and reported anything that happened to him. So when we arrived at the hotel, looking pretty dishevelled, the TV newspeople and the press photographers were waiting for us and for our stories. By the time I reached my room after the party, people had begun calling from the United States to find out what really happened. And I suddenly remembered what Ed Hall had told me that evening years before when he gave me my chart.

For openers the chart said I was born under a numerological sign that meant, put in its simplest terms, that I led a charmed life. Ed tried to clarify this for me by saying, "If you were condemned to face a firing squad and were standing there staring into the muzzles of the ten rifles [I guess he thought I was brave enough to refuse the blindfold], before the commander of the squad could say the word 'Fire!' someone would rush up and say, 'Stop! Free this man!' " The chart even predicted that I might really stand in front of a firing squad. But I'll get to that.

To be honest, I read the chart over and over again, smiling and shaking my head in disbelief at the things it predicted. It said I was going to be known all over the world and that I'd become the matinee idol of television. That was particularly amusing because up to that time I hadn't even *seen* television more than two or three times. So I laid the chart aside convinced that while it was wonderful, it was absurd to think it had any validity. Nevertheless, I liked it. Who wouldn't want to lead a charmed life and become a television idol?

I should add that the chart said some things I hoped would never come true. Funny, I wasn't afraid the good things wouldn't happen. I *knew they wouldn't!* Success, maybe. But triumph!? For a while however, I was convinced I was in for all the bad things. Then the whole incident slipped my mind.

The chart foretold that I would run into danger on a trip to Cuba, a place I had never even considered going. But I did. I made the trip about a year before the yachting incident, and never even connected it with Ed Hall's prophecy until after I returned.

Batista was still Presidente. He invited us to visit Cuba as guests of the government. I never was told exactly why. Our syndicated TV show was playing there and was very popular. Maybe Batista wanted to do something special for his people. Maybe he just wanted to meet me personally. Whatever it was, when you're invited to be the guest of a government you can hardly refuse. Unless you're another government.

I was overwhelmed, astounded, could not believe the reception we got at the airport in Havana. All incoming and outgoing traffic was stopped. The airport was closed. There were salutes with rifles and salutes with little cannons. We got off the plane and marched under an arch of crossed sabers held by cavalry officers all wearing uniforms that put anything I've ever worn to shame. And to top it all off, Ernesto Lecuona had twelve pianos playing "Malaguena." It was beautiful. They sure knew how to flatter a fella.

There was a big reception at the airport, that's one of the reasons they closed it, I guess. They didn't want a lot of tourists trooping through while they were serving champagne and toasting the guest of the country. This was all on Cuban television and was followed by a televised parade to the Hotel Nationale where we were to have the President's suite.

I don't know whether the people turned out of their own accord or whether Batista ordered it, but the highway for the whole fifteen miles from the airport to the hotel was lined with cheering crowds. And as we drove along waving from one side to the other, as if I were running for governor, it all came back to me that the reception seemed to have started in Miami.

As we boarded the Cuban plane in Florida I said to Seymour Heller, "There must be someone very important on this plane. Look at all the military brass." The plane was full of men who looked like doormen at The Plaza but were really high officers in the Cuban army and navy.

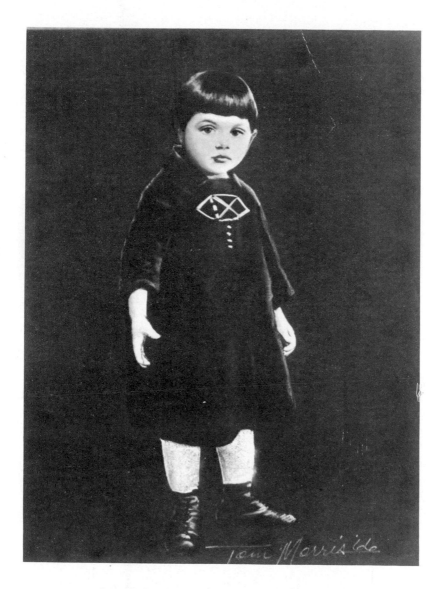

A reproduction in pastels by Toni Morriside
of Wladziu Valentino Liberace at age two.

The high school in Milwaukee Liberace attended.

Lee was a healthy six-footer at seventeen. Graduation picture shows no sign of near brush with death from pneumonia at the age of nine.

Lee posed with fellow graduate at West Milwaukee High's class of '37.

A back injury kept Lee from joining Seabees with George; didn't stop him from entertaining at USO's and in veterans' hospitals.

Liberace in a scene from His Warner Brothers' movie, *Sincerely Yours*.
He was the star of this 1955 film about a concert pianist who goes deaf
just before his long dreamed of Carnegie Hall appearance.

Liberace performing before a capacity crowd at London's Albert Hall.

Liberace, his brother George and their mother Frances on Liberace's first trip to London in 1956.

(Matthews' News and Photo Agency)

Liberace with the young
Shelley Winters in his first
movie appearance in the film,
South Sea Sinner, released in
1950.

Liberace's San Fernando Valley home in the late 1950's. The major attraction here was the piano-shaped swimming pool.

Liberace with friend as guest host of TV series, *Hollywood Palace* in 1965.

Liberace in skit with Andy Williams and Phil Harris.

(Las Vegas News Bureau photo)

Liberace played himself in a special cameo appearance in a film *The Goony Byrds* shot in Las Vegas and featuring chimpanzees.

Liberace on set of London TV program called *Showtime*. Liberace was guest host and this appearance led to his own 1968 variety show, which was also filmed in London.

Liberace as guest co-host on the Emmy Award winning show with blind children.

Liberace on set of 1968 London TV series with star of movie, *Oliver!* Jack Wilde, who played the Artful Dodger.

Liberace discussing costumes on the *Engelbert Humperdinck Show*.

Liberace portrayed an unctuous casket salesman in MGM's *The Loved One* in 1965.

Liberace as he appeared in a guest appearance on the TV series, *Batman*; he played twin brothers, one of whom was good while the other was a villain.

Liberace in one of his frequent appearances on the *Dean Martin Show.*

Liberace in comedy skit with Red Skelton on the *Red Skelton Show.*

Liberace with friend Phyllis Diller in London.

Mae West and Liberace at premiere of *Les Poupees de Paris* in Hollywood.

(AP Wirephoto)

I kept looking around to see what VIP was getting the lavish display of military ceremonies. When we got to Havana and I saw myself walking through the arch of sabers I realized with surprise that the whole show was in my honor. It was sort of embarrassing.

And it became more and more embarrassing. But it was the kind of embarrassment you can learn to live with. What I mean is, no matter where we went—everyone in my party, whether we were in a restaurant for a meal or a department store to buy gifts to take home to our families and friends, when we'd attempt to pay, they wouldn't accept our money.

Until you're someplace where everything is on the house, you have no idea what it's like. The closest I can think of anything like that happening in America is what happens to a really high roller when he shows up in Las Vegas. There it's, "You're a guest of the management." They get it all back later at the table. With us it was, "You can't pay for anything. You're guests of the government." And they didn't get it all back. They wouldn't even let us use our own money to buy chips in the casino.

It was all very flattering but a grown man doesn't like to be escorted everywhere. I felt too old to have a Nanny with me even if the Nanny was the power of the government.

So one evening after all the escorted entertainment was over and we were back in our hotel suite, I said to Seymour, "Wouldn't it be fun just to sneak out and see what this town is all about?"

He said, "I don't know. They seem awfully insistent on the guards. And if they make such a thing of it, there must be a reason." So I didn't say any more. But like the little boy who once ran off and got lost in the Wisconsin State Fair Grounds, I sneaked away all by myself to find out what was doing. I walked around Havana and dropped in on some of the night spots and had a ball.

When the authorities found out about it the next morning, they were terribly upset. I imagine the men who were assigned to guard me had a pretty bad time, having let me get out of their sight. Still I couldn't understand all this. "Why all the fuss?" I asked. "No one bothered me. I had a good time. Everyone was very nice and helpful."

So they said they were glad I was safe and dropped the whole subject because, after all, even a government can't scold its guest for enjoying himself.

Everyone who knows anything about me knows that I enjoy the

trappings of pomp and ceremony. I like things to be regal and exciting. So you can imagine what a time I had when we went to El Presidente's Palace to meet Juan Batista, himself. I'm not a very political person, so I didn't know anything very much about his politics, but I admired the way he lived. I guess it was his politics that made such high living possible. Whatever it was, he sure enjoyed it when he had it.

We did a television show from the Palace all in Spanish. Nobody had yet thought of cue cards, at least in Havana. So I had to learn the whole show in a strange language, by heart.

To help me the government gave me a newspaperman who translated my act into Spanish and then rendered it phonetically so I could memorize it. It was awfully hard to do and I don't think I did it very well. But the people loved it. There were 7,000 of them in the audience. The show was done live. So when I made a mistake, we couldn't go back and shoot it over.

A couple of times my memory went blank and I got stuck. But I was in luck. Maybe it was part of that "charmed life" Ed Hall told me about. A beautiful little Cuban girl who had studied in the United States was playing first violin in the orchestra. I was at the solo piano and she was right behind me. When I got stuck I'd say to her *sotto voce,* "What's the word I'm looking for?" And she'd whisper it in Spanish. That would start me off again. I wish I could remember her name because she saved my life and I got through that Spanish TV show successfully. The first telegram to arrive was from Batista. He was aboard his yacht, but I wasn't invited to visit him there. Obviously that wasn't the yacht that was slated to give me trouble. I had to wait a year.

It was not until I returned to the United States that I found out from the Cuban Consul why the government had kept me under such heavy guard and why they were so concerned when I sneaked out into the streets alone. The Consul called me and said, "You really gave us a lot of headaches when you were in Havana."

I apologized saying I didn't know what I'd done to cause him to say that. He said, "Of course you had no way of knowing, but there had been several threats that if you came to Cuba you would be kidnapped and held for ransom. This would cause an incident that would embarrass the government and they could not take any chances that the threats might really be carried out."

"Why should they want to kidnap me?" I asked.

"Your television show has made you a national hero in my country," the Consul told me, "so you figured to be a ripe personality for a snatch." It was very flattering. But I didn't feel like a national hero. I just felt glad that there had been no "snatch." I remember being amused at the Cuban Consul General's use of American underworld slang. But maybe slang is the same all over the underworld. I don't mean to imply by that that the Consul was a citizen of that world, just that we all enjoy using the colorful language of people we don't know, just as the slang that musicians use has crept into the casual conversation of those who wouldn't know a four bar rest from a flatted fifth.

Again the Consul spoke of how the Cubans appreciated that I spoke to them in Spanish. "Even though you didn't speak perfectly," he said, "you honored them by trying."

I realized years later, when President John F. Kennedy went to Germany, how people take you to their hearts when you speak their language. Just as a thunderous ovation followed when I acknowledged the applause of the Cuban audience by saying, "Muchos gracias, señors y señoras," President Kennedy won the hearts of the West German people when he said, "Ich bin ein Berliner."

One thing that Ed Hall's prophecy didn't mention was airplanes. I probably wouldn't have given this a thought until one night over Buffalo, New York. There was one of those fierce electrical storms that make you think the world is coming to an end. The lightning, as I looked out the window, fascinated, came dangerously close to the plane. And when the copilot came to where I was sitting and with a flashlight tried to look out the window at some part of the wing which I supposed was not functioning properly, I thought to myself, "This is it!"

I began to search my mind for some mention of aircraft in my numerology chart; I could think of none and reconciled myself with the bit about leading a charmed life. Well, if I ever needed that consolation it was then.

The copilot's exploration with the flashlight had not been overlooked by the other passengers, none of whom, like George and myself, had been given any information on what might be the matter. The turbulence was pretty bad, and the lightning continued to play around the wing tips. Then, suddenly below us, we saw the lights of Buffalo. I never loved anyplace as much as I loved

Buffalo at that moment. We began to descend and then to circle the airport for what seemed an eternity. I wondered why we were so close to the ground and circling. On the field we could see fire trucks and ambulances being assembled along one of the runways.

Finally the announcement came from the captain. Due to some malfunction in the landing gear mechanism we were going to have to make a crash landing. We were told to put our seats in an upright position, remove all sharp objects from our pockets and put our heads between our knees. Everyone on the plane was suddenly gripped with that icy numb sensation that is felt by the bravest people in the face of known danger. Out of the corner of my eye I could see some of my fellow passengers moving their lips in prayer. These were the same people who, only moments before, had been joking about the inconvenience of air travel and saying things like, "Next time take the bus and leave the driving to us." It wasn't very funny when they said it, and it had suddenly become macabre.

I began to pray. But even as I prayed, all bent over with my head between my legs, I thought to myself, "This is an awfully undignified way to die."

The tension mounted as we came down, closer and closer to the end of the runway. When you fly a lot you get a feeling for such things. I knew the moment of impact must be at hand. Then, all of a sudden, I heard the most beautiful sound in the world, the landing gear dropped and locked in place and we made a safe landing.

Ed Hall's chart had done it again.

Like the shock of being abandoned in the Mediterranean Sea, the shock of the experience didn't take full effect right away. George and I spent some time talking to the press about the escape we'd just had and then we went to our rooms for the night. It was then and only then that I suddenly began to shake, just the way I did on the deck of Aly Khan's yacht. I had to call the hotel doctor who gave me a sedative. The next day at my concert, my opening line was one of the truest statements I've ever made, "Ladies and gentlemen, I am so very, very happy to be here in Buffalo." Some of the audience must have read of the near crash in their morning papers and applauded. They understood.

I've flown hundreds of thousands of miles, but I'm really not crazy about it. I have never boarded a plane without a feeling of trepidation. I always say a silent prayer at takeoffs and landings. And often, as I arrive safely at my destination I say to myself, "Well, I made it again." I hope I keep on saying those words for many, many years and will always do anything I can to make sure I do.

For example, we were in Johannesburg, South Africa. We'd just wound up a strenuous three week tour from Capetown to Durban to Pretoria to Johannesburg and everyone in the company was really beat. No one looked forward with any joy to boarding a plane for the States immediately after our last show.

I went to Seymour and begged him to change our reservations so we could all get a good night's sleep and then start the long flight the next day. Seymour said it was impossible to change our reservations. There weren't so many flights out of Jo-burg for the USA. There was a whole company of us and to get that many seats at the last minute just couldn't be done.

I can be very persistent when I want to be, and I wanted to be that day and it paid off. Seymour actually came up with another flight, going a different route, that would get us home only a few hours later. Everyone in the company agreed this was the best thing to do and thanked me for thinking of their comfort.

The next morning when we got the local papers with our breakfast there, in big black type, were the headlines saying that the plane we were supposed to have been aboard crashed a few minutes after takeoff and all one hundred and twenty-seven people aboard were killed. To this day everyone credits me with having received some divine message that saved our lives.

Again I thought of Ed Hall's numerological charts and the words "charmed life." But I'm not letting that go to my head. I never board a plane if I have the slightest premonition that all is not well. And because of the incident in Johannesburg, no matter how much trouble it causes to change our reservations no one ever questions my judgment. I hope I continue to bat a thousand. I always think of that gag, my *number* may not be up, but what if the pilot's *is*.

9

When I'm on the road, which is thirty or forty weeks out of every year, it means a show every day with two on Thursdays and Saturdays. Sometimes we're in a town only one night, sometimes three or four days, occasionally as much as a week or two. Those longer stands are almost like a vacation to my musical director who in addition to conducting the show bears the burden of selecting and rehearsing the orchestra in city after city. It's a hard job and takes a lot of advance planning.

As I'm writing this, I have a brand-new musical director and I'm happy to say he's great. Of course this isn't an accident. His name is Bo Ayars and I didn't pick him because he just got out of Julliard and wanted to be a musical conductor. He's had a lot of road experience and yet is young enough to know where everything is at musically. He's "today," he's "now" and I couldn't be happier. Because, as I've said, there's a lot more to the job than just standing in front of eighteen men and giving them a downbeat.

That's why I felt a sort of sinking sensation in my middle when "Dr." Gordon Robinson came to me at the end of the tour in 1972 and told me he was planning to retire. He isn't really a doctor. He has a couple of college degrees. But his doctorate was conferred on him by me. In introducing him one evening, he looks so much like a professor I called him "Dr. Gordon Robinson" as a joke. He's been called that ever since. He tells people he's an LLD, Doctor of Lee Liberace.

Gordon had become my right hand when we were on the road, so

I took the news of his retirement with a sense of personal as well as professional loss. You can't travel around the country with a man and work closely with him for twenty-two years without becoming very dear friends. Had it been otherwise, there would not have been those twenty-two years.

At first I tried to shake off his retirement plan the way everyone tries to make something unpleasant go away by pretending it doesn't exist. "Everyone plans to retire," I said. "But when the time comes they change their minds."

"I'm not changing mine," said Gordon, "I've been on the road as a musician, arranger and conductor for the better part of every year since I was seventeen years old—twenty-two of them with you—those last twenty-two years have been wonderful, but the time has come to quit and just enjoy the goodies all that work entitles me to. I want a home that I can really live in and enjoy. I want lots of time to read and study. And I want to have the time, when the mood strikes me, just to listen to all the music of all the great composers performed by all the greatest artists and to do that listening just for the sheer joy of it without ever thinking what help it might give me professionally. I've never had time to do any of that."

There could be no doubt that he'd really made up his mind. I had to accept the inevitable. And I've found out that when you're faced with an irreversible situation the best thing to do is to accept it as gracefully as you can. So I said, "I understand. It's a hard life. Rewarding but hard. You've earned retirement. And to be perfectly frank with you, if everything goes well, I won't be far behind you." I said that but I didn't mean it. It was just a little white lie to relieve the tension.

Maybe some of you who read this book will have had the experience of coming to see me when I played in your community and been surprised when the curtains opened, to see that there was someone you recognized in the orchestra. I'll tell you how that happens. His or her presence there was part of Gordon Robinson's job. You see in every city and town in the country there's a pool of musicians. Naturally the bigger the community, or the more cultural minded it is, the more musicians there are . . . and the better they are. This fact—that the United States is carpeted ocean-to-ocean with people who play all kinds of instruments is a very lucky thing for performers like me. It's economically impossible to travel around the country with an orchestra of eighteen men anymore. That's one of the reasons for the disappearance of the big bands. So what we have to do is plan our itinerary far in advance and then alert the musical contractor in every place we are to play that we're coming and what we need, how many violins, how many trumpets, how many strings, how many reeds. (I play the piano.)

A contractor in the music business is just like a contractor in any other trade. He's the man you hire to shape up and manage your work crew. Most of them are musicians themselves, and they know just which men and women are the best and which ones are better for our kind of job. So when we let a contractor know eight or ten months in advance, it means that we're reserving the best musicians there are for our engagement.

Of course we do travel with our own key men. For us these are a drummer, a guitar player and, generally, a trumpet man. The reason is that if one man in a band comes in wrong, the rest will follow him. So we have a drummer for a strong beat, a guitarist for solid rhythm and a trumpet player who gets them off to a solid start, because he knows the book better than they do.

The local men are all ready when Gordon Robinson—or Bo Ayars now—gets into town. He sets our book in front of them and rehearses as long as necessary to get things right. In big cities like Philadelphia, for instance, where there's a great pool of wonderful musicians, this generally can be done in a couple of hours. In other spots it takes a lot longer. Sometimes it just can't be done at all.

Back in the early part of 1960, when we were doing one-nighters, we played Chanute, Kansas, a very rich little town. It was rich because there had been a lot of oil there. Most of it had been pumped off. But the smell of it remained in the town, and there was that warm comforting glow that comes from a concentration of big money. But money doesn't make musicians, and there weren't a lot of those to choose from. In spots like that the men and women you get are generally moonlighting. They are really doctors, lawyers, bank personnel, insurance salesmen, shopkeepers, people who did fairly well on an instrument in their youth and have kind of kept it up. But they're never great. Sometimes they're truly terrible.

Normally, on one-nighters Gordon would play a second piano and we carried drums and bass for rhythm. But this time in Chanute, the promoter had taken us out on a limb by advertising "Liberace and Orchestra." So we had to try to meet the terms of the advertisement by recruiting an orchestra from the local talent. Well, it turned out to be more local than talent, and after trying all afternoon Gordon gave up. He couldn't make the few school-teachers and marching band musicians sound like anything but a disaster rushing someplace to happen. And the worst of the lot was a cornet player who must have hated music or he would have stopped trying to make it. If the group ever got started right, he was the Judas goat that led them astray. His name was Cecil. I remember this because he became an obsession with Gordon, his name almost a swear word. For days after, Cecil would pop into Gordon's mind and he'd start talking about the incredibly wobbly tones he could produce. He said he sounded like the second cornet in a Salvation Army street corner band, who had frostbitten lips and looked like a movie actor named Franklin Pangborn, who played ribbon clerks and floorwalkers and interior decorators.

Finally, exhausted and distressed, Gordon realized that a way had to be found to keep everybody honest, and fulfill the promise of the ad without producing music that would drive *me* out of the theater. So he rehearsed his little group of moonlighting serenaders in nothing but the play-ons and play-offs. All the rest of the music was handled by our drummer, bass player and Gordon himself, while the orchestra simply sat there and enjoyed the show.

But things like that didn't happen often. In all the years of traveling I must say we've had very little trouble with musicians, amplification system, sound men or light men. Contrary to what I've heard some people say, I think they're all generally great, and they're getting better and better as the whole country grows more show-wise and sophisticated.

Of course, Gordon was a lot of help to me in many other ways. When I'm working on the stage, playing the piano, talking or singing, I'm so involved in what I'm doing that I seldom take any notice of what's going on in the auditorium. Gordon always watched because there was a time when we had a lot of trouble with people suddenly trying to get up on the stage to get into the act. And you'd be surprised how many ladies actually did get past stage doormen and wandered out from the wings or found the stairs that led from the auditorium to the stage and used them to come up and talk to me or sing with me or play the piano with me. And when we were playing in night clubs the access was even easier.

Gordon handled these problems marvelously. In the first place, he's a very tall, handsome man and any woman would be happy to have him put his arm around her waist and talk softly to her. So when he saw someone coming onto the stage from any direction, he'd go to meet her. And he had the greatest "bum's rush" technique in the world. He'd put his arm around her waist where he could exert some pressure and whisper in her ear, "What's your name, dear?"

While she was telling him and he was talking to her, she was being propelled off the stage, and that generally worked fine. I really don't know what else he might have said to her. He never told me. But we never had any bad reaction from anyone. Of course, no plan works all the time. Once a lady, more determined to get her way than Gordon was to defeat her, wound up standing next to me at the piano. I saw her out of the corner of my eye and heard Gordon whispering, "She wants you to play 'Stardust.' It's the only way to get rid of her." I segued from the Chopin piece I was playing into the Hoagy Carmichael tune, the lady smiled happily, patted the top of my head as if I'd been a good little boy and walked off under her own steam.

We don't get that kind of "happening" very much anymore. I don't know whether it's because the women who used to do that sort of thing have gotten too old to bother about it or whether I've gotten too old for them to bother about.

Actually, there was nothing really embarrassing in those little incidents of intrusion from well-meaning fans. The real embarrassing things are too awful to think about. One night at Harrah's Club at Lake Tahoe, I was wearing a full dress suit made of mohair that was very crisp and shiny and sparkling. Besides that it was embroidered with beads and jewels. It was very elegant.

My mother was in the audience at a ringside table and after introducing her I bent over to give her a little kiss on the cheek. You've probably guessed what happened. Women have told me what it feels like when they get a run in their stocking. That's what it felt like when I got a run in my pants. Run? The whole seat split wide open.

It was impossible to continue the performance. It was even hard to figure out how to get off without exposing my flanks. So I started to back off saying, "Thank you very much. You've been very kind," and things like that and they thought I was crazy because they had

139]

no idea what I was thanking them for. They hadn't applauded or shown any kindness. So they did what all audiences do when a performer confronts them with the unexpected. They applauded. I guess I'm the only performer except maybe Buster Keaton or Charlie Chaplin who ever got applause for ripping his trousers.

One of the weirdest things happened in Dallas, Texas. We were playing an intimate little room in the Adolphus Hotel and on opening night, seated at ringside was a young man with a red rose in his lapel. He was alone at the table, handsomely dressed and very enthusiastic about everything I did. I always look to see what a person is drinking when he or she becomes what I think might be overappreciative. This gentleman was always accompanied by a bucket of champagne.

Well, you can't knock that kind of music lover so I guess maybe I kind of played to him. This, of course, made him even more responsive to every number. He would shout, "Bravo, Liberace!" after every number.

When we came off the floor Gordon said to me, "How about that guy with the rose?"

I said, "Maybe we'd better put him under contract. Any audience can use a guy like him."

We both laughed. But when the following night the same character, dressed to the nines and wearing a red rose in his lapel, was at the same table, Gordon looked at me as much as to ask, "Did you really hire him?"

Again this fan was enthusiastic about the show. Each show was as if he were seeing it for the first time. And that went on for our entire run at the Adolphus. Every night he was there at the ringside with a rose in his lapel and his bucket of champagne. I began to think it was some sort of publicity stunt.

When we moved from the Adolphus to the Fontainebleau in Miami Beach you could have knocked me over when I saw who was sitting at ringside. Same man. Same rose. Same champagne.

Well, I couldn't ignore him anymore so when I came on I nodded to him and said, "How are things in Dallas?"

He just smiled and continued to enjoy the show as if every minute of it were new to him. And night after night, just as in Texas, he came back for more.

Finally he came back stage. The Krofft Brothers puppet act was on the show and he especially loved them along with everything else. We had a nice visit in my dressing room. He was very refined and intelligent. And when he left he said, "I'll see you tomorrow night." He made no explanation for the rose, the champagne or his excellent taste in entertainment.

A couple of days later I got an invitation to a gala dinner being planned by my rose wearing friend, whose name I'm not using for reasons you'll understand when this incident is closed. The invitation said the dinner was planned to include the finest delicacies from all over the world, which he had ordered specially flown to the Fontainebleau. The dinner was to be accompanied by strolling violins. The scuttlebut around the hotel was that he'd insisted that only the top men in the kitchen be permitted to participate in the preparation of these rare viands.

Well, if I tell you I could hardly wait for this feast, you had better believe me. Then, the night before the banquet was to be set before us, Gordon came into my dressing room and said, "Did you hear? The dinner for tomorrow night is off."

"Why?" I asked. I felt like a kid who'd just heard Christmas had been canceled.

"He won't be at the show tonight," Gordon said.

"Why?"

"A couple of FBI men, some Dallas policemen and two cops from Miami Beach just picked him up."

I suppose I knew it was sure to happen. "But for what?"

"Transporting money that didn't belong to him across state lines," said Gordon. "He absconded with about a quarter of a million dollars in cash from a Dallas bank."

"Gee," I said, "he must feel awful."

"Yes," said Gordon. "But I'll bet the bank feels a lot better."

"Did he leave any explanation for us?" I asked.

"No. But the gossip is that when the police showed up he was very philosophic about it. He just said, 'Well, the honeymoon is over. Am I allowed a telephone call?' he asked."

Thinking he was going to call his lawyer or a well-needed friend, the FBI agreed. Instead, he dialed the operator and asked for the Le Ronde (the room where I was appearing) and said, "Cancel my ringside table for tonight, I'm sorry but I'm afraid I have another commitment." And he really did. I understand he got ten years.

He had done a terrible thing, but I felt kind of sorry for him. He was the nicest embezzler I ever met. Come to think of it, he was the only one . . . that I know of.

From the strangest to one of the most embarrassing things that ever happened to me, we move to The Terrace Room of The Statler Hotel in Boston. As I think about it now, I'm sure it wouldn't be so embarrassing today. But *then,* for a young performer just on his way up, it was simply awful.

As everyone who played The Terrace Room knew, or was told the moment he came to rehearse, the room was planned by an architect who either didn't know anything about show business or hated it. The only way those who came to dine and see the show could get in or out was to cross the dance floor, which was the only place where anyone performing in the room could work. It wasn't exactly the greatest setup in the world, but you learn to live with a lot of things.

At that time Boston was quite a show town. Lots of plays used to try out there before coming to Broadway. So the management warned me that there might come a time while I was on the floor doing my act that some of my audience would get up and walk out. They said I shouldn't let this bother me, that I shouldn't take it as criticism. It just meant that they had tickets for whatever show was in town and had to leave to make the curtain. Even when you're aware of this it doesn't thrill you at all and it sure doesn't help your act, to have ten or twelve people suddenly rise and start filtering out while you're doing your best to entertain.

Well, I have a theory that if there's something terrible that you can't get rid of, try to figure out if possible how to make it work for, instead of against, you. The show that was playing in Boston at that time was a revival of a play about a star on her way to Hollywood who was being bamboozled by a crazy director into signing a contract she didn't want to sign. Because the action takes place on that now defunct but once grand old train The Twentieth Century Limited, the play was called *Twentieth Century.* I think John Barrymore starred in the picture as the mad director. The star of this show was none other than the wonderful Gloria Swanson, and of course, she knew a lot about how to play a glamorous movie star, so she was very, very good in the part.

When anybody got up and started to walk across the floor during my performance, walking in front of the spotlights and casting funny shadows all over the place (to say nothing of distracting the audience), I'd just lean over to the microphone and say out of the corner of my mouth, "Enjoy the play and say hello to Gloria Swanson for me." They didn't know that at that time I didn't know Gloria. But it didn't make any difference, because they didn't know her either. The line served to bring the attention of the audience back to me and sometimes got a laugh.

At that time I had a little audience participation sequence in my act. I'd get someone from the audience who didn't know how to play the piano and bring them up and teach them to play a concerto with me. Generally it would be some nice outgoing lady who wanted to have a little fun. Anytime I could get a child to join me it was even better. But you don't see many children in rooms like I played, except occasionally at the dinner show when someone is traveling with a kid and doesn't know what to do with it.

What I did was show an audience volunteer the few notes of "Night and Day" to hit with one finger while I supplied the accompaniment, concerto fashion, to her one finger plunking. Anybody who did it with me would always get a big round of applause, but particularly if it were a child. Then I'd reward her with a kiss, a corsage and a miniature piano with my autograph on it.

Sometimes the children didn't react as well as might be expected, but one night I found a precocious little girl who seemed almost to have planned on joining me. She spoke in a loud, clear little voice and responded amusingly to everything I said to her.

I said that stupid thing so many grown-ups say to children, "Do you know who I am, honey?"

She said, "Don't *you* know who you *are?*" But, clearly she didn't mean it to be fresh. She just seemed a little sad that this grown man didn't even know his own name. Of course that got a howl and applause. There were some other exchanges which I have forgotten and then she played her simple little part of the music just perfectly. In short, she was a smash hit. I rewarded her with the prizes I've mentioned and went on with my show wondering whether it might not be a good idea to get that kid for all the rest of my performances in Boston.

Several minutes later I was in the middle of Debussy's "Clair de Lune" when I sensed some figures walking across the floor. The

143]

theater crowd had already left. I looked out of the corner of my eye and saw it was my little girl partner leaving the room, hand in hand with her mother. So I called out to her, as I kept on playing, "Where are you going, honey?"

And as she left the room she turned back and yelled in a loud clear voice, "I'm going to take a piss!"

The mother flew out of the room pulling the kid behind her like a scene from Alice in Wonderland.

Naturally the audience in The Terrace Room simply fell apart. They were positively convulsed. And, when *they* went, I went too. I broke up completely and had to stop playing. When everything began to settle down and I was able to get in a word, I yelled after the little girl who was now well out of sight, "Say hello to Gloria Swanson," and the audience exploded again.

But I think the little girl's mother had the last laugh. She was so embarrassed by the whole episode that she never returned to pay her check. The child had done so much for my show that I told the management to put it on my bill. I wonder if her mother planned it that way?

It isn't because of that little girl, however, that I hold a warm spot in my heart for the Statler in Boston. I made some very dear friends there.

I'm constantly running into people who claim they discovered me. This is simply because they happened to be in one of my audiences at an early point in my career when, to quote them, "Nobody ever heard of you." If that was the case and they came to see me, I guess as far as they're concerned, they did discover me. But they all want to take a bow for my success and I'm happy to let them. There are enough bows to go around . . . now.

On the other hand, there have been certain people who really *did* help me when I needed it. They are people that I've met along the way up and who I still see and love. For instance, a gentleman named Clarence Goodwin. He was in Boston representing the French, Shriner and Urner Shoe Company at a shoe manufacturer's convention being held in the hotel. I'd seen him at the show and later in the lobby he handed me his card and said, "If you're ever out in Hollywood look me up. I'd like you to meet my family, my wife and children."

I filed the card away, but I noted that he became a regular member of my audience as long as the convention was in town.

And he'd frequently stop and talk to me and give me encouragement which is a great help to a young performer. So when I did go out to California, I looked through my cards and found the one Mr. Goodwin had given me. When I called him up, I said, "Do you remember the pianist you met at the Statler Hotel in Boston?"

"I sure do," he said, enthusiastically. "It's great that you called. Where are you staying."

I told him I was at the Ambassador Hotel in Santa Monica.

"Well, I'm going to send the car for you," he said, "And you're coming to the house to have dinner with us."

I was really thrilled because I'm kind of a home boy even now, and of course, I was a lot more like that way back then. You can have all the wonderful, gourmet restaurant dinners in the world; as for me, give me a good home-cooked meal in a nice comfortable happy home where you can feel surrounded by love. That's the kind of a home I found when I got to the Goodwins. I guess it was more than merely a "comfortable" home. The family picked me up in a beautiful car and took me to their exquisite house in Hollywood—a place that was exactly what I'd expect a Hollywood star to have, swimming pool and everything. But this man was no star. He was in the shoe business. But what impressed me most about the Goodwins was that they were such a closely knit family, a beautiful mother, handsome father and two grown sons who, with their fiancées, had dinner with us. And the delicious home cooked dinner made me feel homesick for my mother's cooking after all the hotel food I'd been eating.

We had a grand time. They asked if I'd play their piano for them, and I was delighted to because such a warm feeling had grown up between us. I even fell in love with their piano. And before the evening was over Mrs. Goodwin said to me, "Why should you stay in a hotel? We have this big house. Why don't you make our home your home for as long as you're in the Los Angeles area?"

The invitation came as such a shock to me that I immediately started to refuse, and they kept urging me to accept, and I kept thinking of their lovely piano and how good it would be to get away from hotel living for a change and live in a comfortable home with the chance to do a little practicing in the morning. So I accepted their invitation, and the next day I moved in bag and baggage. It was the smartest move I could have made. I actually became part of their happy family. And that made *me* happy.

Mr. Goodwin, the West Coast representative of that shoe company, was, of course, a very good businessman. He was also very kind and generous. He began to sort of take a fatherly interest in me and appointed himself, unofficially, as my business manager. He asked me how I was doing and I told him I thought I was doing rather well, but no doubt, I could do better. He asked me how much I was getting and when I told him he said, "I don't think they're paying you enough money. Let's hold out for more. The next time you agent calls with an offer just tell him it's not enough, that you think you deserve more. Better still, if you want me to, I'll speak to him. You're an artist. You shouldn't have to talk business."

"Great!" I said. What did I have to lose? If I didn't work I still had a good home to live in and if Mr. Goodwin's idea didn't work, I could always go back to the salary I was getting, which wasn't all that bad.

So when the first call came, Clarence Goodwin got on the line and said, "Liberace appreciates your offer, but it really isn't enough to tempt him to change his present plan to just relax and practice for a concert he's preparing to present at Carnegie Hall in New York."

I had no such plan. But Mr. Goodwin's plan really worked. Everybody thought that I'd been doing so well that they became embarrassed to offer me the salary I'd been getting. They'd call a second time and a third time until they really were offering more money than I could afford to turn down. So I graciously was persuaded to take certain jobs.

I stayed with the Goodwins for an entire year, except for the time that I was away playing an engagement, and to this day they refer to me as "the man who came to dinner," but even Sheridan Whiteside didn't stay a whole year.

Because I'm not afraid to talk to people when they want to talk to me, because I'm not suspicious of people, I've made a lot of wonderful friends like the Goodwins who have made things a little easier when the going was tough; they are people with whom I've been able to share my good fortune, people I'm still friends with today. Although we sometimes don't see each other as often as we'd like, because of the strenuous schedules I follow, we keep in touch and when we can get together we enjoy the blessing of giving and receiving friendship.

Around this same earlier period in my career between the late 40's and the early 50's, a few years after meeting the Goodwins, when I was doing my syndicated TV show, I met for the first time one of the most fascinating characters in the world of entertainment—a legend in her own time—Mae West.

It all came about on account of a gag when she, in her own forthright way, had actually asked to meet me. Some friends of Mae's asked her what she'd like for a birthday present and she said, and I can almost hear her saying it, "Just bring me Liberace."

They decided to do just that. They got in touch with me, told me their idea and asked if I wanted to go along with the gag. They said it would only take a few minutes of my time, and it would be a wonderful surprise for Mae. It sounded like fun to me and besides it would give me a chance to meet her, so I agreed.

We went to the luxury apartment building in which she still lives on Rossmore Avenue in Hollywood, rang the bell and put a red ribbon on me that said "Happy Birthday" in gold letters. Then they pinned a big red bow where my tie ought to have been. By the time the butler came to the door, I was standing all alone—gift wrapped—waiting to be taken in. The man looked at me strangely, as who wouldn't, and finally I said, "I'm Miss West's birthday present." His perplexed expression changed to a grin. He chuckled and said, "Just a moment, please. I'll get Miss West." He left me standing there for a few moments, and when the lady, herself, came to the door, I said, "Happy Birthday, Miss West. I'm Liberace. I'm the birthday present you said you wanted." She laughed out loud and said, "Come on in. Glad you could come up to see me."

The guys who'd thought up the gag were hiding down the hall and let out a hoot and pretty soon we were all having a fine time and I was getting acquainted. She was absolutely charming, and we sat for hours as she told stories about her life in the business that was just beginning to accept me.

One of the things I found fascinating about her, as she talked, was that she always referred to herself in the third person. She spoke as if she were talking about someone else. Instead of saying, for instance, "When I signed my contract at Paramount, I made it clear to them that I was to have this and that or I wouldn't play,"

147]

she would say "When Mae West signed her contract with Paramount she made it clear that she was to have this or that or she wouldn't play." I thought it was very grand and very queenly. But I wouldn't think of doing a thing like that for the world. It removes you too far from the one you're talking to to eliminate the personal, eye-to-eye feeling you get from the more intimate "I" or "me."

After that first bizarre meeting our paths crossed from time to time when we both happened to be working in the same city, or we both happened to be "between engagements" in Hollywood or Palm Springs. But the meeting that was the most fun after I became her "birthday present" also took place in Los Angeles in connection with a glamorous Hollywood type opening. I guess it was the only one at which everyone in the audience would admit without hesitation that all the actors were dummies . . . at least puppets on a string being manipulated by people higher up. It was the Hollywood opening of *Les Poupées de Paris* which millions must have seen a little later when it became the great hit of The New York World's Fair.

It was produced by good friends of mine, Sid and Marty Krofft, the puppeteers, and the cast included puppets of a lot of show business characters such as Maurice Chevalier, Mae West and me speaking lines specially recorded by the people themselves. I'm sure there were many others whom I've forgotten. But this story deals only with Mae West and myself.

To get as much publicity as possible out of the opening night doings a la Hollywood with kleig lights, audience bleachers and all the trimmings, Sid and Marty suggested that since we knew each other anyway and were both represented by puppets in the show, it would be a good idea if we attended the opening together. We were agreeable, so it was arranged for me to escort Mae West to the opening. It got a lot of newspaper space because it seemed to the gossip writers and the newsmen to be a rather strange coupling.

Since Mae—I guess I'd better call her Mae West as she always speaks of herself—since Mae West was living way out on the beach in Malibu and I was living in Hollywood, it made more sense, and was much more convenient, for her to be chauffeur-driven in her beautiful limousine to pick me up at my home in Hollywood. (For those who don't understand the geography of this: If I had called for her, I'd have had to drive about twenty miles down the coast to get her, bring her back twenty miles to Hollywood and then drive twenty miles back down the coast to take her home and then bring myself back that same twenty miles. I make that to be about eighty miles. By having her pick me up, we cut out half that mileage.

When she arrived, looking absolutely smashing as she always does, I asked her if she wouldn't like to come in and spend a few restful moments before going on to the excitement of the opening. She, being wiser in such matters and more experienced than I was, decided it would be better to go directly to the theater and give the photographers and the television and newspaper reporters a chance to see and talk to us before curtain time. But she promised, on the way to the theater, that if it weren't too late after the show, she'd come back to my house and have me show her around. I guess she could tell how eager I was to show off the place because I don't think I talked about anything else. You see, having been in her home, I was familiar with her taste in furnishings and appointments and I had an idea that my place would appeal to her since it had a lot of the elegance she admired. I told her about all the unique things and spoke most proudly of the beautiful gold motion picture theater pipe organ that I had.

I must have done very well with the description because she showed great interest and said how much she hoped it wouldn't be too late after the show to come back and see all the things I'd talked about.

Of course, when we got to the theater, as Miss West had anticipated, there were hordes of photographers, movie and TV cameras to fulfill the whole purpose of the opening, which was to spread the news to everybody that there was an amusing and different type of show in town. Well, when we stepped out of the Cadillac, both dressed as beautifully as we knew how, cameras started grinding and flash bulbs started popping and people started clapping and it was very exciting.

Before we arrived at the theater she had asked me to stay very close to her and help her with any steps or stairway that we might encounter. She explained that in a situation like this one she didn't like to look down while walking. So I was to whisper sweet nothings to her as we walked, things like, "There's a step coming. Be careful." Or, "We're coming to a little incline in a moment." It was very effective, and she looked simply out of this world in a long white satin dress with a short train. The dress, her furs, her hair formed an ensemble that was the final definition of glamor.

149]

After we finished with the press in the lobby we started to move to our seats in the theater. Mae West can't enter a room or a theater without attracting attention and so all eyes were turned in our direction. Suddenly, halfway down the aisle, she stopped and gazed around the room like a queen giving her subjects a chance to get a good look at her. "She's really enjoying this adulation," I thought to myself as I stood there and waited for her to conclude her gracious pause for admiration. Then, out of the corner of her mouth, in a stage whisper, she said to me, "You're standing on my train."

You can imagine my embarrassment. I looked down and sure enough, she was right. I stepped off, and we proceeded down the aisle as if nothing had happened and Mae West had made a grand moment out of what could have been a disaster.

Naturally we both loved the show, having recorded every word the puppets said. Seeing ourselves represented and being able to judge from a third-person vantage point how the public was accepting us was a new and interesting experience. And when the show was over we were all invited to a reception on stage. As you might expect, the reporters tagged along firing questions at Mae West and probing for the kind of quotable statement she was always able to supply.

Finally, the big question came. One of the reporters asked, "Miss West, where are you and Liberace going after this reception?"

She smiled and said, as only she could, "I'm going over to Liberace's home to see his gold organ. I've seen every other kind, but I've never seen a gold one before."

"May I quote that?" the reporter asked.

"If it's all right with Liberace, it's all right with me," she told him. And from then on we were free to enjoy the party. When it was over she did come back to my home and she loved it. As she walked into one room after another, she kept repeating, "It's me. It's me."

"No," I said, "it's me!" We became very close friends and, as I showed her around I asked her if she'd like a drink. "No," she said, "I don't drink and I don't smoke, but I wouldn't mind having a little something to eat, something light."

I said, "Marvelous. My housekeeper, Gladys, is a wonderful cook and she's made some super rice custard. Would you like some?"

"I'd love it. How did you know I adore rice custard?" She adored it so much she had a second helping. And then we continued the tour of the house. I showed her my piano collection and my antiques and she thoroughly enjoyed herself.

And for the finish I showed her my gold organ. I not only showed it to her . . . I played it for her.

10

I have already written about the giant step backward my career suffered when Don Fedderson and my agents, MCA, decided I should go from prime time to daytime TV. And the look of austerity. No candelabra, no fancy clothes, none of the showmanship, that, it turned out, was responsible for my first big success.

It didn't take long to find out that the viewers resented the plain look. Letters began pouring in saying the music was still beautiful, but all the charm, the glamor, the fun was gone out of the show. They told me, "It isn't the real you." At the end of the year when the ratings had fallen off and, worse than that, my gross income had dropped almost 50 percent, it was obvious we'd made a bad mistake and something had to be done.

It wasn't hard to figure out what. Gradually I began to bring back some of the exciting wardrobe. The candelabra came back, and as the word got around, so did the audience. But I got fed up with daytime television. For one thing, they seemed to be putting commercials right in the middle of my numbers. It wasn't really that way, but the advertising spots came so fast, that's how it seemed.

As I think I've indicated, I'm not against commercials, nor do I think the general viewing public is against commercials. It is against the misuse of them and, occasionally the stupidity or lunacy of some of them. Frequently they notice a combination of all three . . . a crazy, stupid spot, run many times too often. What bores me, as a viewer, is seeing the same commercial again and again in which someone is surprised. How many times can a person be excited by how wonderful Puffo works? Then there are the comedy commercials. No matter how funny the jokes are, they're not funny more than once. And after you've seen the same gag three times in an evening, and maybe twenty times in a week, it stops being funny.

Then, of course, there's the bad taste. The careless insertion of commercials into a show in such a way that they spoil the impact or the intent of the entertainment and jolt people entirely out of the mood of what they're seeing. I remember late, late one night I was watching a movie. The film was about a tanker that had been torpedoed. Men were floundering around in the sea. The surface of the water was on fire. At that point they cut away from the picture to a commercial of a bunch of boys and girls splashing around in a swimming pool. It was either for a soft drink or some brand of bathing suit.

The whole impact of the picture was lost. When we were doing a Thanksgiving Day show on my daytime program, I had a set built that was an exact copy of my own dining room. I had the entire cast seated around the table. In this setting we did the beautiful song, "Bless This House." And as the turkey was brought in and placed on the table before me, I gave a special blessing.

We even had a real turkey. Mom actually did all the cooking at home and she and Gladys, my housekeeper, brought it to the studio. After the song, we all enjoyed the for real and wonderful Italian-Polish, typically American Thanksgiving dinner right on television. So I really had a Thanksgiving dinner with my viewing audience.

I was very happy with the way the whole thing went until later when I saw the playback of the show. I couldn't believe my eyes. Just as my lovely blessing ended, on came a commercial . . . for Drano. It made me want to vomit. I'm sure the people who make Drano wouldn't have wanted that to happen. It was just poor taste—"poor," it was inexcusably bad taste . . . on someone's part.

I went to the heads of the studio and complained. I told them that they could have endeared themselves to their viewers by saying that in honor of Thanksgiving Day all commercials were being eliminated. That would have given the viewers something to be thankful for right away. I didn't say *that* but that's what I thought.

They had their own thoughts. They thought I'd gone crazy. Leave out a commercial? Lose all that money? Clearly this goofy piano player had flipped his lid. I think maybe I did. A few days later I begged off the show and it was canceled. It wasn't that we weren't doing well. It was that I wasn't happy. And if I'm not happy with what I'm doing, I can see no reason to do it.

The truth is, I think, I'm not a daytime performer. Daylight is bright and plain, matter of fact, and very real. The sun shows things as they are. Nighttime is different. The stars twinkle, the moon casts a mysterious white light, the shadows take on beautiful shapes, everything becomes more glamorous and that's the way I like it. The clothes I wear when I'm working are not daytime clothes, they're nighttime clothes because the night is when people like to dress up. There's a little bit of make believe in every night and it's reflected in the gowns the women wear and the more imaginative clothes the men wear. The night is full of mystery and vibrations. It's show business. And to pretend that it's not is like putting Marlene Dietrich in a Mother Hubbard.

I'd resent that. I don't care if she's a grandmother, a *Hausfrau* in her spare time. To me she's a star. And what's wonderful about it is that *she* never lets me forget it. She lives up to her talent. You never see Joan Crawford *schlepping* around in a mu-mu. She, too, knows the meaning of glamor and its importance to the people who—without any themselves—love to look at it in others.

I worry for those young movie stars of today who don't realize this. I mean the ones who mooch around in tattered jeans and baggy sweat shirts. They are taking some of the "show" out of the business.

As must be clear, I'm a star-gazer from way back in the days when I was much younger and very new in the world of glamorous entertainment. But I've never lost the fascination that success holds for me. I don't think that if I live to be a hundred I'll lose the excitement of meeting someone I admire, a celebrity . . . someone who has written a great book, painted a great picture, written a great play or made a great movie. When I see one of these people I sometimes do childlike things.

I was having dinner one evening at The Four Seasons, one of

New York's great restaurants, and sitting across the room I saw Alfred Hitchcock. I wanted to send him a note to tell him how much I admired him, but I wondered if he might not think it an intrusion on his privacy. Finally I decided to take a chance and on the back of one of the menus I wrote, "Dear Mr. Hitchcock, I'm truly and sincerely one of your most ardent admirers." I signed my name and drew my little piano sketch and asked the captain to take it over to him.

In a few moments the captain came back with another menu. On the back of it, Alfred Hitchcock had written the one word "Likewise," and signed his famous profile caricature. I framed the menu and it now hangs in a prominent place among my most cherished mementos. But occasionally when I stop and look at it, I'm not sure whether he meant that he is one of my admirers of that he, too, is one of *his!*

I love pomp and ceremony . . . heads of state . . . Presidents, Kings, Queens, Princes. I've played for three of our Presidents, Truman, Eisenhower and Nixon, when he was running for the Presidency. (Or doesn't that count?)

I've entertained for Queen Juliana and Prince Bernhard of the Netherlands and for everyone in the British Royal Family. These are the kind of people I respect most deeply. I respect what they represent and admire the way they go about representing it. And I think the British people, as a whole, feel the same way I do and hold their royalty in generally high esteem.

For they inject beauty and pageantry into the lives of those who yearn for something better . . . those who can only dream. It's showmanship of a very high order. The changing of the guard, the Beefeaters' old uniforms, the velvet, fur-trimmed robes of state, the impractical but luxurious quality of everything . . . the gold.

The Catholic Church has never lost sight of this. They value the mystery of flickering candles, the glory of statuary and art. They know a ceiling by Michelangelo surpasses any other ceiling there is. They know that people want to escape into another kind of world.

I try to help them do this for a little while, to help them forget work and problems and enjoy, vicariously, a folderol of fun, good music and fancy dress. I give them a little recess from the humdrum.

A psychologist once tried to explain to me what it was that gave the late Adam Clayton Powell such a hold on his constituency in

Harlem. It was shown time and again that he lived outrageously. But his people didn't care. At least one of them was really making it. They admired Powell's daring. It was his very outrageousness that they, themselves, could not indulge in, that they looked up to in Powell. Through him they did what they wanted to but couldn't. Through him they defied the power structure that was trying to submerge them. Through him they lived a vicarious life of luxury and maybe sin. He had fun and they loved him for it.

When I ride onto stage in a Rolls-Royce there's something of the same association. Who wouldn't want to do that? Or if he didn't actually do it, be able to afford to do it. Men are beginning to break out of the colorless fashions that they used to think were their emblem of masculinity. But these same men who were afraid to wear anything but white shirts, somber ties and plain blue or gray suits during the day got their kicks wearing the craziest pajamas you ever saw when they went to bed. Man has to have some release for his need to be a peacock and, thank goodness, he is beginning to seek it. It makes the world a pleasanter place to walk around in. But it makes it harder for me to stand out.

It worries me when I'm on a plane and someone with me says, "You know who's on this plane?" Then they mention some name that I may have read about. "He's just made his third gold record." That means he's sold over 3,000,000 records. I think that's exciting. I look around and there's not a star in sight. Too many young performers have forgotten that the most important part of show business is not the second word, it's the first. Without the show there's no business.

Not only do my clothes give people something to look at and laugh at, if they want to, they make good copy for the newspapers and that makes good publicity. Even serious writers sometimes get into the scene. I remember a piece several years ago which pointed out that the reason for my popularity was not that I could play the piano, that I had good people with me on my show, that it was a wholesome happy show but that my clothes, my costumes represented a satirical look at the absurdity of fashion. Now how do you like that?

I liked it. I'd never thought of it that way. But if that's his view of my style, good for him. I don't believe that anyone looks at my gaucho outfit and says I'm making fun of the fashion designers who are trying to bring back bloomers for women. I just don't believe it and for a very good reason. I don't think it makes a damn bit of sense.

I had not intended to get off on what I'm now dealing with at this point. But I've learned that when you have a good thing going, don't try to change it. So I'll get back to television later. As a matter of fact, television was possibly the impetus to the clothes "scene" and here's why. The few TV appearances I'd made locally in Los Angeles had attracted enough attention to get me booked into the Hollywood Bowl. At the time this happened it was the realization of all my dreams.

You see, when I first came to Hollywood in the late 40's my main ambition, the one thing my life was pointed at, was to play the Hollywood Bowl. The trouble was that nobody knew me. The problem was to get them to know me. The solution turned out to be television. But I had no idea it would work out that way.

One afternoon, as a tourist, I went to look at that beautiful outdoor amphitheater. It's open to tourists—or at least it used to be—so I wandered onto the famous band shell and looked over the vast auditorium of empty seats. As I did so I promised myself that someday I'd be on that stage again, but playing the piano with all the seats occupied.

A few years later, in 1952, I kept that promise and played the Hollywood Bowl for the first time setting a modern attendance record that has never been broken. The reason it has yet to be broken is that after my first concert, the Los Angeles Fire Department made the management take out 2,000 seats because they considered certain areas, where too many seats had been installed, to be hazardous in case of any sort of emergency. There wasn't much chance of fire out there in the open, except, possibly a brush fire in the hills that could have swept down into the bowl. But I think, maybe, they also had in mind the ever present possibility of an earthquake that exists in the L A area.

Anyway, that's the reason nobody has ever been able to attract that many people into the Bowl since my first concert there.

What a night that was! One of the greatest thrills of my career. There was such a traffic jam leading to the Bowl that I got caught in it. Would you believe that? I got caught in my own traffic jam! I was forty-five minutes late starting my own concert because I had to get out of my car and make my way on foot to the stage entrance of the Bowl. I probably would never have made it at all if it hadn't been for a couple of husky Los Angeles policemen.

What an ironic situation: So many people came to see the concert that the star couldn't get there so there was no concert. But they couldn't get home because of the traffic jam. Fortunately that didn't happen. And it was that first appearance in the Hollywood Bowl that started my love affair with attention grabbing garments.

As I've said, it's an enormous amphitheater reaching up into the hills. People who sit at the top of it must feel like mountain climbers. To the performer on the stage they're almost indistinguishable as individuals.

Well, it was perfectly clear to everybody that if I sat there, wearing the conventional black tails of the concert circuit, with a whole orchestra behind me in black tuxedos, I'd just blend into the "blackground" and lose my identity. So it was suggested that I wear a suit of white tails. I did and all kinds of wonderful things began to happen and all kinds of semi-funny things were said about it.

I was called "the new Cab Calloway . . . the hidey-ho man of the Hollywood Bowl." One thing was for sure. The white suit did not go unnoticed. And what's more, I noticed that it didn't.

I saw the showmanship there is in daring to do something different, in challenging the conventional. I realized that just with the white suit I had lightning in a bottle . . . or, at least, in one of the pockets. It turned out to be the kind of lightning that would fill what was then the country's most prestigious shrine of music—-Carnegie Hall in New York.

But that was just the beginning of the snowballing of one suit of white tails. The success of the Bowl and Carnegie Hall concerts got me signed as the summer replacement for the *Dinah Shore Show*. Remember how she used to close each show by throwing a kiss. Well, this is a kiss to Dinah. After my eight weeks in her time slot, Carnegie Hall in New York was no longer big enough. I went into Madison Square Garden and other mammoth arenas like the Cow Palace in San Francisco.

Maybe if I played the Cow Palace now, which is twenty years later, I might include in my outfit mink chaps or some other type of cowboy gear such as a blue workshirt that lights up. Or maybe if I did Madison Square Garden I'd wear something that suggests

159]

sports. But I don't think I'll ever do either, again. I don't like such places that are better suited to political conventions, hockey games and prizefights than to the kind of entertainment I offer.

It's not easy to be glamorous, the image that I always strive for, when nobody can really see you. To enjoy the clothes I wear the audience must be close enough so that their eyes can almost feel the texture of the fabric. My inclination to this sort of sensuous thing goes back, I suppose, to my childhood background, the hand-me-down clothing I got from my brother George and training I got from my father.

Dad kept pounding into me the importance of never being caught at a disadvantage. To be successful your "presence" must dominate wherever you happen to be. Why do you think high army officials dress up like that? He said, "These are the rules. First, always have a neat appearance and, second, have a good piano because a musician is only as good as his instrument."

I didn't dare talk back to my father, but occasionally I'd throw in something that bothered him. Like when I asked him if he wouldn't rather hear a good musician on a bad instrument than a poor musician on a great instrument. To this day I don't know what I would answer to that question but my father's answer was simply, "A poor musician desecrates a great instrument."

Of course all that stuff that Dad drilled into me made my life harder when I started to work. Frequently I had to play on lousy instruments. Often I had to work in rooms and auditoriums (or is it auditoria?) that were architecturally unsuited to the kind of show I do. Their acoustics were often very bad and poor sight lines deprived some of the audience of seeing the show they paid for. I find that today many Johnny-come-lately performers, who cut a record in a garage and find they have a hit on their hands, don't know how important it is to play in, how shall I say it, sympathetic surroundings. They make a fast buck but they shorten their careers. Of course, there are some to whom one freak hit *is* their career.

If a theater isn't suited to the type of show I do, I won't go into it. Sometimes this makes me settle for houses with fewer seats. And this usually means that I have to do extra performances to accommodate the demand for tickets. But I feel that having things just right for the audience, makes them just right for me. And when things are just right I give a better show.

And the show is not only the wardrobe and the theater. There are all sorts of elements of lighting, staging and sound amplification that have to be worked out in careful detail. The performer who's not careful about these things, who just comes out and "does his stuff" any old way, won't continue to come out and do that stuff very long. Audiences feel it, somehow, when they're being shabbily treated, and they have a way of showing they resent it by not coming to see you the next time you hit town. They can even tell if you're leveling with them, being sincere in what you say, or not.

So, when you get all the mechanical things worked out and put together, then, the last but most important detail is that you look distinguishable from everyone else in your field.

Again I say, perhaps it was my humble beginnings that gave me my penchant for expensive, exciting stage clothes. Maybe it was an eagerness to eliminate in some way those drab surroundings of my youth and the dull clothing that was all we had. In my act I jokingly refer to the days when I had to wear my brother George's hand-me-downs, which isn't really a joke because they weren't really hand-me-downs. He was also wearing them. We took turns.

It's a laugh, when I tell about wearing George's old clothes, for me to say, "Now he wears my linings," and to flash the lining of whatever coat I'm wearing. These linings are generally such that they'd get a laugh if I just flashed one and didn't say a word.

I can remember going to school wearing one of George's old band uniforms. He played in a lot of the big bands during the famous big band era and, of course, when he went with another band his uniform was no longer any use to him. So he'd give it to me. My wardrobe represented some of the greatest musical aggregations in the country. I looked, to say the least, a little different from the other kids in school, and anybody who looks different from other people takes a lot of kidding. Believe me I know. And I'm glad.

The big problem since I started on this wardrobe kick has been to keep topping myself each year. So the whole costume thing has become a very expensive joke. Some cost over $10,000. But as long as audiences enjoy seeing me, I'm glad the joke's on me.

Somebody once said, you can wear the most beautiful and expensive clothes in the world but if your face is dirty, and your fingernails uncared for or your hair untidy, you're a bum. All true! On the stage your face is "dirty" if you're not properly made up.

The lights will make it look that way. Or else, you look pale as a ghost, a living walking example of warmed-over death. And even if the words about fingernails weren't true about anybody else, they're true of a pianist who plays to an audience with their eyes focused on his fingers.

As for the hair, the way hairdos have changed for both women and men just within my memory is something to make your hair stand on end. When that happens you'll have a "natural" which is fashionable in some circles as I write this. Later on, in a more appropriate place I expect to tell about an incident involving me and a wig. But for now let me tell you that my own hair, not a wig, has been the subject of a certain amount of confusion and controversy.

Early in my career, I thought it would make me look more distinguished and more sophisticated, more mature and worldly-wise, if I had a little gray around the temples. So I sprayed my hair with silver to get the suave, debonair look I thought I needed. Everyone thought that silver temples looked so great, I got a little carried away. If just the temples did all that, how wonderful would I look if I sprayed the whole head? And I actually have a picture of me when I was a very young gray-haired old man.

Then I suddenly realized that this silver hair was making me look like a candidate for some sunset city retirement settlement so I stopped spraying it, rinsed that gray right out of my hair and went back to looking my age. But you can't stop the clock. Pretty soon a little gray that hadn't been sprayed on began to show and I now began to cover it up with a dark rinse because youthfulness, I guess, will always remain the thing that fans want to see in their favorite performers. They don't like to see them grow old. Possibly because it reminds them that the same thing is happening to them.

Haven't you suddenly run into someone you haven't seen in a long, long time and your first reaction is, "My! Hasn't he grown old!" Did you ever stop to think what he's saying about you? You can't stop the aging process, but you can slow it down a little by using rinses in your hair and all kinds of cosmetics and that's what I do. I don't mind telling the world I want to look as young as I can for as long as I can.

A man came up to me a few months ago—maybe a year ago, time goes so fast—and he said to me, "I met you when you were a gray-haired old man. Now you're a young man. What did you do, have your face lifted?" Anybody who isn't in the public eye would have given such a guy a sock in the teeth and told him to mind his own business. Performers can't do that. I told him politely that I was just getting younger as the years rolled by because, I said, "I've learned not to burn my candelabra at both ends."

Of course I could have told him that my real name was Benjamin Button. He probably wouldn't have known what I meant but it would have been fun to see his perplexed expression. In case you are now wearing such an expression, the great F. Scott Fitzgerald once wrote a story about a man named Benjamin Button who was born a bearded old man and grew younger and younger, until he just sort of baby-ed away. And I'll bet you thought I didn't have time to read.

It's one thing to look young but it's another to feel young. To live young, eat the proper foods, get the proper rest and the right type of exercise and, whatever you do, do everything in moderation. That's a very important word in my life. Drinking, smoking, sex . . . all in moderation. The joy of that is that you get to do everything longer, particularly sex. I've seen guys who have had a hell of a sex life and they look it. They look like hell.

There is a yarn I heard about a man who went to see a doctor because he could no longer make love. The doctor took one look at him and said, "At your age, what do you expect? Exactly how old are you?"

The guy said, "Twenty-eight."

It can happen. Not to me. I want to enjoy myself as long as I can. And if I have any credo I'd say it's thinking young, surrounding myself with positive thinking people who also think young and avoiding things that drain my energy. It's over-stressing mind and body that cuts you down before your time. And in show business just not keeping up with your time . . . or ahead of it . . . can kill you. You have to keep topping yourself. No matter whether it's films, the Broadway stage, the circus, anything, something new has to be added. Some new gimmick, some new spice. When business began to fall off in the film houses and theaters because people were becoming disenchanted with what they were seeing, producers began to throw in a little nudity. But pretty soon a little nudity became dull and they had to throw in a little more nudity until there was nothing very interesting about it. Groucho Marx said of the first all nude show, *Oh! Calcutta!,* "I didn't buy a ticket. I went

163]

home, took off my clothes, stood in front of a mirror and saved fifteen dollars." Nudity doesn't show anything that everybody hasn't got. We dress to improve out natural endowments.

Velvets, laces, satins, feathers, beads, furs, these are the things men and women have used to adorn themselves for centuries. So I guess I come by my love for them naturally. Angie tells me that even when I was a little boy I was fascinated by the feel and look of fine fabrics. And I guess I loved them all the more because I seldom got a chance to get my hands on any.

If you like materials and you like to draw as I do and you like to show off a little, as I do, you'll probably wind up designing some clothes. I don't have time to do much drawing anymore except just enough of a sketch to show my tailor, Frank Acuna, what I have in mind. He then makes some suggestions and we work it out. Recently we've had to add an electrician to the designing staff now that I have a suit that literally lights up.

As I've said, those costumes cost plenty. And, because they're all so expensive, even the simplest looking ones, I soon got in trouble with the IRS. I'm not the only performer who's had that kind of clothes problem, either. I was told that Dinah Shore, who wears beautiful dresses whenever she appears, and was then appearing on her own show for Chevrolet also had trouble. The Internal Revenue people wouldn't accept the fact that all those expensive gowns she wore on her show were a business expense. To prove it, Dinah had to model them all. The proof was that they all fit so snugly that they could only be worn on the stage. She couldn't move in them. She couldn't sit down. The dresses wouldn't bend. The seams would split.

The IRS challenged me the same way. They claimed that my clothes could be worn socially, hence they were *not* costumes, not deductible as a business expense. There was only one way to prove our case. I went down to the meeting to discuss the matter wearing one of my most elaborate outfits.

It doesn't take long for a crowd to gather when a guy dressed as I was steps out of a limousine in front of the Federal Building. A crowd began to form at once. It grew and grew. The people in back wanted to see what the people in front were looking at so they began to push. The people in front pushed back. And pretty soon there were a lot of policemen pushing everybody.

I managed to run into the building with the crowd following me, held back a little by a few cops. The crowd followed me right upstairs to the IRS office for what turned out to be the shortest income tax review on record.

My lawyer said to the examiner, "You people claim that my client, Liberace, can wear these clothes on the street; therefore, they are not deductible. Look out the window at what's happening downstairs. That crowd began to gather when Liberace stepped out of his car. The crowd's waiting for him to come out. People are banging on doors to get into the building. The police have had to lock it. In view of this, do you still think that costumes like this one he's wearing, which is from his stage wardrobe, can be worn on the street? Let me go further, would *you* wear it on the street?"

"Hell no!" said the examiner.

"Then it must be tax deductible," said my lawyer.

"Case dismissed," said the examiner.

The next problem was to get me out of the building. The police sneaked me through the back door. The result of that meeting was that ever since then I've made sure that there was something about every outfit I wore on the stage that was so outlandish it could be worn only in a stage performance, in a film or on a TV show.

Actually, it was my wardrobe that was responsible for what is, I think, my most famous line. And it isn't often that a piano player makes up jokes that live for years and are used by many people.

I was appearing at the opera house in San Francisco. This was where the critics, used to seeing very straight artists in the opera house, got their first look at my imaginative clothes. They didn't like them. They didn't think such things should be worn in an opera house. You have never read anything like what they wrote about me. I was almost afraid to go back to do the show the next evening. It's embarrassing, you know, to play to empty chairs, One critic, whose name just happened to be Frankenstein, wrote as if he were Frankenstein's monster himself. But the cream of the jest was that those critics were so flabbergasted that each, in his own way, conveyed the thought that my clothes had to be seen to be believed. Well, Ripley made a fortune with "Believe It Or Not," and so the challenge to credulity attracted wide attention. There had, of course, been a full house on opening night. When I walked on the second night and saw the place packed I asked the stage manager to turn on the house lights. I said, "I want to look at all those wonderful people out there." Then I turned to George and said, "Isn't that something? Did you count 'em?"

Then I motioned for the house lights to be dimmed again and thanked the audience, saying, "I was really worried that you wouldn't come to see my show after you read the reviews. I thought I'd be out here alone just playing for George. Honestly, I felt so terrible when I read those reviews yesterday that I cried all the way to the bank."

So every knock has been a boost for me. By learning to turn a nasty crack into a gag on myself, I got sympathy. It's a little like judo, using the other fellow's attack to throw him off balance and make his own weight work to your advantage.

I've gotten so I can almost guess what an audience is thinking and say something that will reply to that thought. I've already told how learning to read lips for some work I did in a motion picture helps me respond to my audience.

I may see a woman staring intently at my hands, and I know she's interested in my rings, not in how I finger the keys. So I say to her, "Want to see the rings?" Then I walk down to the edge of the stage and show them to her. "You're entitled to look at them," I say. "You paid for them."

That sort of thing works a lot of different ways. People like to touch a performer. In fact, touching has become a sort of cult among some people. I don't mind being touched, if the hand isn't a fist.

This tactile contact with an audience is easiest and most effective when you're playing in the round. I've been doing it almost since in-the-round theater was revived. When something new comes along, I'll try it. And I found the round stage made it easier for me to make contact with my audience. Buster Bonoff, who books my shows in Rhode Island and Arizona, calls me "The King of the Round." I find it much easier to bridge the gap between performer and audience when there are no footlights, no orchestra pit to divide us. And it can be done without losing any of the excitement I love.

It's easy for me to understand why President after President, when he's on any kind of a trip, likes to break away from the secret servicemen who surround him, and shake hands with the people. It's a feeling no one can understand until he experiences it. And don't think politicians aren't performers. Toward the end of the 60's and in the 70's, show business has practically rewritten the political book. Each office seeker finds his own techniques, or has them taught to him. This is particularly true when it comes to humor. Luckily I found that I was best saying what came naturally to me. I talked to my audiences just the way I'd talk to friends and guests in my home.

When I was doing my syndicated TV shows I was sponsored in over two hundred different marketing areas throughout the country by a lot of different sponsors. So when I appeared in concerts, or in a night club, I did a whole routine about these sponsors. They ranged all the way from undertaking establishments, banks, and biscuit companies to a well-known manufacturer of paper products. As sort of an afterthought I'd say "Everthing but writing paper." (Pause) Then I went on, "It was customary for all these companies to send me samples of their products." At this point some of my audience would begin to anticipate me and start to giggle. "Naturally," I told them, "I didn't hear from the undertaker—fortunately. Nor the banks—unfortunately. However, I did hear from the biscuit company and the paper manufacturer. We had more cookies than the Girl Scouts ever dreamed of. And toilet tissue to match every bathroom in the house . . . the wallpaper, that is."

Just talking about these sponsors in a chatty way enabled me to get hearty laughs from my audience. Often I got bigger "yoks" than many professional comedians are able to get with their well-prepared material. This was entirely because what I said seemed to come out of me, not out of a joke book or some gag-writer's typewriter.

I know this to be a fact because once in Las Vegas Seymour Heller thought it might be a good idea for me to try getting the help of a professional gag-writer. So we invited one of the best in the business—name withheld to protect the innocent—who had written for men like Bob Hope and Jack Benny (if there are any men like either of them). We asked him to attend one of my shows and see if he could come up with some fresh, sparkling lines. After the performance he came back to the dressing room and confessed that he didn't think he could write any funnier material than I was using. He very seriously encouraged me to continue using my own personal, special brand of humor.

Whenever I appear as a guest on a TV show, the writers of that show try to write funny lines for me. Nine times out of ten it doesn't work because it doesn't suit me. So I usually talk them into letting me do my own thing. This was especially true when I did my English TV series in London in 1969. They had hired two comedy writers to help me. But after giving their material one or two tries it was agreed that, given an idea, I could come up with better lines that were not only suited to the show, but also suited to my personality. This worked particularly well when I had special guests.

On one show I told Phyllis Diller, with whom I've always had a great rapport, that the stuff written for us wasn't right. So at our first tea break, which is what the British call our coffee breaks, we worked out some situations and lines that were much better suited to each of us and we got great big laughs with them.

I had this same experience with another guest, a man named Jack Benny, whom I've worked with many times both in the USA and in England. I seem to be the perfect straight man for his marvelous slow "takes" when he just turns and stares at the audience. All he has to do is look at me and what I'm wearing, then turn and look at the audience and they break up. He doesn't even have to say, "Welllllllll!"

The fact that Jack played the violin automatically put him in the minds of my audience, in the same category with my brother George.

Most people don't realize this but in those one hundred and seventeen syndicated TV shows that I did, George never uttered a word. He became sort of the Harpo Marx of the violin. As usual, I did all the talking. All he did was react with his expressive face and winning smile. It always worked. When I'd ask for the house lights and turn to George and say, "It's a wonderful audience. Did you count 'em?" he'd just nod in the affirmative and the lights would be blacked out. To this day there are many people who think that George was (as they thought of Harpo) a mute.

My mother once received a letter when my brother Rudy was with the Army in Korea, saying, "Dear Mrs. Liberace, What a wonderful mother you must be to have such talented sons. But what a cross to have to bear with one son in Korea and one who cannot speak."

Often I get wonderful laughs talking about articles that were written about me or my shows. I still do. A reporter once came to my old home in Sherman Oaks, California—the one with the piano-shaped pool—and wrote that practically everything in my house was shaped like a piano. Commenting on this, I said to my audience, "This is utterly rediculous. It would be downright uncomfortable if *everything* was shaped like a piano." What a laugh!

Then I quoted his tacky line. "He probably makes love on top of his glass-top piano." I said, "This too is ridiculous. Anybody knows it would scratch the hell out of the glass and besides"—I made a broad gesture at the precarious angle of the piano top—"anybody can see it would be extremely dangerous. Isn't that right, George?"

George would look at the piano, think about it, and then nod his head knowingly in the affirmative. Blackout!

I never give the names of the people who write the awful things about me. As I said during my libel trial in London, "I don't want to make them famous."

11

Hardly a day goes by that I don't hear someone knocking the United States mail service. "It's not like it used to be." "It took three days for a letter to get across town." "The rates go higher and the deliveries grow slower." Everybody gets in his crack. But, as far as I'm concerned I owe the US mail a big favor. I think it's the best agent I ever had.

To explain my reason for saying this, I have to go back a few years to the days when you could send a postcard to a friend for one penny. Today it costs six cents to send the same card. Maybe if the Postal Service had collected 10 percent for the job they got me, and all that it led to, an increase of five cents might not to have been necessary. Just think of how much money the service would make if they got a salesman's or agent's commission on all the sales and all the deals that were initiated by mail.

To be more specific. Back in those penny-postcard days (that sounds like a song title) I used to send a lot of them to entertainment buyers all over the country. By "entertainment buyers" I don't mean those who buy a ticket to a show because they want to be entertained. I mean the people—wholesalers, I guess they'd be, in any other business—who decide what shows will play in what night clubs and theaters all over the country. All it said on the card was, "Have you heard Liberace?" Then there was a note of where I was appearing and could be reached.

In those days it was the cheapest way to remind the entertainment market of your availability. Radio appearances didn't seem to do it. At least not for me. Actually there were no important radio shows you could get on unless you were already a star. And if you did get a booking with Rudy Vallee, Bing Crosby, Al Jolson or one of those topflight radio variety shows you didn't have much chance to let people get the full impact of your work. You did one number, a little chitchat with the host and then an encore. Everybody got the same treatment. In short, you got heard. But not much more.

It wasn't until television came along, and you could also be seen, that a performer like me got a real break on the so-called "desk and sofa" shows. On these you can really get across your personality, as well as your talent. It's a much better way to advertise than by postcard.

Among those who got one of mine was the Entertainment Director of the Last Frontier Motel in Las Vegas, Nevada. Although it didn't seem funny in 1943 to write "Las Vegas, Nevada," it does now. Today when you say Las Vegas, everybody knows you're not talking about the one in New Mexico or anywhere else. It's like when you say Paris, nobody thinks of Paris, Texas.

The Entertainment Director at the Last Frontier turned out to be Miss Maxine Lewis. It was while I was playing the Normandy Roof of the Mount Royal Hotel in Montreal.

In passing I'd like to call your attention to the fact that whenever anything really significant in my life happened . . . anything that was, or signaled, a big change . . . I remember a lot of details that I wouldn't otherwise remember.

Miss Lewis, I guess now I'd have called her Ms. Lewis, called me long distance, and when I came on the phone she said, "Yes, I have heard of Liberace. And I am calling to find out if you would like to play Las Vegas?"

Without a moment's hesitation I answered, "Yes, indeed. I sure would like to play Las Vegas. I've heard so much about it."

She said, "Well now that we've got that straight, the next step is, what kind of money do you want?"

The conversation from that point reflects, I think, two things. One is the prevailing money values in the early 1940's. The other is how much I needed an agent who knew what the market really was.

Every performer bad mouths his agent for not getting him a job, for getting him the wrong job, for not getting him enough money and a lot of other little show business problems. But the truth is, no matter how many mistakes they make, agents can never make the colossal boners that an entertainer, speaking and bargaining for himself, is likely to make. The reason is that the performer primarily wants to work. And it's not just his ego or his exhibitionism. Money is important but being "on" is more important. The longer you're "off" the less you'll be known and the shorter the dough will get. I don't know what my starting salary in Vegas might have been if I'd let an agent speak for me. Instead I tried to do something I'm not good at. I tried to bargain.

When Maxine Lewis asked how much I was making, I said, "Well, I get an awful lot of money." This was marvelous because at that time I had no idea what "an awful lot of money" was. Now I do.

What I was actually getting in Montreal was $350 a week. But from what I'd heard of Las Vegas, I knew I could expect better there. So with all the strength I could muster, I took a deep breath, and lied that my price was $750. (Come to think of it, the post card rate has risen six times. At that same rate of inflation that $750 would be $4,500—still not an awful lot of money as I know it.)

She said, "Seven hundred and fifty a week?"

"Yes," I answered, "I must have seven hundred and fifty dollars a week."

There was a very short pause that seemed like two and a half years. Then I heard, "You've got yourself a deal, boy. When can you open?"

Right then and there on the phone we set an opening date with her saying, "I'll get the contracts in the mail in a few days. And by the way, you may be interested in knowing that you're following Sophie Tucker."

Knowing the stature (no pun intended) of Miss Tucker at that time, this should have told me immediately that I'd asked too little or that they planned to make up on me what they overpaid her. But none of that ever crossed my mind. I was elated at the thought of playing Vegas.

Of course Las Vegas was very different when I saw it for the first time than it is today. All the "action" was down in the town. There were only two hotels "way" out on the now famous "Las Vegas Strip." One was El Rancho Vegas Motel, the other The Last Frontier. Both were sprawling one story, early-western motel-style architecture. Promoters must have had in mind how they hoped "The Strip" would develop. But I'm sure they never, in their wildest dreams, foresaw the high-rise hotels that now line it. Nor could I guess that I was destined to work in the very first of these "skyrise" hotels to open.

The name of the show room in The Last Frontier Hotel was The Ramona Room and my opening night there, my very first performance in Las Vegas, was so gratifying to me that I was happy and contented with the whole world. And I knew I had found the most exciting and responsive audience there was. Even the rehearsal on opening day proved memorable. In those days, I was a huge company of one—stage manager, lighting and sound technician, musical director, personal manager, and performer. In other words I handled everything myself, so I was pleasantly surprised when I entered the room for rehearsal and discovered they furnished a light man whom I mistook for the only gentleman seated near the light board. I walked up to him, introduced myself, and asked him if he was the spot-light man—he nodded affirmatively—and then I explained my sheet of light cues to him. Just then Maxine Lewis walked in and saw us talking and said, "Oh, do you know Howard Hughes?" He was already a famous Billionaire in those days, but you'd never have known it to see him dressed very casually with sneakers, looking very much like a light man. He teased me about the incident long afterwards by saying "How are the lights?" whenever he would see me. Of course that was back in the early days of Vegas before he became a recluse.

After the opening show, I hardly had time to get to my dressing room when there was a knock on the door. It was Maxine Lewis.

Her greeting was, "Mr. Liberace, you have found a home for yourself in Las Vegas. There's only one trouble. We're not paying you enough money."

Because nobody had ever said anything like that to me before in my whole life, I just simply didn't understand her. It was almost as if she'd been speaking a strange language. Anyway, what she said sounded strange to me. I have one rule. When in doubt about what anybody says or means, be polite.

I said, "Thank you. But I don't really understand what you're talking about."

"So I'll translate," she said. "We just had Sophie Tucker here. We paid her six thousand dollars a week. After that show you gave tonight, I feel guilty about only paying you sevn hundred and fifty dollars."

This was a new thing to me, too. I'd never heard of a theatrical booker feeling guilty about anything. I knew I had to make some reaction to her statement, however, so I said what I thought was the right thing, "Well, we made a contract and I'm happy with it."

"Not me," said Miss Lewis. "You're worth at least fifteen hundred dollars, twice what we're paying you. So if you don't mind, we're going to pay you fifteen hundred dollars a week instead of seven hundred and fifty dollars."

I was absolutely flabbergasted. It wasn't so much that I was getting my salary doubled as it was that this made it the first time in my life I was able to get into the four-figure salary bracket. Naturally it was the beginning of a beautiful friendship between me and The Last Frontier. In show business the words for beautiful friendship are spelled l-o-n-g t-e-r-m c-o-n-t-r-a-c-t.

It made me very happy that I was lucky enough to come to the Last Frontier first. And that's exactly what I got. I played the Last Frontier over a dozen times during the years the contract was in force. And during that time other hotels began to blossom along The Strip. One of these was The Flamingo.

One evening I'd just finished my show at the Last Frontier and was walking to my dressing room when a man grabbed my arm and introduced himself as Bugsy Siegel. He said he'd just seen my show and wanted to talk to me, privately. I had no idea who Bugsy Siegel was, so I told him he'd have to wait till I changed my clothes. Then, if he didn't mind waiting, I'd be glad to talk to him.

He said, "Okay. I'll wait. But make it snappy!"

When I came out of my dressing room he wasn't there. But when I walked into the hotel lobby, there he was. He started to walk along beside me saying, "Young man, I liked your show very much. How would you like to play at the Flamingo?"

"I think it's a very beautiful hotel. But I think my loyalty is to The Last Frontier. They were the first to discover me in Las Vegas."

"Well," said Siegel, "now I'm discovering you. Let's talk it over." He took me by the arm, very firmly, and kept me moving with him as he said, "Why don't you come over to the Flamingo with me and we'll discuss it?" On the way over he told me he was Entertainment Director.

175]

As many readers will know, Bugsy Siegel was a lot more than entertainment director of a hotel. He was one of the most notorious mobsters on the West Coast at the time and had a big interest in the Flamingo. If I'd known that I might not have been as firm as I was in talking to him. I'd heard lots of stories from old time cafe performers who worked in the prohibition era, so I knew what happened to entertainers who didn't do what the mob wanted them to do.

When we got to his hotel he took me to the main dining room, introduced me to the maître d' and other personnel of the house and told them to give me anything I wanted. Then he left me alone for a few minutes to think and enjoy the courtesy of the house. Finally he came over and joined me at my table and asked, "What are they paying you over at that other place?—And don't lie to me because I can find out the truth."

I felt sure he could. So I told him the truth.

His answer was. "I'll double that if you come over to the Flamingo and work for us."

All of a sudden I found myself in a world where everybody was doubling my salary. It's not easy for a young performer to keep his head under conditions like that. In my heart I felt I should be loyal to the Last Frontier. But, I also felt an obligation to be loyal to myself. Which was more important to me, I asked myself, the stockholders in a hotel or my family and my future? "I'll have to think it over," I told Mr. Siegel.

He said, "Okay. You do that. Think it over. Then let me know before you leave Las Vegas and we'll set a date for you to come and play the Flamingo."

Clearly, he felt that he had made me an offer I couldn't refuse. Whether this was based on his connections or the money offer, I guess I'll never know. Before it was time for me to get in touch with him, the papers were full of headlines, "Bugsy Siegel Shot in Beverly Hills Home."

I must say—and this is how I felt before I knew who he really was—he had a most convincing and ingratiating way about him and, I suppose, had he lived, I might have taken him up on his offer. I don't know. I may just think this because time has taught me that a person owes his loyalties only to other persons—that being loyal to corporations seldom is worth the honesty of purpose that it represents.

So I stayed with the Last Frontier for ten years, until 1954, when The Riviera, "the first high rise in the Las Vegas skies," opened. The building was a nine-story job and they must have thought I could do something to keep it full because the management made me an offer it was impossible to turn down—$50,000 a week.

It was historic because it was more money than had yet been offered to a performer in Vegas and broke that entertainment capital's price ceiling. I have since done better; I recently signed a twenty-week over two-year contract with the Hilton for $2,000,000, which means my salary has reached the seven-figure mark.

Of course, since the Riviera was built, hotels have gone higher and higher and so have salaries. I wonder everytime when I go to Vegas how they can go on building more and more glamorous hotels and paying higher and higher salaries, competing with each other for talent that will lure the tourists to their casinos.

The truth is that Las Vegas, in an effort to keep people coming there, keeps topping itself. The old El Rancho Vegas and the Last Frontier bear no more relation to places like Caesar's Palace and the Las Vegas Hilton than some motel on the outskirts of Atlantic City bears to the Waldorf-Astoria in New York.

And in line with this ever-better-onward-and-upward attitude of Vegas, it was almost part of my contract with the Riviera that I had to wear some clothes that would top anything I'd ever worn before. And since I was making more than I'd ever dreamed of making . . . well, not exactly, but more than I'd ever actually made before, I really wanted to sparkle. So I went from the comparatively simple white suit, which had really created a sensation, to gold lamé. And *that* made the wire services.

From then on, as I heard an old mule skinner say once when I was staying at the Furnace Creek Inn in Death Valley, "It was Nellie bar the door." Over the years I've used fur coats and fur trims, jewels of all kinds and diamond buttons that spell out my name. I've worn star-spangled hot pants and jewel-studded Bermuda shorts. I've dressed as a hillbilly, a clown, a court jester. I've appeared in the styles of famous composers, worn hats, plumes and wigs of various eras. I even have a jacket that lights up and twinkles when the house is blacked out.

It has gotten so that I must always do something to create a larger-than-life image. And even as fantastic as some of the clothes

I've worn were, some are no "farther out" than the costumes I now see on the streets of New York, Los Angeles or any big city.

To be a leader in fashion you have to be a couple of steps ahead of the crowd. I don't pretend to be a leader, but I'm obliged to look more extreme than anybody in my audience because that's what people pay to see and they're entitled to what they've paid for.

While I was playing at The Riviera, one of the nicest things that can happen to a performer happened to me. I was able to give another entertainer the one chance any true star needs. She was only twenty-one years old at the time although I suspect she was really younger than she admitted. That's the way women are, when they're very young they call themselves older, and when they start to get a little mature . . . welllllll! Forget it.

The first time I heard her she was singing in a little spot called Bon Soir in Greenwich Village in New York City. I was very excited by her individual artistry and style, as well as the quality of her voice and a special something of her own that she seemed to add to everything she sang. Apparently I was not the only one who recognized this unusual talent and not too long after seeing her in the Village, I found she was on the same *Ed Sullivan Show* that I was on, although she was a comparative unknown. (Can you be "comparatively" unknown or is that as silly as saying "a little pregnant"? I guess "unknown" means just not known at all and there can be no comparative about it. So I ought to change that to, she was known to very few.)

Anyway, this little-known personality absolutely stopped everyone cold during rehearsal. All the busy people around the theater-studio where the show was done stopped whatever they were doing and listened to her. It was almost electric. She had some kind of magic. Then I began to hear comments like, "Man, that gal can really sing!" and "Tough she's so homely!" Or, "Too bad about that beak." These were all accurate. Pretty she wasn't!

The next time I heard her was at Basin Street East on 48th Street and Lexington Avenue in New York. The word had gone out, and she had them standing in line to get in, all the way to Third Avenue, a block away. But if there had been no holdout waiting to get in to see her, if there were none of the symptoms of impending success surrounding her, if it were only for the way she sang, I'd have wanted her on my show in Las Vegas the next time I opened at The Riviera Hotel.

I took my manager, Seymour Heller, to hear her and after the show he said, "Well, she sings all right. But do you really think she's *that* good?"

I said, "She's fabulous."

"But you've always had such beautiful girls in your shows. This girl is definitely . . . well . . . she's definitely not glamorous."

"I'll agree with you, she's not beautiful. But I feel that there is something glamorous about her. Maybe not glamor as we know it. But there have been some sensationally successful women who never could have made it on that Bert Parks show in Atlantic City."

"Name one," Seymour said.

"Eleanor Roosevelt."

"She wasn't a singer."

"See," I said. "This girl can sing too." The discussion wasn't all nonsense like that. We got down to the gut issue of whether I really thought this kid could make it. And finally we made her an offer of $7,500 which we arrived at as the final figure she couldn't turn down. She didn't.

I must say in all honesty that the night we opened everyone didn't rush up to me to tell me I'd made a great new discovery. Many agreed with Seymour that I'd made a great big boo-boo. Everyone agreed she could sing. Even the management of The Riviera was sort of *comme ci comme ça*. However, I went to one of the big bosses and said, "If you're smart you'll sign this girl for a return engagement, because she's going to become one of the biggest stars in show business."

During her first engagement we did something that's only done occasionally in Vegas. We did a third show one night. These third shows are attended largely by people from all the other shows in town—actually that's why you do the show—who wouldn't normally get a chance to see you. It was at this show that my protégée's great magic really lit up the night. Her performance was brilliant, electrifying, and the show people in town took her to their hearts and made her one of them. She was so great that night the bosses agreed to sign her to a return contract.

So enough of being coy. Unless you've never watched TV, bought an album, listened to the radio, gone to the theater or the movies, you must know that the lady I've been writing about is Miss Barbra Streisand.

179]

After that night in Las Vegas, everything started to work right for Barbra. To begin with she got her first record album and an offer to play the great comedienne Fannie Brice, in the musical comedy *Funny Girl*. She stayed with me to do an engagement at Harrah's Club at Lake Tahoe, and then she left for New York to start rehearsals of the show that then became a motion picture and won her an Oscar.

Incidentally, if Barbra had ever done what she suggested she might have done when she discovered the layout of The Ambassador Hotel's Coconut Grove in Los Angeles, she never would have played *Funny Girl* on Broadway or won an Oscar for the film.

On her opening night at The Grove, she walked out onto the floor. She looked at the crowded table in front of her. Then she looked to her right and saw still more tables full of people. To her left she saw another mass of tables and people. She took a deep breath and said, "If I'd known there were going to be people sitting on both sides of me as well as in front of me, I'd have had my nose fixed."

For those who don't remember Fanny Brice, she had a nose just like Barbra's.

I think the thing I admired most about Barbra when we began working together was that she was a perfectionist. When It came to her performance, her singing, it had to be 100 percent the way she thought it should be. Her arrangements, her lighting, her accompaniment, everything was done just the way she dictated and that's the mark of a successful performer. Those who don't take that trouble, who don't care whether things are right or not will soon find that their audiences don't care very much either.

I found Barbra to be a very kind, generous, sweet person, sincere in her work and her attitudes toward people. The one thing she hadn't discovered about show business was the value of glamor. It almost seemed as if she'd never even heard the word. But this, too, got through to her.

The first time I saw Barbra down in the Village it looked as if she'd just been to a rummage sale and was wearing it. Standing next to Emmet Kelly, the clown, she would have made him look like a well-dressed man.

When she first started to work in my show she admitted to the audience that the dress she had on she had made herself out of an old tablecloth. She said that with the trimming and everything

—including her time—it cost $4. Of course, her whole rather ragamuffin idea got a tremendous howl from the audiences in Vegas because it was such a contrast to the clothes I was wearing. Everything I had on cost more than $4, including my shoelaces.

But with Barbra, kooky clothing was sort of an obsession. It represented no financial problem. She loved to browse around in Good Will and second-hand shops and find discarded old garments, beaded bags, funny shoes with crazy heels and pointed toes, that you knew were discarded not because they were worn out but because they turned out to be just too crazy to wear, except to a Halloween party. She liked to browse around antique shops and pick up pieces of art nouveau. All that this resulted in was that she now has one of the largest and most valuable collections of art nouveau of anyone in Hollywood.

Soon, inspired by the sort of clothes she obviously liked to wear because in some odd way their oddness suited her, the big couturiers began designing things especially for Barbra, and she has become a leader in the fashion world. To me her appearance is a thing of beauty. Her figure, her features, the clothes she wears, the songs she sings and the way she sings them come together to make her one of the most glamorous stars in show business today.

And, incidentally, that first contract Barbra signed with the Riviera Hotel was honored by her after she'd played the International in Vegas at a good solid, six-figure salary. Of course, the Riviera—doing what the Last Frontier did for me—recognized what they had and added some numbers to the original $7,500.

There's nothing Barbra won't try. When we were playing at Lake Tahoe, she decided to throw a birthday party for our stage manager. She was married to Elliott Gould at the time, and they were living in a big house loaned to them by the hotel for the duration of their stay. The whole company was invited to the party.

She said she had a big surprise to spring on all of us when the party was over. Everybody was trying to guess what it would be. I thought she was going to tell us she was pregnant. Then we found out. She'd decided to bake the birthday cake herself. It didn't look like any problem to her. She'd seen how easily it was done on a million TV commercials. The cake always turned out to be not only delicious but better than anyone had ever tasted before.

All through the dinner she kept saying, wait till I bring in the cake. She gave that cake a buildup that lacked only the drum roll heralding a trapeze performer's last "impossible" trick. And when the cake came in, imagine our surprise. There was not one big cake. There were a lot of ordinary-sized cakes. Everyone at the table got his own individual birthday cake with a candle stuck in the middle of it. Naturally, the first thing we all wanted to know was what gave her the idea to make cakes for the house. The explanation made everyone hysterical, but it seemed to make sense to Barbra. "I used the Betty Crocker recipe," she said, "and I didn't know how to break it down. So I made each one of us a whole Betty Crocker cake." Then she looked around anxiously and asked, "Well, how is it?"

Elliott was the only one with the courage to speak, after all she was his wife. "The cake's delicious, Barb, but there's something wrong with the frosting."

Barbra looked hurt and Elliott felt sorry he'd said anything. "In what way?"

"Well . . . it's sort of tough."

"I guess that's because I had a little problem," Barbra explained. "I ran out of confectioner's sugar. So I used flour."

Well, we all peeled the frosting off and ate the cake—a little of it because she'd obviously done some substitution on that, too. We took the rest home with us saying we'd eat it after the show. I still have mine in Palm Springs. It makes a great doorstop.

Knowing how Barbra felt about antique articles of clothing, when *Funny Girl* opened I sent her a beaded bag that I picked up in a Good Will store for $3. It was absolutely filthy. I brought it home, washed it in sudsy water and hung it out in the sun to dry. I was glad this turned out okay, because it was the first beaded bag I'd ever washed. When it dried I packed it nicely and sent it to her as a gag. But, she told me that the gag bag was her favorite and that she carried it when she went out in the evening. And she returned the gag by saying, when people asked where she got it, "I stole it from Liberace."

As this book is being prepared for the printer, I will be back in Vegas again at the Las Vegas Hilton, which now has me under an extended contract. So if you're thinking of going to Vegas for whatever happens to be your idea of fun, find out when I'm at the Hilton and say hello. If I'm not there, I'll be back soon.

I try not to return to any one place too often. It is possible to suffer from overexposure. I know. I have. So usually it's at least eighteen months before I play any return engagement . . . except at Las Vegas. There, the tourist turnover is so terrific there's almost a whole new set of people every day. And they come from all over the United States, Canada and Mexico . . . from all over the world for that matter. The French, who love Monte Carlo, say that it pales into nothingness beside the opulence of Las Vegas. I agree.

So Las Vegas can be returned to as often as you can get bookings. You don't have to worry at all about a local audience. The "locals," as they're called in Vegas, hardly ever attend the shows unless they really love you or the word gets around that you're wearing star-spangled hot pants. *That* they had to see to believe. They've seen them all. Sometimes, in the case of such "locals" as Totie Fields and Shecky Green, they've *been* the shows. As for the rest of the citizens of Las Vegas it's just a place to live and work. Most of them don't even gamble.

I think the most wonderful thing about Vegas is that it's actually a place where you can enjoy yourself no matter what you like to do. I've had people ask me, "Why should I go to Vegas? I don't gamble." So what? There's golf, tennis, swimming, boating and water skiing on Lake Mead. And what's wrong with just lying around in the sun during the day and seeing the shows at night? A lot of people who go to Vegas don't gamble. I'm one of them. No matter how often I go back, I'm always sure of a new audience.

Speaking of audiences, I think my favorite Nevada engagement is John Ascuago's Nugget in Sparks, just four miles from the center of Reno. With all due respect to the magnificent show places of Las Vegas and Lake Tahoe, this has to be one of the most unusual places I have ever played. The audiences, which I would describe as unsophisticated family type, are the most attentive and responsive in every way. When they give you a standing ovation, it is spontaneous and sincere. If I ever had to hire an audience, I would hire them any night of any week. First of all, The Circus Room is not too large—about 900 capacity—and the atmosphere is intimate and friendly. It has a U-shaped balcony which makes it more like a theater than a nightclub. And it has as a permanent feature in every show (are you ready?) two elephants, Bertha, a big one, and Tina, a small one, and they open the show with their amazing tricks and are truly "Superstars" in every sense of the word.

Then after their act there is a slight pause to reset the stage and the regular show begins. I don't know if you have any idea what it's like to follow elephants in a show, but let me tell you it can be great funb. For example, about three-quarters of the way through my part of the show, I make some flattering comments about the Nugget and The Circus Room, and then after a brief pause, as sort of an afterthought, say that I might consider buying it. Another pause is followed with, "But I've got to get rid of those damn elephants! How would you like to share the dressing room with that? [Laugh!] Besides the big one has eyes for me! [Howl!] She's not getting near me with that trunk!" [Scream!]

They say elephants never forget; well, I hope they can read because I want to go on record as saying, "Bertha and Tina, I'm only kidding, I really love you even if you are big showoffs!"

12

I don't know why it is that every place I went, I find as I think back, the press took pot shots at me. I use the past tense here because happily this sort of thing is no longer sporting and is almost a thing of the past considering my press today. Even in Australia. I didn't go there expecting to find a great vast wasteland inhabited solely by kangaroos and koala bears. If I'd thought that I'd never have gone. I went expecting to find interested and interesting intelligent people who would be entertained by what I do. And that's what I found. I also found the usual hostile press corps. All of them heavily loaded with prepackaged quips they'd picked up from papers in other places I'd played. None had ever met me before. It was my first trip Down Under . . . oops!

I'm sure I didn't make that slip when I was in Sydney and Melbourne. They don't really like the expression Down Under. To them, we're down under. Not one Australian ever speaks of the United States, although they admire us, as being "up over."

I'll get to the hassles and the pot shots later; there were immediate problems on my arrival. For one thing, there was another attraction in town the same day. You know, in show business, it's not the best thing in the world to move in against a hit. That's what I did. The Queen Mother was on a tour of Australia and she happened to be in Sydney when I got there. Not that we do exactly the same things. But she figured to get the bulk of any newspaper headlines. And there's no use kidding yourself; when you're on tour in a foreign country, headlines mean bread

185]

and butter . . . longer lines at the box office. Nevertheless, I did have a "hot time in the old town" of Sydney. For openers, according to the newspapers the day I arrived was the hottest day in the hottest February they'd had in over twelve years. That doesn't mean it was rather warm for late winter or that spring was coming early, as it would in New York or London. They were having their summer and when you think of their December as being like our June, then you come up with February being like August and that's, as the kids say, hot.

In the past fifteen years since that hot February day, air conditioning has grown as popular and become as general in Australia as it now is in the United States. Back in the late 50's in Sydney, America's "common cold," which it does so much to encourage, had not yet struck and the best way to keep cool was to drink tea, shower and change your clothes a lot.

I had hardly stepped off the plane when the reporters began to fire the usual barrage of usual questions. By that I mean such old standard zingers—even way back then—as "Do you really have a piano-shaped swimming pool?" Of course a question like that means more in Sydney—or did then—than it means in the States where having a pool in Connecticut, much less Los Angeles, was not such a big deal. Of course when you have a piano-shaped pool, before you can dive in you have to find out what key you swim in. So just to have a little fun I told the pretty young girl reporter who asked the question that I had to get rid of the piano-shaped pool because the piano tuner almost drowned.

You can't imagine how delighted I was to find an invitation to the Royal Garden Party for the Queen Mother—to be held that afternoon at Government House—waiting for me in my hotel room. I can't tell you how excited I was. The Queen Mother was the one woman in the world I wanted to meet and I must say that meeting her convinced me that I knew how to pick wonderful women. So it was the thrill of thrills to be told that I would be presented.

Well, I figured I'd better wear my most conservative clothes, a dark suit and all that understated elegance that is British all over the Empire, even in Australia where they're really more like Yanks than Limeys. What else do you do when you're going to meet your idol, the Queen Mother?

Since this was my first trip to Australia and my TV shows had

[186

not yet played there, the people knew me only by my recordings which had been selling very well throughout the country for several years. The Aussies are big record buyers. And they'd seen my one starring picture, up to that time, *Sincerely Yours*. This, I figured, was very limited exposure so I was flabbergasted to find that the crowds outside of Government House—waiting to see the Queen Mother—recognized me and gave me one of those typical English-type cheers that start with "Three cheers for Lib! Hip! Hip!" followed by three "Rah's" with a "Hip! Hip!" in between. Even the constabulary controlling the crowd and protecting the Queen greeted me like a pal. They're very friendly, the Australians. But, said a Sydney PRO man (that means Public Relations Official), "We're a no-nonsense lot. They really like you, Lib. We don't get rocked off our feet by ballyhoo."

I was interested to hear that but hoped they'd get rocked off their feet enough to come to the Trocadero where I was opening the next day.

Inside Government House and through to the garden, I walked into one of the prettiest scenes I'd ever seen. It was as if I'd made an entrance into the second act of *My Fair Lady*, which not only had not yet reached Australia, they hadn't even heard the music . . . which I was to find out to my dismay and despair.

It was charming. Lots of lovely ladies strolling around carrying parasols to protect them from the hot February sun. And in the midst of the swirl of upper-echelon Australian elegance there was the Queen Mother being gracious and charming to everyone . . . but me because I was not presented.

I never did find out what the foul-up was and it made me very unhappy. But imagine how unhappy I became when I got the word that I was about to be "slung out." That means in Australian slang, exactly what it sounds like. I was going to get the bum's rush. They said I was an imposter, that I didn't belong there. I showed them my *carte d'entrée* but that made no difference to the hot heads who wanted me ejected.

They might have gotten their way, too, if it weren't that the young lady I was escorting to the party was a reporter on the Sydney *Daily Mirror*. As the situation began to grow a little sticky—I didn't want to leave at any cost because I still had hopes of meeting the Queen Mother—it passed through my mind that maybe we could switch roles and I could become the person she, as a member of the press, was escorting to the party. In show business, all passes are for two.

When the charge that I'd sneaked in was disproved by my *carte d'entrée* with my name and the crown on it, they then charged that the invitation was a forgery. I was later told that the real trouble was that some super-patriots were trying to avenge the Queen Mother for something I'd casually said on TV in America several years before, something that Cassandra brought up in his libelous column and was again rehashed a year later during the trial in London.

The young lady reporter I was with, who signed herself with the one name Andrea (giving us one eccentricity in common), was immediately outraged at what was happening. She went right to work to do something about it. And the very first thing she did was to seek out and introduce me to a friend of hers by the name of Mrs. Delaney. Mrs. Delaney told me what a fan of mine she was and how grateful she was to Andrea for bringing me over to meet her.

Andrea then told Mrs. Delaney about the nasty thing that was happening and she went immediately to tell this to Mr. Delaney. They were one of those legendary, ideally married couples, so he, naturally, wanted to do everything he could to please his wife. And since he was Chief of Police there was a lot he could do. So everything was quickly straightened out. But the truth then turned out to be that there were people who had gotten in on false credentials. Andrea, good newspaperwoman that she was, found this out in a little while when she discovered three people with phony invites within a few yards of where we were first challenged.

But innocence is no excuse when newspaper people are out to get a sensational story, as I've discovered time and time again. So the fact that everything was cleared up did not deter the papers in Sydney, as well as in Melbourne, where I was also booked to play, from running nasty headlines like: LIBERACE CRASHED ROYAL PARTY—THEY WANTED TO THROW HIM OUT.

That little dandy is the way the Melbourne *Sun* phrased it. There were variations on the same theme in all the other papers.

Right after the garden party I was scheduled to meet the press at the hotel. But people who plan such schedules never seem to allow enough time, so naturally I was late. Well, I might have been late anyway, but I was really later because I hung around as long as I could hoping against hope that in some way I could pay my respects to the Queen Mother.

It was not bad enough that I had kept the newspaper people waiting, but the publicity types who had arranged the press conference weren't honest with the reporters. They told each one of them that he or she was to have an exclusive interview. Naturally, when I finally arrived at the hotel I found a very hostile group of men and women waiting for me. The fact that they didn't cut me up any more than is usual everyplace I go convinces me that what I once said in an interview in an unguarded moment is the truth, "People can't help liking me."

I believe that. If it's possible to be chemically allergic to things . . . to automatically hate things . . . why can't the opposite be true? Why can't there be something about you that attracts? Anyway, as someone who signed himself merely Staff Correspondent, wrote in the arts Department of the sophisticated Sydney weekly *The Observer*, "We were all ready to make mincemeat of this pompadoured sissy. Then a black car drove up, Liberace walked over to us, smiling, calling us each by name after the introduction. Our mouths fell open. No publicity man could have manufactured that smile."

One of the women journalists at that interview later wrote that I was the only person she ever saw who could smile and talk at the same time. Clearly Don Ameche had never been to Sydney.

My anonymous friend on *The Observer* continued, "He was just a good-mannered, pleasant bloke. That's more than can be said for many other celebrities who get a much better deal from the press. So it was that when the bombshell dropped, none of us really cared."

" 'I'm sorry,' he told us with a winning smile, 'but I never give exclusive interviews. Life is too short and I just haven't the time.'

"You can't blame a man for not wanting to spend the rest of the evening talking to newspaper men," wrote this newspaper man. "If Liberace is publicity hungry, he definitely did not show it then when he risked offending the press."

The next day I opened at the Trocadero and that very same day I got bombed in a weekly magazine that corresponds roughly to our *TV Guide* or to the TV and radio program magazines that come as supplements to our Sunday newspapers. It was a two-page article dealing with me "pro and con" that must have been written at least a week before I arrived. On the left hand page an Australian music critic, Julian Russell, tore me to ribbons and summed up his sizzling critique by saying, "His music is slovenly and sentimental enough to disgrace a mediocre high school student."

On the opposite page I was "defended," if that's the right word, by a man named Peter Sainthill. His strongest defense was, "Liberace's genius lies not in his ability to play the piano but in his capacity to gauge the taste of his audience with unfailing accuracy. It is quite probable that in the course of his recitals, Liberace heightens the musical appreciation of his audiences by introducing them to music of which otherwise they would be ignorant."

Well, even I know that's not very good writing but it does say what I try to do. I do not, nor have I ever, played to please critics and that is certainly why, as Julian Russell points out, "Liberace seldom gets a good press."

That isn't quite true either. While the critics tear my music-making to pieces, blast my singing, deplore my dancing and the feature writers make fun of the things that I want them to make fun of . . . things that I have surrounded myself with so they'll have something to write about, rarely does anyone who actually meets and talks to me say anything unpleasant about me, personally.

But there is always one spoilsport in the group who comes up with something like this, "In 1956 when you first went to London, the *Sketch* said, 'Liberace will make thousands of pounds in this country. He deserves every penny he gets. Such shameful exhibitionism must be rewarded.' " Then he looked up and smiled and asked, "Do these remarks hurt you?"

I said that it was partially due to remarks like that, that I had become (at that time) the highest paid entertainer in the world.

The man then asked, sarcastically, "Exactly what is it you do that gets your audiences eating out of your hand?"

"I don't encourage that," I said, "I've been bitten too often."

Then some smart reporter asked if it was true that at one of my concerts I snatched a pen knife and scratched my autograph in a woman's ankle bracelet. I had to tell him that was nonsense.

I wouldn't dare do that, even if someone suggested it. The knife could slip and I could be sued for performing an illegal operation.

And so it was in Australia, everything going exactly as anticipated ... the usual knocks, the usual boosts and the usual capacity audiences.

Even an unusual thing happened a propos the running battle between the press and me. A producer of a rival show came to my defense.

Harry Wren had a musical comedy called *The Cherry Blossom* coming into Sydney at the same time I was there. Yet Harry, whom I did not know, had this to say to the newspaper people, "Although he is in direct opposition to me, I am prepared to say Liberace is the greatest showman I have seen.

"We are so far away, it's hard enough to get topliners here. If the critics keep up their vituperative tactics we'll be left with only the abos to entertain us."

"Abos?" you ask. That's Australian slang for the aborigines who still live deep in the heart of Australia.

Then something even more unusual happened. I was told that I could not do—had to cut out—one of the most effective numbers in my act. I was actually served with a legal order to cease and desist from playing any of the great songs my friends Alan J. Lerner and Frederick Loewe wrote for the Broadway hit show, then in its second year on Broadway, *My Fair Lady*. It was like telling Judy Garland she couldn't do "Over the Rainbow" or Al Jolson that he had to quit singing "Sonny Boy" or maybe eliminating Beethoven's Ninth from the New York Philharmonic's Christmas repertoire.

I think there's only one way to explain, fully, frankly and completely the deplorable situation that left me stunned, surprised and exasperated. It was a situation I would not have thought possible. It took me so by surprise that I misunderstood the motivation behind it and made an awful mistake. As Mayor LaGuardia of New York City once said, "When I make a mistake, it's a beaut!" Well, the Little Flower can move over and make room for me.

I went off half-cocked, misjudged and maligned the Australians and said things that fifteen years later I'm still ashamed of and apologizing for.

Perhaps the best way I can continue that apology is to tell the story just as it looked to the Australians, as it was reported in their papers, and not sparing myself any of the embarrassment atten-

191]

dant on the things I said or the things they said about me.

It was one of the few times in my life that I have lost my temper. I can remember no time since. Maybe that incident was a lesson sent to me by whoever handles adult education up there on high to show me how easily temper can cause you to make a terrible mistake.

The Sydney *Telegraph,* of March 6, headlined BOOING CROWDS HELD BACK FROM LIBERACE.

The Melbourne *Sun* of the same day headlined LIBERACE WALKED OUT–THOUSANDS BOOED.

The Sunday *Morning Herald* of that day started its story with the head LIBERACE TO CONTINUE AUSTRALIAN SHOWS. And here is the story in its entirety just as it ran . . . nothing changed . . . nothing omitted.

Liberace, the American entertainer, decided last night to continue his Australian tour after his promoter had threatened legal action against him.

Liberace, the pianist, cancelled two Sydney performances yesterday because Chappell and Co. has begun a court action to prevent him from playing numbers from *My Fair Lady.*

The company claims that it holds the exclusive Australian rights to *My Fair Lady,* an American musical based on George Bernard Shaw's *Pygmalion.*

Mr. Lee Gordon, promoter of the tour, said last night that after legal action was threatened because of alleged breach of contract, Liberace telephoned his lawyers in America and then agreed to continue his tour.

The American composers of *My Fair Lady,* Lerner and Loewe, were trying to get special permission for Liberace to present numbers from the show.

Liberace will give a show Thursday night to make up for missing yesterday's performances.

Yesterday's ticket holders could obtain refunds from the agencies, where they bought their tickets or the tickets would be honored at the performances next Wednesday or Thursday.

10,000 POUND OFFER REJECTED

Chappel and Company yesterday rejected an offer of 10,000 pounds by Mr. Gordon to allow Liberace to present numbers from *My Fair Lady.*

[192

Liberace's refusal to appear yesterday followed the serving of a notice of motion that tomorrow Chappel and Co. would seek an extension of a Supreme Court injunction restraining him from presenting any numbers from *My Fair Lady*.

A capacity audience of about 2,000 at the Trocadero in the afternoon heard Liberace read a statement that he would not give any further performances in Australia until, "I am once again permitted to perform any and all music of my country."

About 40 people waited outside the Trocadero last night. A sign informed them, "Liberace performance postponed. See tomorrow's paper."

Liberace walked onto the Trocadero stage in the afternoon to a fanfare and introduction.

When the applause subsided he said, "I, Liberace, an American-born citizen of the United States have been restricted by law from playing any of the compositions from *My Fair Lady*, which constitutes a portion of my program.

"Any laws that prevent my democratic right to perform the music of my country are in violation of the doctrines of my government and its people and must be interpreted as Communistic.

"Never before in my entire lifetime have I been prevented from expressing myself as an artist, to exercise my democratic freedom of musical speech.

"If necessary I will call upon my government of the United States of America to assist my defense.

"Until I am once again permitted to perform any and all music of my country without any further restrictions, I am compelled by my American convictions and beliefs to refuse to give any further performances in your country.

"I am truly sorry."

Then Liberace left the stage. A brief silence was followed by murmuring and then loud boos.

That was the mildest and most straightforward story of all that appeared. Most made fun of my speech, and I presume they had a right to. As I have said, it was headstrong, ill-advised and rather pompous.

Having said that, I'll exercise my right to criticize what I consider to be one of the most amateurishly written, repetitious, unprofessional news stories I have ever read anywhere. And that was the best of the whole Australian lot.

This is the first time I've ever criticized a newspaper, but maybe it's about time I should and I certainly feel better for it.

If you want to read how a professional newspaper handled the story, and at the same time find out what the action really was, *Variety*, which has been called the show business bible, ran this story:

FINE LIBERACE FOR UN-"FAIR" TUNES

Liberace received a $450 rap for infringing an Australian copyright by playing tunes from the musical *My Fair Lady* during his Down Under engagement. The fine will be split by Liberace and Lee Gordon the promoter of the Australian tour.

Fine will be paid to Chappel & Co. Ltd. of Sydney, which has the sole Australian copyright to the Alan Jay Lerner-Frederick Loewe score and the sole right to the performance of the songs in public or authorization for their public performance. The tuner is scheduled to open in Melbourne in August.

That's the whole story. There was one amusing footnote to the affair, one that shows that all over the world, no matter where you go, there is always someone ready and eager to seize the opportunity to make a buck by bucking the law.

A syndicate offered me the use of the Sydney Harbor Showboat, the Kalang. They said they could beat the ban on singing the *My Fair Lady* selections by performing outside the three-mile territorial limit.

Because of all this I thought long and hard before returning to Australia and particularly to Sydney. I figure there's no use pushing your luck, and if the Aussies have long memories or like to hang onto a grudge, I'd be about as popular as a sore throat epidemic in a traveling opera troupe.

On the other hand, if you don't take a chance, as Bing Crosby used to sing, "Old Rockin' Chair's Got Ya." So we decided to take another crack at a country that has the strongest beer I ever drank. And they drink a lot of it.

After all, thirteen years should have given them enough time to forget and forgive, at least the latter. So in 1971 I went back with what I think was the most outrageous wardrobe I've ever had. But by then the young people had made what I used to wear look conventional. So when I stepped off the plane in red, white and blue trousers, I didn't look much different from a lot of kids in the Sydney discotheques.

And it was sheer joy, and a big relief to hear the crowd at the airport calling, "Hi, Cobber." In Australia, if a digger calls you cobber, you're his pal, his chum, his buddy. So you can believe I was delighted and felt that I was home.

It got even better when they sort of gave me a nickname that adapted their two friendship words "cobber" and "digger" and started to call me Libber. I liked it a lot better than my London nickname, Libby. That always sounded to me like some kind of tomato juice.

But the test of all this "love" from the Australians would come, I felt, when I made my first appearance in my satirical answer to the garment that had everyone in America talking about it—or is it them? Hot pants!

They too were red, white and blue. There was a reason for that, too. The kids in the United States at that time were all featuring those colors in their clothes and there was a big flap over whether or not it was traitorous or treasonous to wear any sort of suggestion of the flag. Well, the way I felt was if the government shows the flag by flying it on warships and painting it on bombers . . . anyplace you show the flag has to be better than that.

There's no question about it, that hot pants outfit was certainly the campiest one I'd ever worn. I meant it to be! It had everything on it . . . a jacket hung with American Indian-type fringe . . . sequin-studded, knee-length sox and the kind of two-toned oxfords that used to be spiffy back in the 30's. To top it off, I came on strutting like a majorette and twirling a baton. It should have lit up. Now, I think of it!

Just let me quote what one of the critics, Neil Mitchell, wrote, "The great moment came soon after the interval." (We call it intermission.) "The glamorous and talented Liberace pranced on-to the stage in a patriotic red-white-and-blue hot pants suit complete with baton. For anybody else, it would have been a poor attempt at drag humor. But the crowd loved it and the star loved it even more."

And that's the truth.

The pants were the only thing that could have topped the long, gold embroidered coat I wore over a pair of lace pantaloons and patent leather boots. I told the audience it was a little Argentine outfit I'd picked up in a gaucho surplus store in downtown Buenos Aires. I lied. I'd never been to Buenos Aires.

One of the things I'm unhappy about is that on these trips all over the world, the play-dates are so tightly scheduled that there's never enough time left over to meet and get to know some of the people and talk to them and find out what they think and how they differ from our thinking. And to make it even more complicated, as it did in London, we crowded in a television special called "Liberace in Australia."

Maybe someday I'll put all those together and become sort of a latter-day musical Burton Holmes or J. J. Fitzpatrick whose ship was always slowly sinking into the sea . . . or was it the sun?

Mom used to take me to see Burton Holmes' illustrated lectures when I was a very little boy. Maybe they were what gave me the desire to travel. But at the time I was seeing the world's wonders through the eyes of Burton Holmes, I just didn't believe that there was anything in the world like the stuff he was showing us. Now I know there is, and it's even greater than I thought.

I did, fortunately, get to meet some of Sydney's high society before we trouped out of town for our second visit to Johannesburg. I was lucky enough to be asked by the local hostess with the mostest, Lady Fairfax, to be guest of honor at one of her fabulous parties. I was tipped off that she had told the rest of her guests to try to top anything I might wear. So I showed up looking very conservative in a plain blue blazer with plain white dots in it, a plain white shirt, with plain ruffles at the cuffs, plain stars-and stripes necktie and plain red, white and blue shoes. That's not three shoes. Just a pair of the usual three-tone jobs that any banker might wear to work.

Talking to the people at the party I found that the ladies all wanted to talk about my clothes and most of the men, who knew we'd broken our long jet flight by stopping off in Tahiti for a rest, asked about the total nudity they heard was being achieved by the strippers there. Luckily I could give them a rundown on one of them I met on the beach.

One man said, "They go pretty far, don't they?"

"The one I met walked about a half a mile down to the beach to say hello to me and borrow my suntan oil."

"What happened?" he asked, leaning forward the way guys do when they expect a real juicy one.

"I gave her the bottle of suntan lotion. I figured it would have a better time with her than with me."

"Didn't you go see her show?"

"Sure. After all, I'd supplied her costume . . . the suntan."

But of all the things that were said and done during that trip to Australia in 1971, just six words at the finish of a review of our opening night in Melbourne's Festival Hall gave me the most pleasure. They were, "He made eight thousand people happy!"

I really am looking forward to many more tours of Australia, especially the one in 1974 which will include right consecutive performances in the long-awaited Sydney Opera House which took over thirteen years to build at a cost of over one hundred and ten million dollars. What a thrill to be the first American artist to be signed to play in this super magnificent concert hall. Believe me it's opportunities like this that make my life so constantly exciting and unpredictable and the reason I never think of retiring when there are so many new challenges to face and so many new audiences in this world to conquer.

13

You may feel, as you read the following chapters about my libel case, that there is a certain amount of repetition. Strange as it may seem, I have written it that way on purpose, much as a composer repeats various themes in different contexts to give unity and emphasis to a work.

This repetition spotlights the fact that all testimony from all witnesses, friendly and otherwise, demands that the accusations be repeated again and again in the framing of counsels' questions.

It shows the dulling repetitiveness of a trial that must have its effect on a jury, and it illustrates what the principals in the case must go through.

What's more, as the trial with its constant repetition of the same evidence (or non-evidence) goes on, the newspapers keep repeating the same unpleasant charges and countercharges.

So if you become conscious of the repetition, remember it's there to help me show how I felt—suffering much more of it than I would dare include between these covers.

I made my second trip to England on the same *Queen Mary* I crossed on three years earlier in 1956. That wonderful ship is now a tourist attraction in Long Beach Harbor in California and the thought of it makes me a little sad. I hate to see such depressing proof that "the old order changeth."

Among the invited guests at the Captain's cocktail party on the first evening out, was a New York police official with a very vivacious and charming wife. She had a marvelous sense of humor and became the life of the party. She was short and sort of roly-poly, and before the party was over everybody, including me, loved her and found her very amusing.

During our conversation I asked if she was going to London and she said, "Yes."

So I invited her to my concert at Albert Hall. She accepted and looked pleasantly surprised and delighted as she said that she, too, was going to give a concert at Albert Hall and would I be her guest at that one.

I said, "I'd love to. What do you do?"

She said, "I sing."

I asked, "What kind of singing do you do?"

Her answer was, "Operatic."

"Really," I said. "What kind of of operatic?"

"I'm a Wagnerian soprano," she said.

"I'm sorry," I said. "I didn't quite catch the name." She had been introduced to me as Mrs. So-and-So, so her name came as a big surprise when she said, "I'm Eileen Farrell of the Metropolitan."

I apologized for not having recognized her and she just laughed and said if she didn't have on her Viking helmet and wasn't wearing her solid-steel finger bowls nobody recognized her.

We became very good friends during the crossing. I didn't tell her that besides my bookings in England, I was also going to be the plaintiff in a libel action that was coming to trial on June 8. I figured she'd find that out soon enough after we got to London.

We did several informal shipboard concerts together in the private dining room after most of the passengers had gone to their cabins and only the swingers were around to enjoy it and cheer us on. It was during one of these concerts that lasted way into the wee small hours that I discovered that Eileen, besides being a Wagnerian soprano with the Met, could sing the blues like I never heard the blues sung before. She just laughed it off and told us that in her student days before the war she'd even sung on a radio show with Bob Crosby's Bobcats.

Everyone including me urged her to record an album of her blues songs and show the world her amazing versatility. And not long after returning to the States she did. The album was called *I've Got a Right to Sing the Blues* and it wound up on the charts as a best seller.

But all the joy of shipboard fun disappeared from my mind as I waited for the morning of June 8 with growing apprehension over whether or not I'd done the right thing in suing Cassandra for libel.

By this time you've seen lots of evidence that the ballpoint pen is not my best instrument. I can do certain simple things with it, express a few thoughts, write checks and put down superficial memories. But the emotions I am about to try to describe, I could express much easier if I could just sit at the piano and improvise.

I find it very difficult to put into words how I felt that Monday, June 8, 1959, as I sat in an English courtroom, Queen's Bench Number Four, surrounded by black-robed, white-wigged gentlemen, and prepared to hear myself vilified, as well as defended, and waited to find out whether I'd done the right thing or the wrong one in following the insistence of my conscience and the confirmation of my attorney.

Just as civilians (that's show biz slang for people not in the profession) often ask me questions that seem foolish, I ask similar questions of men and women in other professions. I've even stooped so low as to ask a writer where he gets his ideas. He happened to be a very honest writer who said, "Frankly, when I'm absolutely stuck I turn to Shakespeare."

Being, at this point, in trouble, I decided to try this idea myself and it works. It's a good way to start your mind turning over. Shakespeare gets into your head and makes you think. In Hamlet's famous soliloquy he says, "Conscience doth make cowards of us all." It occurred to me that my conscience might be going to make a martyr of me. But enough of that. Plain, simple, ordinary fear is what I think I felt. And I say "think" because I know how memory has a tendency to tidy things up, correct and orchestrate the facts.

All I can honestly say, these many years later, is that I had put myself on the block of public opinion in defense of one of the three most important things in a man's life . . . perhaps all of them. They are Life itself. Manhood. And Freedom.

Naturally my life, as such, was not at stake. But the attack on me had threatened my mother's health and so, her life. And, perhaps, the quality of my life had been put in jeopardy. Certainly my manhood had been seriously attacked and with it my freedom . . . freedom from harassment, freedom from embarrassment and most importantly, freedom to work at my profession.

At the very least I had done something that every man has to do.

I had taken steps to defend my good name. In an earlier day I might have fought a duel. In lieu of that I was sitting in a court that was to judge whether or not I had been maligned and, if so, the extent to which I had been damaged. In a matter of days, I'd know whether it might not have been wise "to suffer the slings and arrows of outrageous fortune," to have taken my lumps and suffered in silence. I'd been doing that for a long time, however, and everything must some day come to an end. But I had a secret feeling I was about to get clobbered.

I had every reason to hold this opinion. It was formed almost the moment I met my English lawyer by whom I had to be defended in Queen's Bench where no American attorney may practice, just as a California lawyer can't practice in the state of New York. Lawyers all over the world have things pretty well sewed up for themselves.

The Queen's Counsel who was to plead my case against Cassandra was a man who looked as if he needed someone to plead for him. He was seventy-six years old and appeared to be more befuddled than even the most outrageous stage prototype of an "English gentleman" had any right to be. He was sort of a combination of Nigel Bruce, C. Aubrey Smith, and Basil Rathbone, with a little bit of Hugh Herbert thrown in. What I had hoped for was a 100 percent Ronald Colman who would do a "far, far better thing than [he had] ever done before."

You see how my movie memories go back? I thought to myself, is this the man to trust my reputation with? He seemed slow and pokey, hard of hearing, as if he needed someone to take care of him. I thought I ought to have a more aggressive man, someone more pugnacious. I said to John Jacobs, who had selected Mr. Beyfus . . . "I'm not being sued. I'm suing, I don't need a defender. I need an attacker. This man seems old and feeble."

John assured me that Gilbert Beyfus was the best in the business. "What you've seen of him is just a pose. He lays back and lets the enemy walk into his traps. His nickname is 'The Fox.' "

I accepted John's judgment, but I said, "He doesn't look like any fox to me. He looks like a toothless old lion."

And when the trial started I watched him fumbling with papers, creating an atmosphere of confusion. He acted like a man who suddenly found himself in a perfectly strange place with grave responsibilities he knew nothing about. My heart sank. I knew then and there that I didn't have a prayer. But when it came time for him to go into action I watched "The Fox" come to life. It was miraculous. He hadn't missed a word that was said. He worked like a skilled fencer, feeling, thrusting, parrying and poking hole after hole in Cassandra's case.

He said that by bringing this action against Cassandra and the *Daily Mirror* I was offering a helping hand to a host of people that Connor and the paper he worked for had attacked cruelly, needlessly, unfairly and unjustly.

That "host of people" was a very impressive list, starting with the Royal Family. Cassandra had poked fun at Queen Elizabeth for being "old" and "matronly." Prince Philip had felt the cutting lash of his quips. And the hack had the audacity to call Princess Margaret an "old maid."

I was astonished that the Royal Family had to suffer this sort of nonsense. But they do. They have no defense. Freedom of the press, you know.

After the Royal Family, my case was cited as a surrogate for a long list of celebrities, Brigitte Bardot, the BBC's well-known Richard Dimbleby, Maurice Chevalier, Ted Shulton, Elizabeth Taylor and my Queen's Counsel said, "Here's a TV piano player giving these people a chance to fight back." Day after day the scurrilous and snide things that Cassandra had printed about them were aired in the courtroom to establish the venality of the man. And day after day the courtroom was jammed with spectators.

Lady Salmon, Justice Salmon's wife, and other celebrities, together with members of the general public, sat and listened aghast at the enormity of the man's literary bludgeoning. And, of course, day after day there were banner headlines in papers all over England and Scotland; all, that is, except the London *Times* which carried the story in full, but with its usual gentility, sans headlines.

Every day the papers all ran long stories, because in addition to the sensational nature of the case, they felt it was also to establish that there existed not only "freedom of the press" but freedom of the oppressed, the right of the attacked to counterattack.

But let me "take it from the top." As I sat there that morning in June, looking down on me from the bench was the man in robe and wig who was, with the aid of the jury, to be my judge. How he charged those ten men and two women that faced me could, when all the evidence was in, weigh heavily on how they would find.

The man was Sir Cyril Salmon, a member of one of the oldest

and most respected of England's Jewish families. He had only been on the bench two years. But in that time he had made a name for himself by the tough and forthright way he handled the case of some young hoodlums. It seems kids like they were were generally let down lightly. Salmon gave them four years.

It served as a warning to all future young vandals to think before they got themselves brought up in court. Luckily I didn't know this until after the trial or it would have made me even more apprehensive than I was. Knowing the judge was tough, I'd naturally expect him to be tough with me.

After the usual formalities that open any case, Cassandra's article was read into evidence. It was headed "Yearn-Strength Five."

It began with a description of a drink, *Windstarke Fünf,* that Cassandra called "the most deadly concoction of alcohol that the *Haus Vaterland* can produce." He then went on to say, "I have to report that Mr. Liberace, like *Windstarke Fünf* is about the most that man can take."

At this point my Queen's Counsel, Mr. Beyfus, pointed out that it was not just recently, although that's how it read, but way back in 1939 that Mr. Connor had sampled that lethal drink. It was a most insignificant detail. But it was a foxy legal jab to point up the fact that Cassandra might, occasionally, tell the truth but not necessarily the whole truth.

Cassandra's article about me was then read in full. It said "But he [meaning me] is not a drink. He is Yearning Windstrength Five" (which is the translation of *Windstarke Fünf*). "He is the summit of sex—Masculine, Feminine and Neuter. Everything that He, She and It can ever want."

Papers all over England that evening and the next day picked up on that "Summit of Sex" phrase and headlined it in many ways . . . even in the provincial *Northern Echo* of Priestgate, Darlington, the headline read LIBERACE CALLED THE "SUMMIT OF SEX" and in Liverpool the *Daily Post* headlined NEWSPAPER SUED OVER "SUMMIT OF SEX" article. But here I am getting ahead of myself again.

After saying that I was everything "He, She or It can ever want," Cassandra continued with,

> I have spoken to sad but kindly men on this newspaper who have met every celebrity arriving from the United States for the past

thirty years. They all say that this deadly, winking, sniggering, snuggling, giggling, fruit-flavored, mincing, ice-covered heap of mother-love has had the biggest reception and impact on London since Charlie Chaplin arrived at the same station, Waterloo, on September 12, 1921. [That's me he's describing. But that's not the end.]

This appalling man—and I use the word appalling in no other than its true sense of "terrifying"—has hit this country in a way that is as violent as Churchill receiving cheers on VE Day. He reeks with emetic language that can only make grown men long for a quiet corner, an aspidistra, a handkerchief and the old heave-ho. Without doubt he is the biggest sentimental vomit of all times.

Slobbering over his mother, winking at his brother, counting the cash at every second, this super piece of candy-floss has an answer for every situation. Nobody since Aimee Semple MacPherson has purveyed a bigger, richer and more varied slag-heap of lilac-covered hokum. Nobody anywhere ever made so much money out of high speed piano playing with the ghost of Chopin gibbering at every note.

There must be something wrong with us that our teenagers longing for sex and our middle-aged matrons fed up with sex, alike fall for such a sugary mountain of jingling clap-trap wrapped up in such a preposterous clown.

How'd you like to pick up your morning paper and read *that* about yourself? Imagine making my love for my mother a nasty thing just because I acknowledge her presence. Making your family part of the act is nothing new in show business. Eddy Foy was famous for it. As soon as one of his many children was old enough the child was introduced. The act finally wound up with "Seven Little Foys" lined up all across the stage.

Milton Berle always had his mother in the audience and talked about her, and so does Don Rickles at the end of all his shows.

And I've read that the great George M. Cohan whose "beg-off" line was, "My mother thanks you, my father thanks you, my sister thanks you and I thank you," made his first theatrical appearance when his mother carried him on stage to take a bow when he was only two months old. If a mother can carry her two-month-old baby on for a bow, why can't a thirty-five-year-old man give his Mom a bow in the audience?

In reading what I've just written, I realize you may not know what a "beg-off" line is. When you have stopped the show and taken repeated bows, possibly even done an unscheduled encore, and the audience continues to applaud, you need a "beg-off" line. It's something to say that will satisfy the audience that you will do no more but does so without making them resent you. I usually say, "You've been a beautiful audience, bless you!" Then I pretend to "Bless" them with my wireless microphone which always gets a laugh. And I follow with, "I've had so much fun myself that honestly I'm ashamed to take the money—but I will!"

I'd like to insert right here something relevant to all this that I read in this morning's New York *Times*. "This morning" happens to be the morning after peace was declared in Vietnam. (I hope there is still peace by the time this is in your hands.)

There was a story in the Sunday *Times* that quoted from the diary of a young medic with the 101st Airborne. He was a seminarian who did not believe in war, but a man who, though reluctant to do so, became a soldier and gave his life trying to help a wounded soldier in a rice paddy in Vietnam.

His name was Charles Stockbauer and he was born and brought up in the very heartland of the United States, St. Joseph, Missouri.

On June 28, 1970, a few months before his death, he made an entry in his diary that said, *"Narcissus and Goldmund* by Herman Hesse ends beautifully: *But how will you die when your time comes, Narcissus, since you have no mother? Without a mother one cannot love. Without a mother, one cannot die."*

That touched me very deeply because like millions and millions of sons all over the world, I know, and feel, the truth of it.

Mr. Beyfus opened my defense with a rather comprehensive summary of my career up to that moment. He told of my childhood, my interest in music almost from babyhood. My father's and mother's interest and how the whole family worked together to make it possible for me to receive the musical education they all felt I should have. He sketched the early struggles of my family and my early struggles as a musician. And then he began to explain the background for the showmanship that helped build the popularity that I enjoyed.

Submitting that people made fun of the candelabra that I use in my act, he said, "It serves as a trademark, something like Maurice Chevalier's straw hat." He told how I had done some early television shows that were not at all successful. Then there came the night I was told to wear a white tailcoat instead of the conventional black at a concert in Los Angeles at The Hollywood Bowl. It was the turning point in my career. I applied this dress-up technique to my regular act and brought it to television. Then and only then, did everything begin to click for me and every place I played demanded that my wardrobe top the last spot. Beyfus pointed out that other performers started copying me. He mentioned Elvis Presley.

Then he summed up about the way I dress by saying, "Before we jeer at the American public [he didn't mention the British public, who also liked my clothes] for enjoying this added glamour or at Liberace for acceding to it, it is well to remember that less than one hundred and fifty years ago in the Regency period our men dressed up and one of the greatest arts was tying a necktie.

"In these days of somewhat drab and dreary men's clothing, remember the Guards at Buckingham Palace, The Horse Guards at Whitehall, The Beefeaters at The Tower, the uniforms of the Privy Counsellors at a Levee, Knights of the Garter and Peers of the Realm at the opening of Parliament. Look at the Hunt Ball when tough hunting men prance around in pink coats with silk lapels of different colours." [That's the way they spell it in England]. Some add dignity. All are glamour."

Then speaking directly to the judge, Sir Cyril Salmon, he concluded, "Look at me, My Lord, and my learned friends dressed in accordance with old tradition which lends dignity to our proceedings. Because we dress like this here, it does not mean we dress like this in ordinary life, nor does Liberace."

And he was right. I have a newspaper picture which shows me entering the courthouse wearing a dark suit. I think it was dark blue. The lapels were narrow and so was the tie I was wearing with a white shirt. All were fashionable but certainly not flashy or unusual in 1959. I was surprised to see how short my hair was cut.

Actually I remember few of the details of that first day of court fourteen years ago. I think you'd like to read what some of the papers printed about the whole agonizing affair, starting from the very first day.

14

The London *Times* quotes me as saying I felt so strongly about Cassandra's article, "because my mother has a hypersensitive heart condition and further because I know how extremely proud she is of all her children, perhaps a bit more proud of me."

Beyfus asked immediately if I'd tried to keep the piece from her and I answered yes, adding that we'd discovered that she had found it which was why (as I've said) we thought it best to get her out of the country.

The London *Times* then goes on to say, "The witness [that's me] said that when he arrived to do a concert at Royal Festival Hall there was a hostile crowd carrying unfriendly placards outside the hall. He had to stay in his car until police took him into the hall under protection. At Manchester there was a hostile group, mostly composed of young men, outside the hall. At Sheffield when he went on the stage there were unfriendly cries from the audience.

Beyfus asked if this upset me.

"Very much, sir," is my recorded reply, "and it upset the audience, too, because I would say that a good many of the people in the audience were embarrassed at hearing these comments."

"Did you win the audience over?" he then asked.

"Yes," I said, "I worked very hard to win them over, sir."

Then came another steaming question that made me wonder whose side my attorney was on. "Was there ever anything sexy about your performance at all?"

My answer was, "I am not aware of it if it exists. I am almost positive that I could hardly refer to myself as a sexy performer. I have tried in all my performances to inject a note of sincerity and wholesomeness because I am fully aware of the fact that my appeal on television and personal performances is aimed directly at the family audience."

BEYFUS: "Do you ever tell what we know as dirty or smutty stories?"

"I have never been known to tell any dirty stories. I have told of experiences that have happened to me that might have been termed double-meaning in referring to some of my sponsors who have at times given us samples of their products. Among them was a very famous paper company which among its products makes toilet tissue. When I mentioned my various sponsors to my audience I always included them because they were one of my biggest sponsors and the audience found it funny. But the audience in no way found it offensive."

Now, let me jump around a little and pick a few Q. and A. reports on that first day's proceedings.

> BEYFUS: Had you, by 1956, reached the summit of your career in the U.S.?
> LIBERACE: It is presumed by some that I had. I have done 200 TV performances and sold over a million copies of my records.
> BEYFUS: Are you earning a very large income?
> LIBERACE: Yes, sir.
> BEYFUS: Had you acted as a comedian?
> LIBERACE: Yes. I have appeared with Red Skelton on his show. Skelton is one of the top American comedians. I also appeared in films with him as his hobo buddy, dressed in a ragged suit of tails and extremely ill-fitting pants covered with patches. I have also appeared as a beachcomber in a film called in America *South Sea Sinner* but retitled *East of Java* when it was shown in England.

That was part of my first day's testimony as reported by the London *Evening News.*

Incidentally, the front page headline on the *Evening News'* story was, of all things $200,000 OFFER TO WED LIBERACE. This refers to one line of testimony in which, in response to questioning I said that I received on an average of twelve marriage proposals per month and then added that one lady offered to put up $200,000.

[210

The *News Chronicle* included in its opening summation of the first day's proceedings the statement that the day ended with "Liberace denying that in a United States television interview he had referred to Princess Margaret as a marriage prospect."

This was about an interview with the great and famous Edward R. Murrow, on his very popular and well-thought-of 1953 television series called *Person to Person*. Many may remember that Mr. Murrow sat in a swivel chair in a control room full of monitors and conducted the interview electronically by remote control as he talked to a personality in his own home, showing off where he lived and talking about himself and family. It was a great honor to appear on that show with Mr. Murrow, and I was very flattered to be one of the people he thought important enough to include in the series.

Mr. Gardiner, the chief attorney for the defense, quoted from the transcript of that interview pointing out that what I said was, "I was reading about the lovely young Princess Margaret. She's looking for her dream man. I hope she finds him someday.

"I would like to meet her very much because I think we have a lot in common. We have the same tastes in theater and music and besides she's pretty and she's single."

My answer to Mr. Gardiner was:

> I was not referring to Princess Margaret as a marriage prospect, I assure you. If any such interpretation was given I have apologized for it since.
>
> I was referring to her solely on the premise that she had been widely publicized as having accepted the performances of Americans who have come over here to appear.
>
> Since it had come to be a foregone conclusion that I only appeal to matronly women, it would have been very lovely and wonderful to have been accepted in my performance by the lovely young Princess. There is no connection between my views on marriage and Princess Margaret, other than she has been known to be looking for a mate and so have I. No other similarity exists.

Although I could not, of course, tell it in court, I was reminded of a story that was going around show business circles in New York at that time. I think the great Jewish comedian Myron Cohen told it on *The Ed Sullivan Show*.

A marriage broker on New York's Lower East Side brought a

book of photos to show to a mother and father who wanted to pick out a girl for their son to marry. All the pictures were captioned in code so that it was impossible to tell any names.

The parents picked out one very pretty girl and decided she was the one who looked right for their son. Then they asked the marriage broker to show it to him.

He did and started right out by asking, "Do you like this girl?"

"Like her? Sure," said the modern young man. "She's a cute chick."

Getting right to the point, the *shadchen* (which is the Jewish word for the male version of what the character, Yenta, was in *Fiddler on the Roof*) asked, "Would you like to marry her?"

"Marry *her; I* can't marry her."

"You think she ain't good enough for you?"

"Good enough. Who you think you're kidding? That's Princess Margaret."

"So she's not Jewish," said the *shadchen*. "Would you marry her?"

Laughing the whole thing off the young man said, "Marry her? Certainly I'd marry her. Why not?"

"Good," said the *shadchen* and snapped the book shut. "Half the bargain I got."

Mr. Gardiner then cited an article in the *Daily Herald* in which the writer described Liberace as "the most unlikeable man on television screens and stated that his leers and dimples make me heave."

Liberace said, "This emotic language is new to me and certainly not evident in my press cuttings."

He said he had never used the expression "mother-complex" and "Momism" when referring to his love and devotion for his mother. . . .

He agreed that it was still correct to say that he had never extended any marriage proposals because he is still looking for a girl like Mom. . . .

MR. GARDINER: Do you insist that your publicity has nothing to do with sex appeal?

LIBERACE: I have never considered myself a sex-appeal artist.

He agreed that one fan, when asking for tickets for his concert had written, "We want to be so close that we can feel the breeze from your eyelashes when they flutter."

MR. GARDINER: Nothing to do with sex appeal?

LIBERACE: I do not consider that a man's eyelashes could be considered sexy.

Liberace said he had no control over the viewers who watched his shows. They were aimed at family audiences—but if some viewers found him attractive, or something—he had no control over that.

"Are you prepared to let the jury see some of your television shows?"

Yes, I wish they would.

Referring to an unauthorized booklet written about him, Liberace said it was untrue that the Liberace Course of Piano Study had helped pay for the glass lining to his swimming pool. . . .

Going back over all this in my mind and in print, I can't get over how the whole United Kingdom covered this painful and embarrassing legal action. The Liverpool *Post Dispatch* headlined all of its stories "I'M NOT A SEX APPEAL ARTIST," SAYS LIBERACE.

I was on the witness stand for six hours.

Every seat was occupied when the court opened, [the *Post Dispatch* reported] with the majority of the spectators being women. At the back and sides of the court scores of disappointed teenagers peered through the glass doors to get a glimpse of Liberace in the witness box. . . .

Liberace today wore a dark grey suit with grey silk tie and white shirt with a pleated front. . . .

Liberace was questioned about a previous *Daily Mirror* article, by Donald Zec, which gave an account of Mr. Zec's visit to Liberace's home, "I am grateful to Mr. Zec, for at no time during this interview did he use the expression he, she, it, masculine, feminine or neuter or fruit-flavored. These are all expressions which in America are termed homosexual. Therefore I have no reason to take any offense at Mr. Zec's article. . . .

"I would thank him again, if I had the opportunity, for saying I was unquestionably a competent pianist, a pleasant vocalist, a friendly host and that he liked me."

Mr. Connor's barrister, Mr. Gardiner, then quoted from a number of articles, one in the *Evening News,* which referred "to a production that delighted Liberace's fans and sickened his critics."

Counsel then quoted from a publication about Liberace's appearance at the Hollywood Bowl, "The women acted like wild animals . . . we had to fight them off from nine in the morning to six at night." That, asked Mr. Gardiner, "has nothing to do with sex appeal?"

"I would say not," Liberace answered. "These people wanted autographs and I found them very well behaved. That statement came from a police officer, not from me."

Liberace agreed with the statement that no one in years had been the butt of so much criticism. "But," he added, "it was criticism directed at my performance [not me]. There is a difference."

Mr. Gardiner said, "One book described you as the 'hottest personality to melt the TV airways!' Still no sex appeal?"

No. I consider sex appeal as something possessed by Marilyn Monroe or Brigitte Bardot. I certainly do not put myself in their class. There was laughter.

Questioning Liberace about his performance, Mr. Gardiner asked, "Do you go from the 'Ave Maria' to the 'Beer Barrel Polka?'"

LIBERACE: I play music of all types, including religious music which is treated with proper respect. And when I play "Beer Barrel Polka," it is later in the program. I never go from "Ave Maria" into "Beer Barrel Polka."

Of a television programme [that's how they spell it in England] in which, when he played the "Ave Maria," curtains were drawn to disclose a stained glass window and a woman praying to the Virgin Mary while a boy dressed as a choir boy put a candelabra on his piano, Liberace said, "That number was done because it is one of the most highly requested numbers on my programme. Audiences like it, and because they like it I try to present it with proper respect. . . .

MR. GARDINER: Do you think that an honest man, even if he does not go to church every Sunday, might think that profane?

No. If I thought so I never would have presented the number in such a manner. It met with the approval of every church dignitary I have ever met who had seen it. . . . [I was thinking of Archbishop (later Cardinal) Cushing and Pope Pius XII who particularly approved of my television interpretation of "Ave Maria" and the way I programmed my TV show. I had a private audience with Pope Pius XII at Castel Gandolfo (his summer residence) in 1956 and spent twenty-two minutes with His Holiness. I discovered that his private secretary who was a monsignor had attended a filming of my television show, which included the "Ave Maria," while he was in California. It was because of this Monsignor that we were invited to a private audience with the Holy Father.]

Mr. Gardiner said that in another programme about his home, Liberace said that there was "someone else" who lived there with

[214

him and his mother and to whom he spoke. The lights then went out and he sang "Bless This House." Counsel asked who was that someone else?

"It is our belief in our religion that God is in every home," said Liberace. "We hope He is in our home and it is to Him I spoke when I sang, 'God Bless This House.' "

Asked if he thought an honest man might object to God being introduced to make a cue for a song, he replied that no one had ever objected to that TV film which had been repeated more often than any he had done and had been approved time and time again by clergymen as a wholesome tribute to family life, religion and faith in God. . . .

COUNSEL: I am not suggesting that many people might not take that view. All I am suggesting is that there are many people who might object to it. . . .

If there are they have never come to my attention because I have never received any objection to the film. . . .

Referring to a newspaper report that quoted him as saying that everyone had to expect a certain number of non-believers and enemies and he supposed that was why they shot Abraham Lincoln and crucified Jesus, Liberace said those were not his words. . . .

At a press conference he had quoted advice given him by an Archbishop who told him that when a man's head rose above the clouds, some people threw stones at him and said that even Jesus had enemies and was crucified and Abraham Lincoln was shot. . . .

Liberace agreed that winking was a standard item in his act and that he had on occasion led women to come onto the stage to touch him, which usually resulted in screams from a section of the audience. . . .

COUNSEL: Do you use scent or scented lotion?

I use after shave lotion and underarm deodorant.

When you come into a press conference a noticeable odour [that's the way they spell it in England] comes with you. . . .

I would not say it's an odour. I would say it's a scent of good grooming, that I smell clean and fresh and I always smell clean and fresh . . . and I wished everybody did!

I was growing tired under the pressure of Mr. Gardiner's steady attack. I wasn't used to the necessity of evaluating every word I was about to say before I spoke it. I wished there was something Mr. Beyfus could do to help me but I knew there wasn't. I wished for a lot of things. But my one big wish was to get out of the witness box. It did no good. Mr. Gardiner pressed right on.

Still quoting the Liverpool *Daily Post,* Mr. Gardiner read a passage which ran: "He is the summit of sex, the pinnacle of masculine, feminine and neuter. . . ."

I prayed I'd never seen that, never heard it and that I'd never hear it again. That was the passage that decided me to sue. That was the one I was afraid would haunt me all my life.

But my thoughts didn't stop Mr. Gardiner. He went on reading. "Everything that he, she and it could ever want." He stopped for a moment. Again after hearing those words the way everyone in the courtroom looked at me seemed to change. Maybe it was just my imagination but the change was from sympathy or dispassionate interest to contempt.

Then he switched suddenly to my arrival in England with, "Are you saying that the scenes that took place when you arrived at Southampton happened without your having done anything to create them?"

I wanted to ask if he were suggesting that the crowd that greeted me when the boat landed came only because they wanted to meet another "pinnacle of masculine, feminine and neuter." But I knew that would be a terrible thing to do. I'd been warned not to try to make jokes. I knew the witness' place in a hearing and that the court would tolerate sarcasm only from the attorneys.

It took me a moment to compose myself before I answered quite honestly, "It was one of the biggest surprises of my life to be greeted by so many thousand fans. It is a performer's right to create publicity and coming by special train was merely to lend publicity to my appearances in England."

As if mocking me, Mr. Gardiner then said that he supposed there was nothing wrong with me using my sex appeal in any way I chose.

Again I took a deep breath and said,

> My appeal is to the type of people who want the type of enter-tainment I give, which is primarily wholesome entertainment not directed to sex appeal. I use my training as a performer and the musicianship I studied diligently for over seventeen years and my experience of over twenty-five years. I have found the formula I use successful since I was eleven when I was certainly not using sex appeal.

[216

There was, of course, a laugh and I was afraid Sir Cyril would warn me again. But I guess he couldn't. What I had said was a fact. And when a fact is funny even a justice of a British High Court can't put it down.

Mr. Gardiner continued his bombardment with, "Is not the size of your public due to your exploiting simultaneously all the emotions—love, mother-love, love of God—a mass assault on the emotions to arouse the emotional temperature?"

I felt he was trying to get me angry so I made a great effort to keep my cool and answered slowly, "My effort is to create in the audience a series of emotions giving a general feeling of being entertained. I have had my audiences howling with laughter and I have had them crying. That is one of the great attributes that a performer can possess and that ability is based on a serious approach to my profession."

Following this, all the papers that covered the case reported that, "When Mr. Gardiner referred to the sex appeal of Maurice Chevalier, Liberace, with a smile, said he would refer to it as charm."

"But he is a man of great sex appeal," Mr. Gardiner insisted.

"I cannot say whether he is capable of that at his age," said Liberace. "He's a man over seventy."

The paper goes on to report:

> Mr. Gardiner, defending his client, went on to say that the statement that Liberace exuded love meant that he had great sex appeal and that he attracted all sections of the community but not in an improper way. . . .
>
> Liberace retorted: This is the most improper article that has ever been written about me. It has been widely quoted in all parts of the world and has been reproduced exactly as it appeared in the *Daily Mirror.* One paper had the headline, IS LIBERACE A MAN?

I was thinking I am fed up with this. I was asking myself why I laid myself open to such humiliation. I wondered what would happen if I just shouted, "All right, everybody! That's all. Forget the whole thing!" And walked out of Queen's Bench Number Four. What would they do to me? They might hold me in contempt of court. But would that be worse than the contempt everyone would hold me in if this case should go against me?

Then my consciousness took over again, and I heard Mr. Gar-

217]

diner referring to a pub crawl that I went on with a man named Doncaster from the *Daily Mirror.*

My reply was, "I promised to do that pub crawl before I came to England. I made a promise and I kept it." I agreed that I was in Miss Winifred Atwell's dressing room at the Palladium when a Mr. Doncaster and others came to take photographs. I also agreed that a Miss Ambler was there but said that she was not employed by me but by one of the newspapers, *The People,* to edit stories about me.

Mr. Gardiner then asked me, "Did Miss Ambler, 'If Randolph Churchill can get five thousand pounds from *The People,* Liberace should be able to get something from *The Mirror?'* "

I said I didn't remember hearing Miss Ambler say that. I also said I didn't recall Mr. Doncaster asking, "Are you going to sue us?"

Asked if I'd said, "No, I am not." I replied, "No, I did not."

The *Daily Post* then says, "Liberace denied that when appearing at the Cafe de Paris in London on October 18, 1956, he said he would dedicate his next number to the stinking press and in particular to Mr. Cassandra. "I'm going to ask him to lunch. If he doesn't come, I'll know he's one of them. Doesn't he use a woman's name?"

I didn't say that at all. What I actually said was that I was going to dedicate my next number to some of my critics, particularly to one whose name I would not mention because I didn't want to make him more famous.

The cross-questioning then went back to how the Cassandra article had, I felt, jeopardized my mother's life and how we wanted her to go home immediately but she insisted on staying to attend my concerts because she felt that if she did not she would be giving people the idea that she thought Cassandra's article was true.

Justice Salmon interrupted to say (referring to the pub crawl) "You must have been in a very forgiving mood, if, after your mother was taken ill, you still accepted the paper's hospitality."

"You really summed it up yourself," Mr. Gardiner added, "when you said that the secret of your success was that everyone in the world wanted to be loved and you expressed that love and they responded to it."

"I was speaking of love of humanity, brotherly love, the love between people which is sadly lacking in the world."

Gardiner said, "I suggest that is what Cassandra was referring to when he was describing the universality of your appeal."

"Yes, I believe he was."

In response to questioning I also agreed that I was appearing the following Sunday on a program called *Sunday Night at the Palladium*, the highest paid engagement in television variety, and that I was also to appear on a variety performance for the Queen Mother.

I was then excused from the stand. It was an endless six hours, and I felt it had taken years from my life. I'm not used to having to weigh my words. What I say is generally too light for that.

Court was then adjourned, but not until Justice Salmon, acting on a suggestion by QC Gerald Gardiner that perhaps the jury might like to see some of the films for theater and TV that I'd made in the States, proposed that Gardiner and Beyfus get together and decide what they wanted to do about it.

Mr. Gardiner said that they might each choose a couple of films to show to the jury or they could fix a half hour screening for each side.

It turned out that both women on the jury had caught my shows on television, which should have been no surprise to anyone. And as for the men, only two of them had never seen my shows, and they said they didn't think seeing them would be necessary.

I've never figured out just what that meant.

15

The London *Evening Standard* headlined, white letters on black, LIBERACE THIRD DAY and in inch-high letters asked, WAS HE SUGGESTIVE? Beneath that in italics, NO, CICELY COURTNEIDGE TELLS JURY.

The story itself started,

A gasp of admiration came from a crowd jamming the pavement outside the High Court today when American pianist Liberace arrived for the third day of his libel action . . . the reason for the gasp—Liberace was wearing another suit—one made of shining rust-brown material. [Were they surprised that I had more than two suits?] The girls in the crowd, some had been waiting since 7 A.M., tried to approach him but were held back.

The first witness was actress Cicely Courtneidge. She was called into the witness box as Mrs. Hulbert. She wore a white-veiled hat, dark furs and a dark dress.

Mr. Helenus Milmo (junior counsel for Liberace) said to her after she had sworn, "The court takes official notice of very little, but are you Miss Cecily Courtneidge?"

When she replied, "Yes," Mr. Milmo said, "I won't talk anymore about your theatrical career except to ask if you are appearing in the lead in *Fool's Paradise* at the Apollo Theatre?"

"Yes," replied Miss Courtneidge.

I thought it was very nice of my attorney to get in a plug for Miss Courtneidge's show.

221]

The *Evening Standard* goes on to report the cross-questioning as follows:

Have you seen performances given by the plaintiff, Liberace?
Yes.
Did you see or hear in these performances anything that could be described as dirty?
No, nothing at all.
Would it be correct or incorrect to say that Liberace's performance was a sexy performance making an appeal to sex?
No. I would not say that at all.

When she was cross-examined by Mr. Neville Faulks, Senior QC for the Defense, Cicely admitted that she had seen a revue in which a song was sung by comedian Jimmy Thompson that made fun of me.

Mr. Faulks said that the show was called "For Amusement Only" and ran for a year and three-quarters at the Apollo Theatre.

Cicely said that she couldn't remember what the show was about except that it was a burlesque.

Then for reasons of their own, I couldn't see what it had to do with my case, Mr. Faulks and Miss Courtneidge got into a discussion of what constituted success in show business. Mr. Faulks said, "If it ran for a year and three-quarters the houses must have been fairly full."

"I don't know that they were full," said Cicely.

"Could a show run for a year and three-quarters on empty houses?" Faulks asked.

The answer was, "It could run for a long time without full houses."

Since that was about the end of the Courtneidge testimony, just to change the subject for a moment, what Cicely Courtneidge said about a show in London being able to run for a long time without full houses is just as true today as it was back in 1959 when Cicely said it. And that's the wonderful thing about the theater in London in comparison with Broadway. A show cannot run for very long in New York without full houses. And that's too bad. It means that if it's less than an absolutely smash hit a lot of people who might enjoy seeing it are denied the opportunity. Now back to my case.

Quoting again from the *Evening Standard,*

The next witness called was John Jacobs, Jr., Liberace's attorney and business manager who was questioned about a book called *The Liberace Story* published in this country before he arrived here for his tour three years ago.

Mr. Gerald Gardiner, QC for the *Daily Mirror* and Mr, Connor reminded Mr. Jacobs that Mr. Liberace had said in evidence that the book contained a number of inaccuracies.

Said Mr. Jacobs, "A lot of things are grossly exaggerated as they always are in that sort of paper."

"Are any steps being taken to stop the sale of this publication to the British public?" asked Mr. Gardiner.

"No steps at all," replied Mr. Jacobs. He then described various ventures in which Liberace was interested including the ownership of apartment houses. "There used to be a Liberace Partnership in which he and his brother George were involved. But as you know, George has withdrawn and the partnership has been dissolved. We have also had his apartment houses put in his individual name for tax reasons.

Of Liberace's financial sense, Mr. Jacobs said, "He just does not understand that if you speak in net terms these days, you are broke. He always speaks in gross terms."

I said then and I say again I do not know what in the world that had to do with the case but there it was in the record of the trial. Why did he want to make me out to be a dummy about money? People could think that I was like that wife who didn't know why the checking account was overdrawn because she still had three checks left.

I'm still wondering if John was really a "friendly witness" that day. The next witness certainly was It was Helene Cordet, who was the director of a club called Maison de France. She was asked to testify because when I arrived in 1956 I held a press reception at her establishment. I'll never forget it. The reception was to be at 4 P.M. and I'd been on the move since 7 A.M. The place was mobbed. Photographers were falling all over one another and then came the reporters with all the same questions reporters ask all over the world. Sometimes I think it would make more sense if everyone made up a set of answers to all their questions, had them printed on a piece of paper and sent to each newspaper. If any reporter on any paper had any original questions he could call up and ask them. It sure would save a lot of time and energy for everyone.

Anyway, in her testimony Helene let it be known that I was always polite and patient and gracious to the reporters and photographers and that the thing that started at 4 didn't wind up until after 8 P.M. And when she was finally asked that question about whether there was anything sexy about any of my performances that she'd seen, she said, "Certainly not."

But did Mr. Gardiner give up? Not on your life. He asked her if she didn't agree that if artists had sex appeal they were entitled to use it. Helene's answer was, that she thought they were entitled to use it to a certain point but that she didn't think I did.

Then, I guess to establish the point that I had been mimicked and kidded a lot on TV during the heaviest viewing times he asked her if the heaviest viewing times were during the two shows *Sunday Night at the Palladium* and *Chelsea at Nine*.

Helene said she had read that that was so. We performers never know the truth about such things, and I secretly think that nobody else really does.

The next witness they called was Bob Monkhouse, only they dignified him with his impressive full name, Robert Alan Monkhouse. When they asked him what he did it made the people in the courtroom giggle because there could hardly be a person in London who didn't know the work of Bob Monkhouse in all sorts of shows and on the telly. His answer was, "I'm a theatrical performer with twelve years experience."

He then testified that when I arrived at Waterloo Station in London he was present in a theatrical capacity, because he happened to be working for Associated Television and they had been showing my programs.

"So they thought it would be a good idea if I toddled along with the official interviewers," Bob explained. "Don't ask me why. But I can tell you this, it was a terrific reception."

He was asked exactly what he meant by "terrific."

"Well, if you want the bloody details, there were mobs of people, teenagers and middleagers. I never saw so much female-ness all crowding in one place—all pushing and shoving—to get a look at Lee. Some enterprising tradesman had been outside the station peddling bags of red heart-shaped confetti, and a lot of the ladies brought along rose petals to pelt him with. The stuff lay there on the deck, ankle deep. You never saw such a litter. Waterloo hadn't been like that since Napoleon."

Bob's description of the crowd made me think back to what happened a week later when I went to the Palladium Theatre on a Sunday afternoon to rehearse for my first British TV show, *Sunday Night at the Palladium.*

I got there about 3:30 in the afternoon, and I couldn't get out of my car until police were called to get me into the theater. It's wonderful to be loved. But that kind of love gets dangerous.

When the rehearsal was over, the crowd had grown larger, and it was decided that I'd better stay in the theater until after the performance from 8 to 9 P.M.

When I started to leave the Palladium a little after 9, the crowd was still surging around, and the police had brought specially trained German shepherds to help the fifty officers.

An hour later I tried to leave again, and this time the mounted and foot police held the crowd in check until I could get into my car and drive off.

I was really sorry the police had to bring the German shepherds. I hated to think of my audience going to the dogs.

When Mr. Beyfus asked Bob if he'd been present at Waterloo when other famous entertainers arrived, Bob said that although it had happened before he was born, he'd seen movies of Charlie Chaplin's reception and the one for me was comparable.

Mr. Beyfus threw in the comment that he didn't think it was suggested that Mr. Chaplin was dependent on his sex appeal. And when questioned about a reception outside the Palladium for Johnny Ray, Bob said it was quite impressive but a little depressing.

I have no idea what he meant by that unless he was saddened by "Cry," the song that made Johnny into a star. I always thought of Johnny as a sort of doleful Frankie Laine.

Testimony brought out that when I arrived in London, Bob was working at the Hotel Savoy and one of the things he did in his act was an impression of me. That was really why they asked him to be at the reception for me at the station. A couple of nights after I got to town I went to see the act. And when my attorney asked Bob how I liked it he said, "Lee was very complimentary about it and made several suggestions to improve the satire."

Eventually of course, they got around to asking Bob the question they threw at every witness, in one form or another, about whether he'd seen or heard anything suggestive about my performance. Bob said no and then he was asked, "Nothing designed to stimulate the sexual appetite?"

Bob said, "Nothing with that definition."

"When you say, 'nothing with that definition,' " he was asked by Mr. Faulks of the defense, "what do you mean?"

Bob answered, "Any artist with reasonable good looks and who is masculine is bound to give an entertainment, not necessarily sexy, but one in which we know he's of the male sex—he is bound to get more fan letters from girls than he does from men."

A funny exchange of remarks resulted when the defense's Mr. Faulks tried to establish how many people saw Jimmy Thompson's burlesque of me. He started out by saying to Monkhouse, "You heard my unsuccessful attempt to persuade Miss Courtneidge that if a play runs for a year and three-quarters it is reasonable deduction that a lot of people had seen it."

Bob said, "I missed her testimony."

Mr. Faulks sighed. "Would you agree," he said, "that if a play runs for a year and three-quarters a reasonable number of people saw it?"

Bob's answer was, "Comparatively."

"I'm still pressing pathetically for an answer," insisted Mr. Faulks. (I agreed with him that his effort was pathetic.) He repeated the question.

"Certainly more people have seen it than if it only ran for a year," Bob said, getting a laugh. "And surely less saw it than if it ran two years." Then he added, "Some shows do run half empty."

Mr. Faulks then pursued a line of questioning about whether a burlesque of me by a comedian named Jimmy Thompson had ever come to his attention, and after some more legal Q and A-ing, it was brought out that Bob had, and he said it was bewildering to him that Jimmy Thompson's song should have been shown on television. He said he could see how it might have gotten by the censors for the show called *Chelsea at Nine,* but it was baffling how it could have been done on *Sunday Night at the Palladium.* And he added that there was the widest line of separation between the impression he did and the one Jimmy Thompson did.

Actually all Bob did was imitate my voice and exaggerate my gestures and movements, which is the essence of every impressionist's performance. But what bothered and perplexed him about

Jimmy Thompson was the wig Thompson wore, his reference to Mom and a song he sang which included the lines:

> My fan mail is simply tremendous
> It's growing so fast my head whirls,
> I get more and more
> They propose by the score
> And at least one or two are from girls.

At one point, I think, Bob Monkhouse said he couldn't understand why I had not sued Jimmy Thompson. The answer, I told him later, was that I had not caught the act and didn't know what he was saying. The result was that I did sue Jimmy Thompson and we got a settlement out of court.

There were five other witnesses on my behalf, three of them musicians. George Coppersmith, musical director of the Cafe de Paris, George Melachrino, whose orchestra accompanied me on my tour of England, and the famous orchestra leader Monavani all spoke well of my taste and musicianship.

The fourth was the American television producer Don Fedderson, Don testified about spotting me as a television possibility when he saw me performing in a hotel near San Diego. He said that my success was instant and that it went far beyond his wildest expectations and that rather than sex appeal, he felt I used charm, kindness and honesty.

When cross-examined by Mr. Gardiner, Don said my appeal was to families, that I was sponsored by a bank, among other sponsors, and, he added, "our banks, like yours, are very conservative."

But the last and probably the most valuable friendly witness I had was Miss Dail Betty Ambler. The newspapers also thought she was valuable because she was pretty, and they like to print pictures of pretty girls. They all printed Betty's picture. She said she was an author, scriptwriter and journalist. And she testified that on October 25, she went to the home of Mr. Connor at The Rectory, Henley-on-Thames, to get material for a story she'd been commissioned to do about Mr. Connor's cat for a series called "Pets of the Famous."

The writ in my action against Mr. Connor had just been issued and Miss Ambler said that when they were alone, Mr. Connor brought it up. He laughed about it and said it was going to be a bit of fun, she said, and that it was a libel for which Liberace would get a lot of money from the *Daily Mirror*. The libel, she testified Mr. Connor said, was in the "He, She or It" phrase.

Miss Ambler said that when she asked him why it was written and printed if it was libelous, Mr. Connor said, "They [at the *Daily Mirror*] think it will be worth it for a week's publicity," and added, "I don't know who will look the bigger buffoon in the witness box, Liberace or me."

Miss Ambler also said that Mr. Connor said the article could not be defended but that the lawyers were looking at everything that had been written about Liberace to see if that line had been taken before.

He told her they also planned to object to the jury because men did not like Liberace and they could make sure there were only men on the jury. (Well, they got ten out of twelve and they still lost. I wonder what that proves about men liking my work?)

Miss Ambler then testified that Mrs. Connor joined them and said, "Liberace will like it *any* way so long as it's publicity. He is vain."

Betty denied having suggested to me while we were at a party in Winifred Atwell's dressing room that I should bring action against Cassandra.

I've mentioned this elsewhere, when I was on the stand and was asked if Miss Ambler had said, "If Churchill can collect five thousand pounds from *The People,* Liberace should be able to get something from the *Daily Mirror,*" that my answer was that I had no recollection of hearing her say that.

Then the defense tried to impugn Miss Ambler's morals by asking her if she were the author of a book called *The Elusive Husband.*

She said that it might be one of her paperbacks, that they go back a very long time.

Mr. Gardiner said that an author usually knows his own books . . . She replied that people who had done books in the fiction-factory style of 40,000 words a week know that you soon forget.

Good grief! Forty thousand words a week. Well . . . I can play the piano very fast.

Mr. Gardiner then said, "A bookseller in this country was fined for selling *The Elusive Husband* as an obscene book, wasn't he?"

Miss Ambler first said she couldn't remember and finally replied, "Oh, yes. That was just before I went to do the Errol Flynn dialogue. That goes back to 1949 or 1950."

Mr. Gardiner said the date was July 27, 1950, and Miss Ambler said, "If you say so."

Mr. Gardiner then asked if that was the only obscene book she had ever written and asked if her answer (that she didn't remember it) was a genuine one. Her reply to both questions was, "Yes."

He then charged that her answer about not remembering one of her books was dishonest and not remembering that a man had been arrested for selling it was dishonest. She replied to both of these charges in the negative. But that didn't stop Gardiner from saying that if those statements were untrue, wasn't it possible that what she said about Connor was also untrue?

I sat there listening to him and suddenly realized how lawyers put thoughts and ideas into jury's heads just the way advertisers on television put ideas into the viewers' heads with their commercials. And if you think about that long enough you begin to worry that honesty is slipping away from us.

Fortunately the ten men and two women on my jury were too smart to be fooled. Justice Salmon took care to keep them from being swayed by any outside influence. He said he didn't want them prejudiced (although I don't know which way he had in mind) when he suggested that they abstain from watching the telly on Sunday (when the court was recessed) during the time I was scheduled to appear on the *Sunday Night at the Palladium* TV show. But, again, I'm getting ahead of my story.

After all the nice people had helped me plead my case, the defense, naturally, had a few friends of their own who were anxious to explain how right William Neil (Cassandra) Connor was and how utterly unbearable, sacrilegious, vulgar, psychologically upset, silly and unmusicianly I was.

As apparently is the custom in England, the plaintiff is the first to be heard, as I had been. Now it was their turn.

16

According to the London *News Chronicle,* which I'm using to jog my memory, Mr. Connor was on the stand five hours. I was on one hour longer. Could that be why I won?

The paper says, "The highlight of his evidence was his accusation that Miss Dail Ambler, who called at his home, had been sent as a spy."

Mr. Connor's comment on his reference to his speculations as to who would be the biggest buffoon in the witness box, was his only observation about me, apart from a possible reference to an American who also did an article about me. He mentioned no name. The buffoon remark, Mr. Connor declared, "was a jocular one which he regretted."

"I daresay you did," said Mr. Beyfus. "Who do you think now is the biggest buffoon?"

"That," answered Connor, "is a most embarrassing question."

Mr. Beyfus then said to him, "You say the whole of Miss Ambler's story is untrue, in which case the notes she made must obviously be forgeries."

Connor answered, "Yes."

(As I copied that out on paper it made me wonder how notes that she made, herself, could be forgeries. I can understand how they might have been fiction. Maybe that's why I'm not a lawyer. Or maybe I should be.)

Mr. Beyfus, of course, questioned Mr. Connor on other articles he had written for the *Daily Mirror.* He read from a piece written about the famous voice of the BBC, Richard Dimbleby, in which Cassandra described Mr. Dimbleby as "the royal pussycat . . . soused with the mayonnaise of his own unction . . . quietly sizzling and gently bubbling, like an over-rich Welsh rabbit."

"Would it be right," asked Mr. Beyfus, "to say that these words are an expression of a tabloid newspaper expressing its views in a sensational form?"

Mr. Connor replied, "It would be right to say that I said what I thought about Richard Dimbleby."

My man Beyfus then said, "I suggest it was written for the same reason you write all your vitriolic articles in order to boost the circulation of your newspaper."

Mr. Connor said, "No, sir," and was then questioned about the connection between the *Daily Mirror* and the *Sunday Pictorial*. The latter was the paper associated with the *Daily Mirror* that employed Miss Ambler. Mr. Connor's answer was that the two newspapers had different staffs and policies but were financially associated and both were supervised by Mr. Hugh Cudlipp.

Mr. Beyfus noted that the Cassandra piece was written before I arrived in England. He then noted that the highlight of the defense was that I'd made some remarks about Princess Margaret on a television interview with Edward R. Murrow and suggested that this defense was utterly and entirely dishonest.

When Connor disagreed, Beyfus went on to explain to the court and to the jury that, some years ago when the question of whether Princess Margaret should marry was being discussed the *Daily Mirror* conducted a poll among its thirteen million readers (imagine one newspaper with a circulation of thirteen million) to get opinions on whether she should marry Mr. Townsend. Mr. Connor confirmed this and Mr. Beyfus asked him, "Can you imagine anything more distasteful to Princess Margaret and the Royal Family than that poll?"

Mr. Connor said he didn't think it was distasteful, that it was lively and pertinent. When asked about reaction in the trade, he said he couldn't remember that the matter had been brought up before the Press Council and that it was quite possible the *Daily Mirror* had been censured.

The charge was then made that the *Daily Mirror* and the *Sunday Pictorial* were completely reckless in what they did with regard to the Royal Family. Mr. Beyfus referred to a recent issue of the *Sunday Pictorial* which reproduced from an American magazine, a strip cartoon entitled "Bringing Up Bonnie Prince Charlie" under the headline "Thousands may laugh at this, but we call it a stupid insult."

Said Beyfus, "This is a most revolting attack upon her Majesty the Queen."

Connor agreed that the cartoon would never have been seen by anyone in England had it not been published by an English newspaper and said, "I would not have published it had I been the editor of the *Sunday Pictorial.*"

"It was also revolting?" questioned Beyfus.

"No, sir," replied Connor. Beyfus added that he didn't agree that there was nothing wrong with Connor's "song and dance" about a harmless little joke made by Liberace in an ad-lib television interview.

At one point in the cross-questioning the matter came up of girls kissing me through a train window which was closed. Mr. Beyfus asked, "If it had been a good-looking young woman and you were unmarried would you not have done the same thing?"

Mr. Connor said, "My passion, though it has always been strong, never forced its way through plate glass." Beyfus also recalled another Cassandra article in which Connor referred to all ladies who walked along Park Lane with French poodles at the end of a leash as prostitutes. Connor admitted he wrote this and said he believed it was an absolute fact.

Beyfus suddenly addressed the bench: "Justice Salmon, what kind of dog does Lady Salmon have?" "A French poodle," Salmon replied. "Is Lady Salmon a prostitute?" asked Beyfus. "Certainly not!" was the justice's retort.

It made Connor wince, and it seemed the whole courtroom suddenly realized Cassandra had more than once used his exceptional writing talents to degrade and destroy helpless victims.

A lot more was brought out in the defendant's testimony including the opinion stated in Mr. Gardiner's closing remarks that I had "a bee in my bonnet about people charging me with homosexuality."

Mr. Gardiner delivered this opinion with what he clearly considered to be stinging sarcasm.

But much more to the point was the astonishing information

that, I think, even surprised the court. Connor calmly admitted he had never met me and had seen very little of my work. He actually said, "I do not detest Liberace. In his personal capacity he is entirely unknown to me . . . but I strongly dislike what he does on the stage, in the concert hall and on television." And it was learned that the man who had taken such great exception to my playing and staging of the song "Ave Maria" on my TV shows, was an agnostic.

I thought a funny piece of information which was totally irrelevant to the trial came out when Connor's wife, Gynfil Mair Connor took the stand. She said she remembered a photographer coming to their house to photograph their cat for a feature article, and she said it was funny because "Secretly, it just didn't like my husband."

After a few already established things were discussed, denied and reestablished, Mrs. Connor mentioned showing Miss Ambler through her house and garden and was asked why she did it.

For those of you who are taking notes, here is a good one. Mrs. Connor said it was always "a very tactful way of getting rid of guests."

Mr. Beyfus said *he'd* make a note of that. I may say I've found it very successful. "Would you like to see the garden? Well here we are. No use going all the way back through the house. You can step out right here."

A friend of mine in New York City who has a garden was delighted with the idea. His is on the 33rd floor. He said he had some people in mind.

When the defense called James Edward (Jimmy) Thompson to the stand, he said he'd performed a televised skit about me on ITV around the beginning of 1956 in a late-night revue called *Here and Now*. The bit was such a success he said that he used it again in a revue called *For Amusement Only* which opened and ran for a year and three-quarters at the Apollo Theater, as was established in testimony taken from Cicely Courtneidge and Bob Monkhouse.

He said that for his burlesque of me he wore a special wig. Then he admitted that when he met me at the Cafe de Paris in 1956, he apologized, "I don't know how I have the nerve to shake your hand."

I remember he'd sent a floral peace offering, in the shape of a dove, to my dressing room with a card. The card said, "To show I had no malice toward you."

I recall that it made me feel like having a guy punch me in the nose and then say, don't think this means I don't like you.

Mr. Beyfus quoted from the script of Thompson's skit about me, a line from a lyric that said I was sort of a combination Winifred Atwell and Vera Lynn. I really had no idea what that meant when I heard it. And after Jimmy's explanation of how the line got written, it was even more of a mystery. It seems there was a TV personality by the name of Godfrey Winn, who did a sort of homey type TV show. The line originally teamed Winifred Atwell and Godfrey Winn, but Mr. Winn objected so they changed it to Vera Lynn, whose only similarity to me is that we can both play "Chopsticks" on the piano.

I wondered on hearing this why Thompson thought I wouldn't mind a whole skit about me, when Winn minded a mere mention of his name.

Beyfus brought up another few lyric lines—if you'll pardon the use of the word "lyric"—from the skit. They were the same lines that had perplexed Bob Monkhouse when he gave his testimony. Remember? "My fan mail is simply tremendous/ It's growing so fast my head whirls/ I get more and more/ They propose by the score/ And at least one or two are from girls."

When he finished reading the lines, Mr. Beyfus told the court he thought, "That is about as offensive as anything can be."

Mr. Thompson said, "Having thought a great deal more about this now than at the time, that is actually a very old, traditional, music hall joke which I heard at the Halifax Palace twenty-five years ago."

That, I'm sure is the truth. But the joke, when told by music hall comics is, I believe, always done in first person, hung on themselves. It's funny when a man makes fun of himself on such a subject, because you know he's kidding or he wouldn't have brought it up. But when the joke is hung on somebody else, it's a libel.

Another witness for the defense was Donald Zec, the show columnist for the *Daily Mirror*, who had visited and interviewed me at my home in Hollywood. Mr. Zec testified that while in my home he told me frankly that he found my performance "unpleasant and nauseating."

"In order to illustrate that," he said, "I sat down at one of the two pianos in the room, played a few bars of the 'Rustle of Spring,' turned upon him, smiled and winked.

"He sat down at the other piano, seemingly unaffected and played the 'Rustle of Spring' much better than I did."

What did he expect me to do? I took it as a joke. As if I were in Jack Benny's house, saw something interesting and said, as Jack does, "Wellllll!"

Jack probably would have done his "Wellll!" right back at me and certainly much better. As for anything inspiring nausea, I think Zec's playing was more apt to inspire it in me than my winking was to cause it in him.

Zec was then questioned about the article, which he subsequently wrote, in which it was suggested that I sit between my brother and my mother so that they could kiss me at the same time. He agreed that he should have said Mom was sitting between George and me.

He then swore that everything in his article was the truth except that one thing. He added that he liked me and found me a pleasant host but didn't attempt to excuse calling me "the golden boy of syrup."

Mr. Beyfus said, "You say you like him. What would your article have been like if you'd disliked him? Can you possibly imagine?"

Zec replied that he was "writing about an extraordinary home and an extraordinary personality."

When Mr. Beyfus pointed out that Zec had written, "It was a relief to see that all his teeth were white and not black alternately," Zec denied he was trying to be funny. He said there was no sarcasm, but some irony. To me that still means I have black and white teeth, if to say I have not is not sarcastic. And it would surely be ironic if it were true.

It was Zec who complained in print about my "odour" and even peeked in my bathroom to find a few bottles of after shave, cologne and deodorant spray.

When Mr. Charles Reid, one of London's leading music critics was called to the stand he said, "I am most anxious to deprecate Liberace's maltreatment of the classics. Doing this," Reid said, "I regard as a matter of conscience." By "maltreatment" he meant that I didn't always play the whole work.

He was told that my concerts had increased piano sales and the number of people learning to play the piano.

"Learning to play *what?*" he asked.

It was explained to him, as he should know, that on commerical

TV I am only allowed to play pieces that run no more than three or four minutes. So I play "digest" versions of the great works.

"What bewilders me," said this so-called music lover, "is why he should want to."

Mr. Beyfus said, "So you won't accept that in music half a loaf, or a quarter, is better than no bread at all."

"No. I won't," said Mr. Reid, which is typical of the attitude of those who understand music more than they love it and would deny the chance to hear and love it to those they think are incapable of understanding it.

The defense closed by calling Hugh Cudlipp, editorial director of the *Daily Mirror,* who naturally defended his paper's right to print anything it wanted to print and could not see what right I had to object to it. Although he admitted that he didn't wholly agree with what Cassandra had written.

All that was left was to find out if the *jury* agreed with Cassandra.

17

According to the Manchester *Guardian*, "The climax of what has been called 'the case of the year' came at nine minutes of three in the hot, dusty air of Queen's Bench IV in Royal Courts of Justice.

"Even the Old Bailey would have been proud of the turnout of lawyers and their elegantly dressed wives and throngs of middle-aged women. [I have no comment on the latter but if you've ever fought a legal action anywhere, you know why lawyers' wives can be "elegantly dressed."]

"For a full hour before the verdict was returned, conversation buzzed tensely." I can only add that the surface tension in me, for that final hour, was only the smoke rising from the seething volcano that had come to life inside me, and was finally erupting after those seven dreary days of trial.

If you've ever attended a theater party at a Broadway show, you know what it sounds like, people chattering with their friends almost oblivious that they're in a theater. That thought made me wonder how many spectators in the courtroom came to see justice done and how many came to see me undone. As for me, at that time, I just wanted to have the whole thing done . . . settled, finis . . . once and forever.

Unlike the USA where the team that bats first when the game starts still bats first when the final inning is reached, in the British Courts the plaintiff opens the proceedings and then gets to close them. This gives him a chance to get in his last licks as us kids used to say in West Milwaukee.

But, as in our national pastime, the umpire always has the last word that counts, so Sir Cyril Salmon, the presiding justice, closed the show. Fortunately, because of that basic British reserve, the case had not become as much of a "show" as it might have been if it had been held in New York, Los Angeles, or any place else in the USA. We tend to go overboard. Not that England didn't outdo itself in that department. It was jolly big for Britain.

But had that libel hearing gone on in the United States, I'm sure it would have dragged out for more than seven days, the pickets and the crowds would have been rowdier, and I'm sure, someone would have been hurt. I'm not sure that it might not have been me.

Mr. Gardiner's closing summation for his client, Cassandra, repeated his stinging remark about me having a "bee in my bonnet," which was aimed at subtly suggesting to the jury that I was probably a psychiatric case, mild, of course, but to be watched. Then he assumed such an attitude of naïveté and injured innocence on behalf of his client that as you listened to him you knew that when he was a little boy, caught with jam all over his face and an empty cookie jar in his hands, he told his Mum that he was just trying to help her put things back in the cupboard.

From this pose he went into a cloud of pure obfuscation, in an effort either to prejudice the jury against me or, at least, to keep them from awarding me too much of a settlement, his rationale being that I made so much money.

He asked the jury to imagine someone who had been abroad and come home to Britain, being told that there had been a man at Queen's Bench who earned two hundred and sixty thousand pounds a year, gross.

Mr. Gadiner suggested:

> He might wonder if it were the President of the United States. It could not be the Prime Minsiter because we do not value his services that high.
> He might ask if it were the head of some great national or international industry or some famous scientist or surgeon, some great artist whose work will be handed down to posterity.
> What is it [he then asked] to which this civilisation after two thousand years attaches such importance? A pianist on the telly.

This was a tack he'd taken all through the trial, choosing to lump me with all other pianists which is perfectly okay, except that it fails to take into consideration the fact that each performer using the same basic materials and tools as all the others, is a success or failure at what he's doing not because of *what* he does but *how* he does it.

When you've sat and heard yourself denigrated and vilified for a whole week, you finally become insensitive to the effects of insult after insult, accusation after accusation, being heaped on the hot coals of sarcasm and ridicule. I just sat there and listened. Natch! I'd heard it all before and my main feeling was that it was a good thing this was the last time 'round.

Finally Mr. Gardiner was finished, after what seemed like more than the hour and a quarter or so they said he spoke. Then Mr. Beyfus rose to sum up our case for the jury.

He, of course, began with the contradictions in Mr. Connor's testimony, then went on to the inaccuracies in the things he printed about me that, unlike his opinions, were in the finite realm of reality. He said,

> I suggest that all these facts make it quite clear that the one thing on which we *can't* rely is the honesty of Mr. Connor as a witness. He found himself in a position where he had to say his words were meant to convey the universality of Liberace's appeal.
> If that were so they would be a very considerable compliment. That the defendant should select the very kernel of this vituperative article and suggest it was a very considerable compliment was the most complete and utter nonsense.

At the end of an hour and forty minutes, having covered Mr. William Neil (Cassandra) Connor, he concluded with what he thought about the *Daily Mirror* saying, "Might I suggest that this newspaper is vicious and violent, vindictive and venomous, salacious and sentimental, ruthless and remorseless." (I felt he was talking a little like my opponent wrote.)

But then he suggested a way that the jury could put a little remorse in the publisher's pulp paper heart. He asked the jury—"to teach them a lesson.

"Let your award of damages be such a sum," he said, "as will make the directors think when they deal with their balance sheets."

I prayed that the good people in the jury box would read him loud and clear.

It now became Sir Cyril Salmon's chore to sum up the law for the jurors before they made their deliberations.

We are free, he said, to state any honestly held opinions in any way we like ... diffidently, decorously, politely and discreetly or pungently, provocatively, rudely and brutally.

Freedom of speech is the right of anybody to state his honest opinion about any matter of general importance. This is not a right peculiar to newspapers and journalists. It is a right common to all of us.

We are all free to state fearlessly our own opinion, honestly held, upon matters of public interest.

We may not tell a derogatory lie about anyone.

We must not make any untrue statement of fact about anyone which tends to lower them in the minds of right thinking people.

If we state an opinion, it matters not if it is defamatory, if it is our real opinion, honestly held, and is such that any fair-minded man might honestly hold.

In spite of the babble of speculation that went on in the courtroom and the corridors during the three and three-quarter hours the jury was out, the courtroom did not have one newspaperman in it the moment the verdict was read.

The reason for this was the charming widow of an Australian sheepherder, Mrs. Jean Friend. As the ten men and two women filed into the jury box, there was a triumphant whisper racing through the courtroom ... "He must have won! He must have won! Look at the smiles on the faces of those women."

Then Mrs. Friend winked at me. It was the wink that emptied the courtroom of gentlemen of the press. It was all they needed to send them out to talk to their papers, give them the color of the final moments, including Mrs. Friend's friendly wink. They knew with all this started they could then come back and get the facts. The one big fact that staggered everyone, most of all me, was the amount I was awarded. £8,000. At that time it was worth $22,400. Although this was the largest libel settlement ever awarded in the High Courts of England, the amount was infinitesimal to what I might have been awarded had this trial taken place in the courts of the United States, where an individual like me could stipulate damages and costs up into the millions of dollars. However, I did not bring this action forward for the sake of money, but principle.

The *Daily Mail* reported, "As the court adjourned there was chaos as dozens of women tried to reach Liberace. Pale but smiling broadly he was ushered back to the safety of a consultation room by High Court officials and his own lawyers.

"But on the fifteen-yard walk along the stone passage, with people milling around him shouting good wishes, Liberace was jostled against a jurywoman, Mrs. Friend. His hand went to her elbow and he spoke to her in a soft drawl." (I don't know how that reporter knew I spoke in a drawl. But I think I said, "I hope we don't get knocked down." Then I saw who it was.)

All I really wanted to do was to get back to the hotel and have a little privacy so that I could call my mother in Los Angeles and tell her the good news, because I knew she'd been worrying.

Anybody who has ever been in a situation must know what our conversation was about. It's difficult . . . impossible . . . for me to try to reconstruct it at this date. Besides, the honest, heartfelt things that people say to each other in the privacy of their personal relationships come out sounding corny when they're set down in cold type.

But Jonah Ruddy, who covers Hollywood for the *Daily Mail* and other British newspapers, got to Mom and filed this report: "When she heard the news from London, Liberace's mother said, 'It is a sort of answer to my prayers. I have been praying twice a day and I was very worried. I am extremely proud of my son and all our family. I am very pleased that his good name has been cleared and my name, too. Because when I was in London in 1956, the horrible things that man said made me sick.' "

Meantime, back at the hotel, reporters found Mrs. Friend and two friends in the Savoy grill having tea with raspberry jam. She said, "I often come here for tea but I had to give it up during the case because there was the danger I'd run into that darling Liberace."

When asked if she had smiled and winked to end the suspense she said, "Of course I did. Any woman with any feeling would have done the same thing. I've always liked him. I think he's a smasher."

Everyplace I went for the rest of that day people held up two fingers in the V-sign and called, "Good show, Libby."

It seemed ironic to me that the theater I played in that night was scheduled to close a few days later (quel victory!) to be torn down to make way for an office building. It struck me as strange. In

America theaters and landmarks are always being torn down to make way for office buildings or parking lots. But you don't think of any place ever being torn down in London. That's what makes it so charming.

I am being as modest as possible when I say I got a wonderful reception on my first performance after the suit. This is what the *News Chronicle* said I said,

> Thank you, ladies and gentlemen, you make me very happy. And I was very, very happy before you did that. (Come to think about it, that sounds as if I'm telling them they reduced my happiness by one "very." Fortunately they didn't take it that way.) I'd like to express my thanks to those people in this country who have been so loyal and encouraging throughout this anxious time. It has been said many times that English justice is the fairest in the world. I am absolutely convinced of it now.

I then sat down at the piano and said, "It's good to sit on a soft bench for a change."

A woman in the stalls shouted, "Come down here, here's a soft one!"

Of course, after the show there was a big celebration party. Janet Medlin, the singer in my company, and Dr. Gordon Robinson, my musical director, were there, of course, although Gordon claimed to be angry at me for not allowing him to be a witness. I felt people might think he was a little biased. Jack Hurlburt and Cicely Courtneidge were there to help me celebrate, Trevor Howard, and Bob Monkhouse, and I remember there was a great big cake baked in the shape of a grand piano. I wonder where they got that idea? But the biggest joke of all was that the meal of chicken Kiev and dessert of strawberries, meringue and ice cream, that I would call Strawberries Romanoff but the chef called "Strawberries de success," was opened with . . . smoked salmon. With a bit of it in one hand and a glass of champagne in the other Bob Monkhouse proposed a toast to Sir Cyril who had presided so gracefully, so patiently, so fairly and so graciously over a sticky situation.

I find I haven't made any comment on all the cartoons that ran in the British press. One of them showed a very grubby little working man's pub. There are sad, tired looking poor people sitting around at tables playing dominoes and at the bar. At the piano, with several empty glasses on top of it, is a typical "ragtime Joe" type piano player who is probably just playing for drinks. And to this wretched creature a man is saying, "Ya'd get yerself a million quid if I was to tell yer what old Fred said about your piano playing."

Another was a figure of Justice with her scales. Her eyes are crossed and she has columns of newspaper clippings wound in her spiked crown. In her outstretched arms she is holding a candelabra—straight up in one hand—a clef of music, hanging from the other. There is no caption.

A third cartoon was a courtroom scene with Queen's Counsel pointing to the jury and saying to the magistrate on the bench, "We're trying to stop this winking business, my Lord." In the jury box, each member is wearing an eyepatch.

Then there was the one of Russia, France and the USA, each represented by their heads of state, sitting around a table discussing the peace of the world and how to keep it. On the table there stands a candelabra. Representing Great Britain and addressing the other three men, Sir Selwyn Lloyd is saying, "Gentlemen, we've got to make a determined effort to get our fair share of the headlines."

These and other cartoons hang all over my house. There are really an awful lot and hardly enough wall space to accommodate all of them. They're about my smiling, my winking, my teeth, my gentility, my hair, my general appearance and, of course, the flamboyance of my wardrobe.

But none of them bother me very much because they're all done in the spirit of fun. One of the most amusing and, I guess, effective, first appeared when I was playing in Nashville, Tennessee, around 1954. I opened March 31, the day before April Fool's Day, and as a prank the cartoonist on one of the local papers did a retouch job on me and they printed a picture of me completely bald. The caption said something like, "Liberace Goes Yul Brynner One Better." The next day they published a picture of me as I was, with my hair and everything in order and simply captioned it "April Fool!"

Newspaper people tell me that retractions never catch up with the statements they were supposed to retract. And that's the way it was with this April Fool gag. I got thousands of letters from people demanding to know how I could be such a fool as to cut off all my hair. And newspapers wrote comments on how crazy a musician can be, particularly if he happened to be a musician they always suspected was a little nutty.

To this day, almost twenty years later, that gag haunts me. People tell me that someone told a friend of theirs that I was bald and wore a wig. A couple of times when I've been working on the stage and lean over to show one of the ladies in the front row my rings or my wrist watch or something like that, one of them will grab my hair and give it a pull. The first time that happened I said the first thing that came into my head which was, "Ouch!"

The lady said, "Oh, I'm so sorry. I didn't mean to hurt you. But I am glad that you're not bald. They told me that hair of yours is a wig."

Of course, the great climax to all that happened in court in '59 was the Royal Variety Show for the Queen Mother in Manchester. It was, naturally, the biggest thing that had ever happened to me and it was also very big for Manchester because it was the first time such an event had ever been held there. For me it was sort of a Royal endorsement proving that the trial had in no way affected my career or colored the way people thought about me.

During the show I slipped in one little reference to the trial. When I came out I said, "This is the suit you read about in the papers."

At the reception that followed, as I heard myself addressing the Queen Mother as "ma'am," I began to wonder why she and the Queen are called that. I asked a lot of people and none could give me a proper answer, except that it's short for "madam." But what American woman would want to be called that?

"Okay! It's all over! You won! What are you going to do with all that money?" everybody was saying, as if they thought that much money all at once would turn my head, and with never a thought that it was none of their business.

How was anybody to know that I decided when I started the action that if I were successful in getting any kind of judgment against the paper and Cassandra, even if it were only six cents, I'd give it all to charity? I figured this was the safest way to prevent some muckraking newspaper man from cooking up a story full of hypothetical questions, suggestions and innuendos to induce the thought that I'd found an easy way to make a living and would continue to sue anyone who wrote anything about me that wasn't idle puffery.

So when I got back home to California, I gave the whole amount to cancer research. It was appropriate, I thought afterward. My attorney had called what Connor was doing a cancerous growth on journalism.

And, I suppose, if any lesson at all is to be drawn from the whole affair it is that no matter how bad a thing may look, it can turn out to do someone some good. If for no other reason than if the $22,400 I got from Connor meant beating cancer one minute sooner, all the agony and embarrassment was worth it.

I felt good about it. And it wasn't long before I got proof of how London felt about me. Every place I went I got the V-for-Victory sign from the people on the street. And to make it even more exciting there came an invitation from the Queen to join the Command Performance the following year, 1960, to be held in the Royal Victoria Theater in London.

The other Americans to be on the bill were Nat (King) Cole. Another piano player? Well, a little different sort of piano player, different style. And Sammy Davis, Jr., was also to be on the bill. Another singer and dancer? Well, perhaps a little better at both than I am. And then there was to be Robert Horton. Another actor? Obviously no one had seen my performance in *Sincerely Yours*. Or had they?

It was both Nat Cole's and Sammy Davis' first appearance before a London audience. They loved Cole but they absolutely adored Sammy Davis. He became the talk of the town. But, unfortunately for Sammy, this time around *he* was the one who caught all the flack from the sensational London press because he was married to Mai Britt.

Those yellow tabloids in London, in those days, lived on picking the bones of personalities. I felt very sorry for Sammy because I knew what he was going through.

At one point in that show I was playing the piano and glanced up at the Royal Box. I couldn't believe my eyes. I was playing "You Made Me Love You" and the audience began to sing. This happens a lot in Britain. If they like you and they like the piece you're playing, they join in. I couldn't believe what I thought I saw in that quick glance at the Queen's box.

Later when I got the opportunity of viewing the television tape of the Royal Command performance before it was run for the public, I saw that my eyes hadn't played any trick on me! Cameras had focused on the Queen during the singing of "You Made Me Love You," and I saw a wonderful close-up of the Queen of England happily singing, along with me and her subjects, "You Made Me Love You."

She seemed to be having the time of her life. Without doubt that picture lives most vividly in my mind and is one of my dearest memories of all the Command Performances I've done . . . so far.

But the most wonderful part of the whole thing was that I finally got to meet the Queen herself and Prince Philip. The first thing Her Majesty said to me was, "Well . . . at last." She was, of course, referring to the cancellation in 1956 and her inability to be in Manchester in 1959.

I was surprised and delighted at her "girl-like" quality . . . youthful, petite, charming . . . after the show she said to me, "I knew you played the piano, but I didn't know you could sing and dance."

I said, "Neither did I until I tried."

She smiled a very knowing smile that I remember to this day.

18

Whe I arrived at Heathrow Airport, London, on my way to South Africa, I was tickled to death to find a lot of my fans waiting for me. There were a lot of people who aren't my fans. They're called reporters.

Along with the same old jive questions about "Did you bring your Mum?" and all the other antiquities I've answered so often that I can wake from a sound sleep and make a sensible reply, there was a new one. It was, "Why are you going to South Africa?"

I knew right away that question was loaded with trouble. Anybody who knows my personal life knows that the color of a man's skin means nothing to me. I think segregation is indecent and inhuman and I loathe the idea of it. But I don't think that it's the place of an American piano player to try to change the quality of life in the Republic of South Africa. I was asked to come to Johannesburg, Durban, Pretoria and Cape town. Would it be right for me to sound off on how the people there should live? If I'm invited to a man's home do I criticize his life style? This is how I feel.

This is what I said to the reporters, "I do not intend to get involved in internal problems. I'm going there to bring entertainment and, I hope, happiness to people. Their way of life is something they have to work out for themselves."

I guess I just can't see the sense of mixing politics and show business the way some of my friends do. Actually, I was once voted

Honorary Mayor of Sherman Oaks, California, and I didn't like it. So enough of politics. It's not my cup of confusion.

Then came another crazy question. Addressing me directly, one of those guys said, "How do you see Liberace?"

How was I to answer that? I never speak of myself in the third person. I'm a first person person and if I can't be "I," I'll be "me." Only to other people speaking of me am I Liberace. So I was tempted to say, "I see Liberace by looking in the mirror." But I didn't. There's no use starting up with the press. I have trouble enough with them when I'm as polite as I can be.

So I went along with the little game and said that I saw him as a genuine entertainer. (What else would a genuine egotist say?) One who knew his audience and didn't go running off to see the Maharishi like the Beatles did. To myself I said, "You ask a silly question, you get a silly answer."

But I got criticized for criticizing the Beatles. Sometimes I'm afraid to say it's a nice day for fear some farmers, who've been praying for rain, will think I'm against corn. What's worse, if I say it looks like rain, theater managers accuse me of giving out propaganda that's bad for business.

I've written how I feel about London, how I love it and how it's been good to me. Fergus Cashin, a London newspaper writer, said to me as we were riding from Heathrow to the hotel, "Driving through the streets of London with you is like being in the Coronation in your day clothes." I laughed. "Of course," he added hastily, "that doesn't apply to *your* day clothes. And speaking of that, how's for a look at that suit of yours I've heard about that lights up?"

"Come up to the room with me and I'll model it for you," I suggested.

"That'll be too good to miss," he said and this is what he wrote about the incident:

> The next thing I know in comes Lee smoking a seven-inch-long Sherman cigarette and saying, "It keeps the ashes off the suit. They might short circuit it.
>
> "It took seven months to make. And it weighs forty pounds. It cost about two hundred and fifty pounds.
>
> "I wear it at the end of the show. I blow out the candles on my electric candelabra, which I do by pressing a button, and then . . . poof! *I* light up." But . . . poof he didn't. The suit wasn't plugged in.

[250

"You must be the only performer in the world who's lit at the end of every show," I said.

"No. There's Dean Martin. But I don't get the hangovers he does."

"Do you ever suffer from short circuits?"

"Yes," said Lee, "and I'm put out by them." I figured that's enough of being topped by a piano player. But Lee went right on. "I thought up the idea in America, because there the customers are likely to hurry off to the parking lot to go home as soon as they sense that you're coming to the end of your act."

That was the end of the story.

As soon as Cashin left I changed back into something that wouldn't stop traffic on Piccadilly and rushed over to the Palladium for a run-through. It was rush, rush, rush and I found being in London for such a short time a little like waving to your sweetheart from the window of a passing train. A glimpse was better than nothing but hardly enough to satisfy.

I didn't have time to relax and get into the mood of the city. There were the two two-hour Palladium shows to rehearse and then perform and a television show, "Liberace's London," to prepare for. That was fun. (Someday I'll have to do Liberace's Milwaukee. *That* would be some show.)

Then, all of a sudden, I was skybound for South Africa. The rest of my people, Gordon Robinson, Florian Zabach and Gale Sherwood had gone on ahead to get things ready for me.

I feel two ways about air travel. I like it and I don't. It sure gets you there fast, I'll say that. Of course, you're more comfortable on a boat. But then you're on a boat so much longer you begin to begrudge the time it takes. And now they make you so comfortable on planes . . . you can walk around and everything. Some of them even have piano bars. I wouldn't dare go near one. The airline couldn't afford to pay my salary. And such little pianos.

I was awfully unhappy that I couldn't take my piano with the transparent top on the South African tour. They told me it was too heavy. I don't understand that! They transport tanks and all kinds of things in planes. And I had ordered a streamlined piano specially designed by me to be made in Holland. But it wasn't finished in time! So when I opened in Johannesburg, there I was at a plain old—but highly polished—Baldwin.

I guess a piano added to over a ton of other stuff might have run the baggage bill a little high.

One of the things I looked forward to doing in Johannesburg was seeing the diamond mines and maybe buying a few on the premises—an idea I made up. It would have been wonderful, I thought, to go down in the mine, pick up a rock, bring it out and have a diamond cleaned up and cut just for me. Me and my fantasies. I didn't get to visit a diamond mine, but I did go down into a gold mine and it was very exciting although they didn't hand out any samples.

But I did buy some diamonds. But buying them "right where they grow" wasn't like going out to a farm in the country and buying fresh vegetables cheaper. The diamonds in Johannesburg weren't any cheaper. The price is the same all over the world.

Naturally the South Africa press gave me the same kind of "but" treatment I'm used to by now. It's almost standard. The writer lists all the things the reader might dislike about me—meaning all the things the writer thought he'd dislike about me before he saw or met me. The piece then finishes "but you'll love (him) his show." I call them "converts" and it's nice to make them. I'm glad I'm able to.

Apparently it shook them up a little when our gear arrived at Jan Smuts Airport. The Natal *Witness* reported it to be "the largest baggage load belonging to one person that they have ever been confronted with . . . there was an air of secrecy as Liberace's costumes, jewelry and ornaments were loaded into an armoured security van and taken to a destination in Johannesburg that will be kept secret until Mr. Showmanship arrives on Friday." The story said that the stuff was insured for half a million rand . . . so the South African rand, at that time must have been worth about two bucks.

A reporter in Capetown thought we had too much luggage, too. He wrote that we "arrived in Capetown with more baggage than is really decent." I wonder what he considers a decent amount of baggage—a toothbrush and a change of linen?

One of the things I worried about all the way to South Africa was that it's hot there. I hate heat. Even in a cool place like London I have a little electric fan under the piano to keep me cool. Those suits I wear ought to be air conditioned like the ones the astronauts wore to the moon. Particularly the one that lights up. And, believe me, I won't have any more made with beading on the pants . . . at least not on the seat. If the beads are turned the wrong way, it's murder! One bead will do it. But as I say, "My clothes may look funny, but they're making me the money."

Sometimes I make a little joke about my electric fan and call it my own private air-conditioning system. I'd say, "Would you like to see it? Eight ninety-five Sears Roebuck. This is it. . . . Oh, boy"—mopping my brow—"I should've got the eleven ninety-eight model!"

One of the nicest things about Johannesburg is that everyone seems to be very polite. I did something I do all the time, almost everywhere I play. I went and thanked everybody on the theater staff for their help in making my performance smooth and successful.

I got a letter from the usherettes saying that they were overwhelmed that I took the time to come and introduce myself and talk to them. They thanked me and said it made them all very happy. Their letter made me happy. Imagine, polite usherettes. No, I'm joking. I was happy to hear their reactions to our little meeting. It's one way I have of showing myself as I am (not as a showman) to people who otherwise would only know the sly innuendoes that they read in the papers about me.

Of course, on the stage I talk about these. I say I've heard them. "In fact," I say, "I *started* them." This is always good for a laugh. Sometimes I say, "I've heard stories about myself that gave me ideas I've never even had before." This, also, is a solid laugh. But they are laughing at what they now understand to be jokes. When I can talk eyeball to eyeball with people, especially those who meet me unexpectedly, I can make them realize that most of what they read about me is nothing more than nasty gossip. Of course, wherever I go, I get the wildest letters.

On my arrival in Johannesburg there was a batch of them waiting for me. One woman wrote that she'd read that one of my hobbies was collecting antiques. She said she had a wonderful old grandfather clock. She wasn't interested in selling it. All she wanted, she said "was to find a good home for the clock." That's how sentimental people can get about things.

Another letter came from a fifteen-year-old boy who wrote that he was looking for a daddy because his daddy had died. Then he went on to say that his Mum was very attractive and only thirty-eight years old and was anxious to see the United States. A postscript said that he wanted to see it, too. I kept the letter. I think it was very cute and quite sweet . . . of his mother to get him to write it.

One thing worried me. There was one review that appeared in a little weekly I never would have seen if the writer hadn't sent me the clipping. He wrote, "I thought you'd like to know how much I enjoyed your performance last night. This is what I wrote about you." The clipping said, "To open the show Liberace wore a sequin-trimmed lavender jacket. Then he came on in a green sequin suit with polo-neck lace shirt. And he followed that with a black sequin-covered suit with diamond buttons that spelled out his name. He's irresistible."

I threw the review away. It was written by a man. I thought he might have mentioned at least once that I played the piano. Also I think he's colorblind. I wore a yellow suit. It was one that LBJ liked. I had dinner with him and Ladybird Johnson and, you know what, there wasn't another suit like mine in the place. From then on LBJ called me "Yellowbird."

Shortly after we arrived in Durban, Gale Sherwood and Florian Zabach and I were holding the usual press conference. For a change I was asking the reporters questions, like why they never mentioned the fact that Florian was traveling with a priceless 1792 Guarnerius violin instead of talking about one suit I had which cost $10,000. I told them it didn't really cost that much. The actual price was $9,997.50, marked down because it was the only one left in stock.

As we were talking Gale Sherwood let out an, "Oh, no!!"

She waved a little note that had just been handed to her. "The airline people say they've lost one of my bags somewhere between Johannesburg and Durban and it happens to be the one with the dresses I wear in the show." Then she broke into a broad smile.

"What am I worried about? You'll let me borrow one of your suits, won't you, Lee?"

I said, "You're welcome, honey. Be my guest. But the alterations will be murder. I'm flat where you're not. You're slim where I'm round. It wouldn't work."

Of course, I'm only kidding. It was all in fun and we had a lot of that in South Africa. Speaking of which, one of the things that surprised me was that in South Africa, where the newspeople dug up 1959 stories about me, and which sometimes refers to itself as S.A., did not produce one newspaper headline saying, "Mr. S.A. Comes to S.A."

At the end of each hot and hectic day in Johannesburg, Durban, Capetown or Pretoria, I used to relax at night in bed by trying to translate the stories about me in the papers printed in Afrikaans, the language of the Boers. I'd print out the Afrikaans words on a piece of paper and then try to put the English words—or what I thought were the English words for them—under them.

For the name of the paper, *Die Burger Staerdag*, I fell back on what little German I remembered from Milwaukee and got "The Citizen Saturday." "Die" means the. "Burger" means someone who lives in a city. And "Staerdag" I guessed at, hoping that "dag" really meant day (as in "tag" in German).

Having triumphed over the name of the paper, I decided to go ahead on the rest of the article. The first line read, *"Twee van die wereld se beroetdste manne het mekaar gistermiddag in Kaapstad ontmoet: die klaviervirtuoso Liberace, het die wereld se engiste lewende hartoerplantingspasient, Dr. Philip Blaiberg, gaan besoek."*

What I had under the words were "two of the world blank blank men blank blank yesterday in Capetown met the piano virtuoso Liberace blank the world's first blank heart plant patient, Dr. Philip Blaiberg, blank blank." I hoped the last two words, gaan bosoek" didn't mean what they sounded like in English which would mean, "gone crazy."

It was fun and it put me to sleep, but not before I fell in love with two words "klaviervirtuoso" and "hartoerplantingspasient." I'm convinced that all you need to speak Afrikaans, at least understand it in print, is a smattering of Milwaukee German and a lot of imagination. Also it helps if you know that the article is about you and where you were and with whom at the time it is reporting.

The thought of my meeting with Dr. Blaiberg saddens me because when we met, he and I talked about his escape from death through heart transplant and about a brush I had with the black angel a few years before. He was a kind and grateful man, and I'm sure that he contributed to the sum total of medical knowledge in the field of transplant surgery, a discipline that will someday become, I hope, as simple as a tonsillectomy.

To show you to what incredicle lengths some newspapers will go

255]

to get a sensational story or headline, the reporter from one of the papers in Durban wanted to know, in 1968 . . . twelve years after it happened . . . all about my arrival in London in 1956 and my little mix-up with Cassandra. I told him, "The man is dead!" and walked away. But I suppose it could have been worse. He might have dug up my big blunder in Sydney in 1958. As far as I'm concerned it would be wonderful if reporters were never allowed into the morgue of a newspaper. Then they'd have to write about what I'm doing, not about what I *did.*

But we had a big and wonderful time in South Africa, the audiences were sensational and we were entertained royally wherever we went. Nowhere was I threatened with being "slung out" and I shall always remember (because I wrote them down) these beautiful words, some of which you'll have to look up for yourself, that were written by an anonymous reporter in Pretoria: "His music comes embellished with passementerie, baubles, gee-gaws, bejouterie, and trinkets." A nice mess of words. I can hardly say them. But you should hear the way I play them on the piano.

When I arrived in Johannesburg from Sydney, for my second visit to the Republic of South Africa in three years, the news of my hot pants had preceded me so they were no big surprise. As in Australia, the kids on the streets were wearing outfits that in many cases rivaled mine in fantasy, if not in cost, and I don't know whether this was good or bad for me. At least it turned the press to talking to me about other things.

Word had traveled halfway around the world that David Merrick had been chatting with my managers about doing a big Broadway musical for me. He suggested it might be about Louis XVI, who is one of my favorite Louis. No question about the fact that it would be fun to do. And remember how wonderful Bert Lahr was playing Louis XV in *DuBarry Was a Lady*? But I didn't want to be tied down to the Broadway routine, the same thing at the same time in the same place every day. I told this to a man named Venables who writes for the *Daily Mail* in Johannesburg and he asked, "But how can you turn down that Broadway cash?"

People get funny ideas about show business salaries. Venables thought I was kidding when I told him Katharine Hepburn got the highest money ever paid on Broadway and that it was $17,000 a week. That was for playing Coco Chanel in *Coco*. When he said, "That's not bad," I had to confess it was hardly anything com-

(Hollywood Press Syndicate photo)

Liberace in snowy sheared beaver dress suit attends premiere of his picture, *Sincerely Yours*, with his mother, Frances, dressed in furs to match her son's outfit.

Liberace's auditorium-packed audience during a 1971 concert tour engagement—this one in St. Petersburg, Florida. *(St. Petersburg Times photo)*

Liberace standing on edge of pool at Hollywood Hills home.

The highlight of the master bedroom in Liberace's Palm Springs home is the Czar Nicholas desk; this inlaid and ormolued desk is valued at over $150,000 and was given to the Czar after he signed a peace treaty with France.

Liberace in portion of walk-in wardrobe closet in Hollywood home.

(Photo Eric Skipsey)

Liberace's hideaway in Palm Springs. This residence was once a small
hotel; Liberace completely refurbished and renovated the buildings and
grounds.

Liberace's hand-carved bed with white llama spread trimmed in ermine tails, in his Hollywood Hills home.

With his classic Rolls-Royce only seven of which have been made for others, including Queen Elizabeth II and John Lennon. This car has been repainted white and maroon since this photo was taken, and it was used during his 1972 Las Vegas engagement.

Liberace comparing jewelry with Carol Channing.

Receiving award in Las Vegas for his 25th Anniversary in show business.

A packed Hollywood Bowl awaits Liberace; 20,000 people, setting a modern-day attendance record.

Liberace and Queen Elizabeth at his 1956 Command Performance in London.

Liberace the performer—on his feet and at the piano.

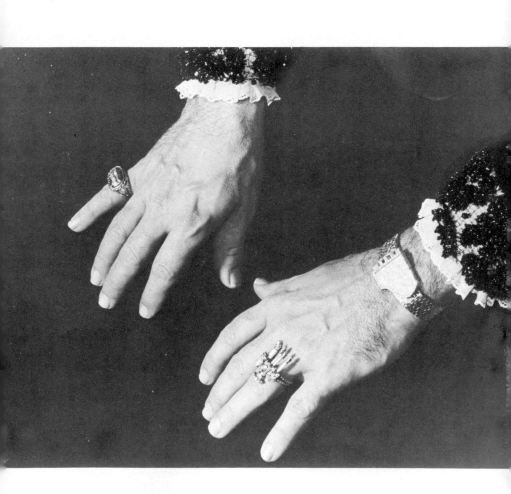

Liberace wearing his diamond rings, one of which is shaped like a candelabra, and his piano shaped wrist watch.

Liberace in Australia.

Liberace and two friends.

Mike Douglas foregoes warm knees to welcome his flashy co-host Liberace in style as Lee joins Mike for a week of *The Mike Douglas Show* in June, 1973.

For his entrance in his 1972 Las Vegas engagement Liberace was driven on stage in a chauffeured Rolls-Royce. His costume, which he had worn for his recent Command Performance in London, was a diamond studded white ermine coat covering a gold lamé jump suit.

Liberace meeting the Queen Mother backstage after his third command performance.

pared to what can be made on a tour like the one I was on or when I play Las Vegas. And both mean more fun for more people and for me.

Actually I hate to talk about money when I'm outside the United States. Show business salaries at home are so out of line with the money paid in London or in Australia or South Africa that it seems vulgar and pushy to talk about it even though it's just as vulgar and pushy to ask a man, any man in any business, how much money he earns. I guess it's because we Americans have no false modesty about success and we generally measure our success in terms of income.

The critics in Johannesburg were particularly enthusiastic about the two other people I had with me in the show and well they should have been. One of them was a boy of ten who I thought, and everyone seemed to agree with me, was one of the cleverest jugglers (of any age) I'd ever seen. His name is Albert Lucas.

And Fay McKay, singing comedienne, who could make Totie Fields look like Twiggy, got almost as much space in the newspapers as I did. Those things please me. I try to discover the best people I can because if there isn't something exciting and interesting when I'm not on the stage, then when I come back . . . what I'll find waiting for me is the backlash of a lull. No performer wants to tangle with an audience that's been turned off.

So, really, the people who thought it was a wonderful thing that I have such good people with me don't know the deep, true secrets of show business. Jack Benny has always surrounded himself with outstanding people who got big laughs by making fun of him. And he's just as wonderful today as he was when I first heard him on the radio when I was hustling for club dates in Milwaukee.

The second time I didn't get myself in trouble in Australia before coming to South Africa and there, again, I got nothing but love even from the press. So, as it says in the song, it's always better "the second time around."

19

A lot of people know how I entertain when I'm on the stage. Not too many know how I entertain my guests when I'm not on tour and have time to invite them to enjoy the beauty and comfort of the homes in Hollywood and Palm Springs that my good fortune has enabled me to create for myself.

They mirror the way I like to live, my love for beautiful things, and my need for luxury and elegance. That was probably psychologically induced by the poverty I knew when I was a child.

It is in my homes that I enjoy the fruits of my labor, the rewards my talents have won for me, the pleasure of companionship and the privilege of privacy. I think anyone who spends as much time before the public on the road and on the stage as I do, has a right to some sanctuary where he can do just exactly as he pleases. Even the wild birds now have sanctuaries.

Although I haven't owned it for many years now, the press and people who meet me for the first time still ask me about my piano-shaped swimming pool. And friends tell me that people who know they're acquainted with Liberace also ask, "Has he really got a piano-shaped swimming pool?" Well, the answer is "No!" Although I don't see why there's anything so completely strange about the idea, there are kidney-shaped pools and free-form pools and pools that look like mountain lakes or desert oases.

After I built my piano-shaped pool, just for the fun of having something different, there was a lot of publicity about it. Not many people had piano-shaped pools and the curiosity to see one ran very high. Tourists flocked to my house in great numbers to get a look at it. And because I think I should always be gracious to anyone who takes an interest in me, I welcomed one and all and made it possible for them to have a look at what some called Liberace's folly. This quickly became too complicated. After all, the pool was part of my home. I built it not to show off but to swim in and for my friends to enjoy. The constant flow of tourists made this impossible. I didn't know what to do. I didn't want to be rude. And I did benefit by the publicity. As the King of Siam says in *The King and I*, it was " a puzzlement."

Finally there was only one solution. I had to get rid of the pool and that, naturally, meant I had to sell the house which I had no trouble doing. It was purchased by Mr. Kerk Kerkorian who thought he got a great thing, something he could show off and talk to all his friends about. He seemed to think that as long as I was no longer on the premises, the spot had lost its main attraction. He was wrong. What a blow that was to my vanity. Nobody had come there to see me. It was the pool!

Finally Mr. Kerkorian had to put up a sign out in front saying "Liberace doesn't live here anymore." But this sign gave nobody the idea that I'd dug up the "crazy" pool and taken it away with me. People kept coming anyway. I actually felt embarrassed when Mr. Kerkorian told me about the trouble he was having. But I didn't offer to give him back his money.

He too had to sell the house. It's a nice place, and I hope the people who are living there now enjoy themselves as much as I did when I lived there. Even if I hadn't had a problem with the pool, I'd outgrown the place. As my fortunes improved and my taste for beautiful things could be catered to more freely I was able to expand. Let's put it this way, I *had* to expand. I needed more room for my growing collections. I'm a born collector. If I see something I like, I have to have it. Then, if I see something in the same class with it, or similar to it, I have to have *that*, too. Believe me it runs into money. But that never bothers me. If I have it I spend it. Pretty soon I have the beginnings of a new collection.

When it comes to those, always remember there's no such thing as "just a small" collection, not if you're a real collector at heart. But I'll get to my collections. Right now I want to talk about where I live.

I've always been fascinated by the carpet of lights that is the international trademark of the sprawling City of Los Angeles, just as the skyline is the trademark of the City of New York. I couldn't see those lights from my home in the San Fernando Valley; the Hollywood Hills were in the way. So one thing I looked for in picking a new home was a view of the "lights of Hollywood." They're not really the "lights of Hollywood." They're actually the lights of the rest of the City of Los Angeles. It's that they're *seen* from Hollywood. Anyway, they're definitely part of the glamor of the place.

But I wasn't about to buy just any house with a view and enough rooms to accommodate my worldly goods. I wanted a house with some history, some color, some background. The one I got was built by an early silent screen star. They told me it was once owned by Rudy Vallee. The kids in the neighborhood said it was haunted. It sure looked like it. It was just a tumbled-down mess.

I must have seen in its location the same thing the original builder did. So I bought it and started to fix it up to suit my taste and needs. It took a long time and it cost a lot of money. The result is what I call my Hollywood Hills home. My family calls it "the palace." They exaggerate.

True, it has over thirty rooms. But it's not a palace. A mansion, maybe. But it's "me" from the red carpet that leads to the front door to every antique, *objet d'art* and piece of bric-a-brac, knick-knack and memento that's in it. It's a far cry from the rather modern house in the valley. This one has strong links with the past. And there's no swimming pool shaped like a piano, because I finally learned that no one can swim a concerto, not even Mark Spitz.

You can really get a good swim in the present Olympic-size pool. It's heated to 70 degrees all the year round and surrounded by formal gardens. I think I got the idea from Versailles, but the carpeting is my own idea. The garden, too, is heated so that it's possible to stroll in it during the chilly evenings we have so often in Southern California. Warm sunny days and cool, crisp nights.

People have described the house in Hollywood as "opulent," and I can't quarrel with that. Sometimes I think I've lived before, that I really belong to another century. I say this because I've decorated the place in the motifs of the fourteenth through seventeenth centuries, although the beautiful 24-karat-gold-leaf-covered theater organ belongs to the early half of my own twentieth century—the movie palace era. It's a wonderful instrument. You can simulate any sound on it—bird calls, drums, tambourines, chimes. You name it, I'll play it. It's like the ones they used to have in the Paramount, Roxy and Capitol theaters in New York and all the big movie palaces throughout the land. Only mine is better. It can use rolls, like the old player piano rolls, and I have some made by the famous organists of the early twenties. There's a CinemaScope theater, and like the second house I lived in as a child in Milwaukee, it has two kitchens. But unlike the Milwaukee place, neither of the kitchens has a wood-burning stove.

I wish I could show you the place. I'm so proud of it. I like to entertain and make my friends feel at home, as if everything is for them to enjoy and appreciate. And generally people who are visiting me for the first time like to go on a tour of the house. I like to conduct the tour. Who else could? I feel it gives people a chance to understand me better as I describe the rooms and their furnishings.

I try to meet my guests personally when they arrive and welcome them into the lovely golden foyer. There is a sparkling crystal chandelier and a stairway that curves gracefully upward to the third level. You come in on the middle level, as is so often the way in hill houses.

The formal living room in French blue and gold is to your right. It is furnished in tapestries and pieces from the sixteenth, seventeenth and eighteenth centuries, upholstered in ivory and the palest of yellow satins and velvet. The chandelier, suspended from a gilded mirror is 18-karat gold and Baccarat crystal. The piano, on a dais, was once owned by Chopin. To the left of this is a small art gallery with some of my treasures.

Up the sweeping staircase to the third level is my office with my huge piano-shaped desk at which I'm working at this very moment. The other wing is where I live, a suite consisting of a bedroom, in which the bed does not look like a piano, nor is it round nor any other exotic shape. But it's a big one. Off the bedroom is a sitting room, a great big Roman bath and a dressing room where I keep my clothes. There are nearly two hundred shirts, several hundred pairs of slacks, a lot of suits, although I don't wear suits very often, and there must be about four hundred pairs of shoes. A lot of underwear, too. And do you want to know something? I've worn every one of them. I'll tell you something else about all those clothes. I have another complete wardrobe in my home in Palm Springs. That's so I never have to pack and no matter where I am, I'll always have something to slip into when I feel like changing. Silly, isn't it? But it's one of the ways I enjoy myself. And I don't want you to think that all those clothes are my stage clothes. I've just told you about the stuff I wear when I'm resting.

The clothes I wear on the stage are, of course, too extreme, too bizarre to wear any place else. I'm often asked who designs them, and I often admit that I do. They're made for me by a Hollywood costumer named Frank Acuna. Of course, when I dream up something that's completely impossible, Frank helps me by figuring out a way to make it possible. Some of my critics say *all* my clothes are impossible. But have you ever seen how my critics dress?

Besides the bedroom, bathroom and sitting room, my own personal quarters in the Hollywood house include a terrace where I can sit and read and get the sun. To make the reading easier, there's a library off the terrace and a bar in case I'm entertaining anyone in the sitting room. Because I know the ladies are interested, I'll add that the bedroom is done in black and red and gold and the furnishings are, naturally, antiques I've picked up in my travels.

Going downstairs from the foyer, to the lower level, you come to what is really a fun room, a work and play room, done in a more modern style. And on the way down, if you want to, you can stop to look at some of the framed awards and commendations, cartoons, letters—all kinds of mementos—that I've accumulated. Then you come into the area where I rehearse for my shows and really relax when I have time. In this room are more trophies and memorabilia.

The room is entirely in black and white, in sort of a piano motif, with a deep red carpet. The ceiling is sprinkled with little stars; there are mirrors on the walls; the lighting is subdued and the first thing that catches your eye when you come in is **my** rhinestone-studded honky-tonk piano. This goes with the bar. There's plenty of space to lounge and the black and white pillows carry out the piano effect of the black keyboard design on the white wall. It's very relaxed, although I know it doesn't sound that way from my description of it. It's truly a pleasant room. The bar sometimes makes it even more pleasant for some people.

But still more fun are the kitchens. One is very large and the other even larger. That's the only difference. I use the smaller one when I cook. It's murder running around a huge kitchen. But the true reason for the two kitchens is that you really need at least two if you have seven dining rooms. There's the informal breakfast room where I have my morning meal when I'm all alone. If it's a nice day I might have it in the terrace dining room right off of it. Then there's another dining room designed specially for buffet dinners. And it's great for those wonderful English manor house-type breakfasts. That's three, isn't it? Sometimes even I can't keep track of my dining rooms. The formal dining room cost a fortune, but it was worth it, because guests are so busy admiring it and talking about it, they haven't time to eat. And I have a dining room that I'm sure every home in America wishes it had. It's designed so you can eat and watch television at the same time. It's a cozy room, everyone gets a good view of the set. That leaves only the lanai by the pool, where we sometimes have informal luncheons, and then there's a counter-type eating spot for people who like to go to diners and places like that, where they sit at a counter, have a beer and flirt with the waitress. I supply everything but the waitress. There is none. Only a waiter. It's me.

Friends have said to me that with all the beautiful, valuable and particularly breakable, things I have in my homes I must be very fussy about whom I ask to visit me. Well, I am, but I'm no "Craig's wife" about it. I'm careful to have only the people I like and know will be as careful about my things as I am. I've mentioned that there is a bar in one of the rooms. But actually there's very little drinking in my homes unless, of course, I'm entertaining the press.

I think the best kind of parties are those where a very few cocktails are served, and by that I mean one or two. Once you get into the third cocktail you're in trouble. They'll ruin the taste buds for a well-planned and well-cooked dinner. And you haven't tasted a well-cooked dinner until you've had one of Gladys'.

With formal dinners, naturally, I serve the best domestic and imported wines. I made a few surveys among my guests, at several parties—informal wine-tasting events. I found that not only could imported wines not generally be distinguished from California wines, but also that the California wines were generally preferred. So now I serve both French and California wines.

When the dinners are more on the informal side, I try to get my guests to help in the planning of the meal or to help me in the kitchen when I decide to do a little cooking. If one of them has a special dish, a dessert or a salad he likes to show off with, I give him a chance to do it.

Another way I have of getting my guests involved is to ask them to pick out the dishes and glassware they'd like to use. And you'd be amazed what beautiful table settings my guests have created. I even give them some flower containers and let them go out into the garden if they want to make a floral centerpiece.

If there's someone who fancies himself a bartender, I put him in charge of the bar, let him create punches or make his own version of sangria, and prepare whatever is his *spécialité*. All this getting involved, I've found, makes for a more congenial gathering. Of course, the whole idea is out of the question unless you're very careful who you invite to your parties.

You may wonder who I invite to mine. Well, they're divided into two groups. One group I call "The Group." These are men and women, their wives and husbands, with whom I'm directly associated in my work or in the businesses in which I'm involved. They include my manager, my musical director, my publicity people, my dresser, my secretary and all the other people who work with me or in my office.

The second group is a little more heterogeneous; they include my family doctor and his family, my lawyer and his family and many, many people outside of show business whom I have met in my travels around the world. Sometimes they're visiting Los Angeles, sometimes Palm Springs. I'm always happy to hear from them, and if I'm free I like to make them welcome with a little party of some sort. And whenever I give a party I like to mix old friends with new ones. This creates widening circles of friendship, like a stone thrown in water. People who have become the dearest friends met for the first time at one of my parties. Because of this outgoing wave of friendship, I try to avoid inviting the same groups of people over and over again. I keep shuffling them around so that there will always be an enlargement of human relationships.

Another thing, I find, it's good to have people with hobbies or professions mingling with those of different interests. This gives each person a chance to talk about his work. I find, for instance, that people in sports mix well with those in show business. And, when I think about it, I guess sports *is* show business, in a way.

Palm Springs is a golfer's paradise. I don't play golf, myself, but most of my friends do. So when I have them visit me down at The

Springs I always get guest cards for them at one or more of the local clubs.

In the evenings, after dinner, I let my guests, whenever possible choose the way the party will go. Sometimes I show a film . . . I have CinemaScope equipment in my screening rooms in both the Hollywood and the Palm Springs houses . . . and sometimes I let the guests select the picture they'd like to see. When the choice is up to me, I try to rent a picture I've missed or a picture that was a hit when I was a boy. Those are great.

For people who like to listen to music, we have plenty of tapes and records. Sometimes I demonstrate one of my pianos or the organ. But I don't like to "give a private show" for my guests. I keep reminding myself of what Oscar Levant said about George Gershwin, who monopolized the piano wherever he went. The line was, "An evening with Gershwin is a Gershwin evening."

I think I like it best when we just sit around after dinner and talk. Somebody's got to keep the conversation alive after what television's done to it in the home. I'll bet there are some families in which the members have not sat down and talked among themselves for years. And I think that's awful. We used to talk among ourselves a lot. Sometimes we even hollered.

Even when I show movies, I try to wedge in a little conversation by having an intermission every few reels. Then there's time for a coke and popcorn. I love popcorn. And when the show's over, if it looks like a really congenial group, I'll try out some new material on the guests without telling them what I'm doing. But I find I have to be careful about that. People who have been well fed and entertained tend to become very uncritical of anything their host does.

All that I've told you will give you the idea that if you come to one of my parties, you're more than a guest. You're also a helper. So if you ever show up, I have a job for you. And don't be afraid to touch and use things. As I've said, I'm no "Craig's wife." And maybe I can give you an example of what I mean by copying the following quotation from a story by Tony Palmer that appeared in the English magazine, *Observer*, early in 1973.

Trying to describe how I love, appreciate, but also *use* the fine things I have, Tony wrote, "One day while filming"—the BBC was doing a film on my life and followed me around with camera and sound equipment for days—

he showed me, with pride, what he described as the largest onyx table he knew of in existence. It must have been all of ten feet long and five feet wide and weighed a ton. Its price, he said, was now beyond estimation.

Later the cameraman asked if he could rest some heavy equipment on the table. Sure, said Liberace, go right ahead. Minutes later there was the most resounding crack. It was almost like a pistol shot. The table had cracked right across the middle from the weight.

Oh, well, giggled Liberace, I now own the largest onyx table in existence . . . that is also cracked. He never mentioned the matter again.

That's what Tony wrote. I felt very badly. But Mom has always told me that there's no use crying over cracked onyx tables.

I feel this way, really, about everything I own. If you can't use it, what good is it? If it breaks, too bad. Use, yes. But don't abuse. I want to tell you about some of the beautiful examples of glassware, furniture and china that I have, but first let me tell you about my place in Palm Springs. Well, really there are *two* places. One of them is the house I live in. The other is "The Cloisters" that houses most of my most precious things as well as my guests when they come to visit me in the desert.

The same urge to save something from destruction that led me to acquire the Hollywood house, made me buy the Palm Springs place. It was an exclusive, small hotel, built almost like a monastery with high walls and lovely sequestered gardens surrounding it. It was a hideaway for big show business stars. None other was ever admitted. And now you know why it eventually had to fail.

Stars don't want to look at other stars. They want to go somewhere to be looked at and admired, not envied by their peers.

So here was that excellent example of early Spanish-Mexican architecture just crumbling away waiting for someone to do something about it, and I came along. You should see it now. Everytime I come back there I'm delighted with what I've done. The pleasure I get out of it makes me want to do some more restorations of what should be landmarks forever.

I'd like to do something to insure the permanence of those magnificent old mansions along the beach at Newport, Rhode Island, that the Vanderbilts, the Astors and the Goulds built in the late nineteenth century and called "summer cottages." Cottages! Anyone of them is so big it could be turned into a Holiday Inn. But that's not what I'd want to turn them into. I'd like to restore at least one of them to the way it was when it was first opened. Make it sort of a museum. A lot of good old American architecture is going to be lost if someone doesn't do something to save it. So let's get back to my own most recent project.

When I first laid eyes on The Cloisters it was surrounded by a high three-foot-thick wall, and the hotel itself sprawled over about eight acres of lush overgrowth where there had been gardens, and tall palm trees that had dropped their fronds all over everything. Well, the wall is still there, the gardens have been restored and the palm fronds have been cleaned up. In fact, you wouldn't know the old place.

There are now ten guest suites, each done in its own decor. One is done entirely in art nouveau with antique wicker. Another is all in carved wood with a Spanish feeling. For tomorrow-people there's a suite done entirely in plastic, glass, steel and chrome. There's a safari suite with animal skins, bamboo fittings and a bathroom with snakeskin wallpaper. The bedspread in this suite is of Nordic sheepskin—a cozy six inches deep. How'd you like to snuggle into that?

The Marie Antoinette suite I've done all in pink because I think that was probably a color she liked. If you don't like any of these, I might be able to let you have the Persian room that's decorated to look like a tent with brightly colored fabrics and a draped ceiling.

Now we come to my suite. It's almost a complete house within a house. The sunken bathtub in the bathroom looks like a little swimming pool. The walls and ceiling are completely mirrored and a beautiful chandelier hangs over the Roman tub. This is no place to take a quick shower. Here you can lie in the warm whirlpool bath and read and listen to music. There's no better way in the world to relax. Of course the suite has the usual rooms connected with the more private aspects of living. My rarest French antiques are in the bedroom. These include an inlaid ormolu desk originally given to Czar Nicholas of Russia after he signed a peace treaty with the French. It's insured for a quarter of a million dollars.

People who have seen the two-story dining room at The Cloisters say it rivals William Randolph Hearst's San Simeon dining room. It's a great place for big formal dinners after which my guests can wander in the conservatory, which is decorated with French bread racks and giant plants surrounding the fountain. I wasn't conscious of it at the time, but I must have gotten the idea for the conservatory out of the picture *Last Year in Marienbad.* If I did, that's all I got out of the picture. I didn't really understand exactly what it was about. But the interiors and exteriors were beautiful.

I'm sure everyone who was around during prohibition, which was repealed before I was old enough to break its law, would love to see the speakeasy. It's a basement game room and the decor is accurate right down to serving the booze in coffee cups.

Then there's the balcony library that's reached from a staircase outside the ballroom. Behind one of the bookcases in the library is a powder room. And for those ladies who need a more extensive repair job, elsewhere in The Cloisters there's a complete hair styling salon.

But wait till you get a load of the ballroom. It's different from most. Not because it has a hand-painted marble tile floor with a glass finish, but because beside being a ballroom, it also serves as a garage for my collection of interesting automobiles, old and new. It's also the only garage with a crystal chandelier. You have to have those in a garage when it doubles as a ballroom.

Besides the big swimming pool and patio around it, there are six other patio areas with orange, lemon, grapefruit, pecan and other food-bearing trees, in case you don't get enough to eat. But that's impossible with my two wonderful housekeepers, who keep the whole place running smoothly and my guests well fed.

And for any of these guests who are interested in things more romantic than food, there's a secluded "get-a-way-area" with an antique Spanish wishing well. It's a nice place to spend an afternoon with a good friend. And nobody will ever know what you wished and whether or not it came true.

My more intellectual friends can play chess on the big board I have laid out for them on one of the lawns. The chessmen stand four feet high and the squares are of black and white terrazzo. I wonder what it would be like to have Fischer down to play chess and Mark Spitz to swim in the pool?

When I decided not to change the name, "The Cloisters," I brought a grotto with a figure of St. Anthony, my patron saint, back from Spain with me. The figure was carved in Barcelona in the seventeenth century, and I frequently go to the grotto to pray and meditate and give thanks for my good fortune.

With all I've written here I feel I haven't done full justice to my desert hideaway. It's really a paradise. But like that other paradise, there's trouble in it. The location has leaked out and it's become as big a tourist attraction as my house in San Fernando, the one with the piano-shaped swimming pool, used to be. Over weekends there are honest-to-goodness traffic jams created by tourists driving by to catch a glimpse of the place. They see nothing but the walls and the flowered hedges growing above them and occasionally me and my dogs.

However, I wouldn't think of not having The Cloisters to come to when I have a little time to rest. But I have offered it to some of my international friends including Queen Elizabeth and Princess Margaret anytime they want to sneak away and take a look at how things are in the colonies.

I'm real friendly with the townspeople in Palm Springs, the people who run the hardware store, the drugstore and people who work in a lot of the other shops. A sort of folksy atmosphere exists in the town. My gardener and his wife call me by my first name. I have been known to cook dinner for my servants on several oc-casions. Can you imagine the gourmet feast I would turn out for such a royal guest as Queen Elizabeth? And besides, I have a Welsh cargi, which is her favorite dog.

It's fun to shut my eyes and picture myself walking into any store in Palm Springs and saying, "Hi, Harry. I want you to meet my house guest, The Queen of England." As for the social life, she'd have a ball. If London Bridge can be in Arizona and the *Queen Mary* in California, the Queen herself would love being in Palm Springs.

20

Christmas is to me essentially a family holiday. Although always including close friends, it's still the time of the year when our family enjoys most being together. But I guess it's that way in all families. I don't really know because I've only been in one family.

During my childhood in the Depression years, when both Mom and Dad were working, it took a lot of getting together, of loving and sharing to make Christmas the memorable occasion it always turned out to be.

I remember one wonderful thing. When Mother worked at the Johnstone Cookie Factory, she used to bring home a large bag of cookies that the company sold to its workers for fifty cents a ten-pound sack. The cookies were seconds that had slight irregularities in them, but they tasted just as delicious as the perfect ones. One of the joys of these cookies was the fun Angie and I had decorating them, disguising the imperfections, and icing them in various ways to make them look festive. We also ate a lot of them, excusing ourselves that the decoration didn't turn out just right and looked ugly. But there were plenty for all. Ten pounds of cookies goes a long way.

I know this extra special love I feel for Christmas stems from my childhood in the lean years when we always managed to pull ourselves up by our financial bootstraps and enjoy some of the things we had deprived ourselves of all year. And this meant more than the outlay of fifty cents for ten pounds of cookies.

I don't know how they did it but somehow my Mother and Father managed to provide us kids with everything we had to do without. And my early recollections of Christmas are of the giving and receiving of loving thoughtfulness. Our family forgot all the little quarrels every family has during a lifetime and we were happy together.

Don't get the idea that Mom and Dad skimped and scraped all year to shower us with luxuries at Christmas time. The presents we got were necessities. And because they were such important necessities they were doubly appreciated. I remember being absolutely elated over getting a new pair of shoes or a pair of sox without any darns in them. I was even thrilled with a new set of long underwear, which I hated. But when you live in Wisconsin you can't completely hate anything that keeps you warm in the winter.

You have probably guessed that toys and games were in extremely limited supply. One or two new ones, if any, had to do us each year. But we saved them from year to year and brought them out again until the playthings under our Christmas tree became an impressive collection. We handled them very carefully, if we played with them at all, and then they were put away until the next Christmas to be hauled out and used again as decorations.

You can imagine how I felt when my toys, that had come down to me from George and Angie, were finally given to Rudy. It wasn't that I didn't want Rudy to have them. It was that little Rudy seemed to have a built-in destruction mechanism when it came to playthings. Things that we'd enjoyed for years lasted only a few minutes when Rudy went to work on them. I remember being in my late teens and actually shedding tears at seeing some of my most cherished childhood possessions disintegrate before my very eyes.

When I complained to Mom and Dad they just told me I was too old to play with them anyway so I should let the kid have his fun. Nevertheless, when my parents weren't looking, I tried to glue some of the broken pieces together. I hate to see anything destroyed.

As the years went on and I began to earn a fairly decent income playing the piano, I tried to provide my family, and our home, with such comparative luxuries as new furniture, new curtains, new wallpaper and the latest things in household appliances. But strangely enough, Mother didn't care too much for these things.

She continued to prefer a coal stove and the old-fashioned ice box to any of the newfangled stuff. Then when food freezers became almost a necessity, Mother wouldn't have one in the house. She stuck to her idea that it was unhealthy to eat food that had been frozen. It took me years to talk her out of that.

I suppose this was the result of her early upbringing on my grandmother's farm near Menasha. She grew up with simple things and those were the things she understood and preferred.

I sometimes find it hard to believe how long it took me to convince Mom that she should have her hair done by a professional. She considered it the height of luxury and an unforgivable extravagance. No matter how I tried to make her see that we could well afford it, she continued to do her hair herself.

I guess it was vanity that finally let her see the light. She appeared as a guest on several TV shows and the people in the makeup and hairdressing departments made her look so attractive that she decided to indulge herself in professional hairstyling. There are so many little things about my Mother that I hold precious. I could probably write a whole book about her. And I feel terrible sometimes that my appreciation and admiration of her as a lovable and very special person has been ridiculed.

I have always felt there was a sort of regal aura around Mother and I found out I wasn't the only one who saw this the evening I was invited to entertain Queen Juliana and Prince Bernhard of the Netherlands at a Command Performance held at the Coconut Grove in Los Angeles. Mother was invited to this affair. And when she and I came down the famous steps at the Coconut Grove everyone in the room was sure it was the Queen herself and gave my Mother a standing ovation. I thought she deserved it and I must say she really looked like a queen that night with her beautiful white hair elegantly coiffed, a white gown, sparkling jewelry and a luxurious fur wrap. To this day I have never told her that the standing ovation she received that night was actually intended for Queen Juliana. Mom thought it was for me. When Queen Juliana really arrived it was almost anticlimactic.

It makes me very happy, and I think it's a lovely compliment to Mother, that she has become so internationally known that no matter where I go the first question I'm asked by famous personages such as the Queen of England and her Mother, the President of the United States, governors and mayors is, "How's your dear Mother?" I never thought of Mother as an "older person." Her vitality often put her children to shame even when we were all grown. I'll never forget her Toast to me on my 50th Birthday: "Well Son, from now on it's downhill all the way!" If you've ever spent any time pulling the handle of one of those one-armed bandits in Las Vegas, you know that it's tiring (and often unrewarding). Well, whenever we were in Vegas or Reno, or Lake Tahoe, Mom would stand hour after hour, pulling the "crank," as they say, without any visible sign of fatigue . . . or success. She did get the $7.50 jackpot one night. Cost her $30!

She lives in the three-story Hollywood hill house and until recently was able to make her presence felt on every floor. She'd go around doing little self-imposed chores such as tidying up after me, cleaning ash trays, turning out lights, which I invariably leave burning, and following those whose job it is to keep the house clean adding a touch here and there to achieve her state of perfection. She even hounds the gardeners as they look after her precious plants and blooms. She has a green thumb and feels no one but God can make things grow the way she can. Her attitude reminds me of the man who asked a parish priest for permission to clean up a vacant lot next door to the church and plant a garden.

The priest said that would be a wonderful thing to do. So the man went to work, cleared the lot of all the rubbish and old automobile tires that had been thrown into it, fertilized the land and planted some corn and tomatoes. In a while the once ugly lot had become a beautiful vegetable garden.

The priest said to the gardener, "You have done a wonderful job here, with the Lord's help."

"Yes, Father," was the reply, "but do you remember what this lot was like when the Lord was on His own?"

Mom has always felt that God helps those who help themselves and that those who help themselves, help God. She hates being waited on. Prefers to do things for herself. So I know how demoralizing it must be for her to recognize old age creeping up on her although we try not to let her know we notice it.

We all do everything we can to cater to her comfort and her peace of mind, but unfortunately, it's impossible to fight the calendar. When Mother was taken seriously ill just recently we were told she might not make it. I used a little psychology on her. Knowing how she was looking forward to coming to Las Vegas at least one more time, I told all my friends, "If you want Mom to get well, don't send her candy and flowers, send nickles and quarters for the slot machines." It worked. She made a miraculous recovery and not only made Vegas but Reno as well!

My father, too, is in his declining years just living from day to day in a convalescent home in Sacramento, which is where my brother George and his wife Dora live. And my only consolation at this difficult time, which every son or daughter faces sooner or later, as parents grow old, is that perhaps Mother and Father will be happily reunited in another life after being separated for so many years in this one.

She enjoyed everybody's love, young and old. One of her dearest friends was a Polish girl who used to like to come and keep her company when I was on the road. Her name was Maryanne Michelski, another of Milwaukee's illustrious contributions to show business.

If the name doesn't immediately ring a bell, it's because Maryanne gained super-stardom through vaudeville, The Follies and the movies as Gilda Gray, The Shimmy Girl. In the beginning there were two contenders for this title. The other was Bee Palmer. They shimmied it out, best two shakes out of three, on the vaudeville circuits of the country. Gilda must have won because nobody but a few old vaudeville buffs I've spoken to remembers Bee Palmer.

Gilda's career in pictures ended abruptly when she sued Columbia Pictures, headed by Harry Cohn, for calling one of their films *Gilda* without her permission. She took the position that her first name had become a trademark just as Tallulah had become Miss Bankhead's. Gilda won. But she never worked in Hollywood again.

She continued to visit us after she had successfully defied Harry Cohn, who saw that she never worked in Hollywood again. And on some of these visits she was hungry. But always she dreamed of a comeback. I tried to help her. But she was unable to make any compromises for the changes in times and tastes. So we were never able to agree on what her comeback act should be.

Finally, proud to the end, she died in the Motion Picture Relief Fund Home. It was around Christmas time. I think the year was 1965. It made Mother very sad.

Because of the love that was lavished on us children at Christmas

I still believe in Santa Claus . . . holly wreaths, mistletoe, tinsel decked trees, yule logs, egg nogs, carol singing, gift wrapping and the exchanging of presents on the world's most celebrated birthday, December 25.

Like everybody else, I get a big kick out of gifts—opening them and being surprised. And I don't mean just receiving them. One of the greatest joys I get after selecting something I think someone would like to have and gift wrapping it is watching his face when he opens it. And I prefer to open any present I receive in the presence of the one who is giving it to me. This makes it possible for me to thank him right away and for him to see the pleasure I get. Childish? Maybe. But there's a song called "Christmas Is for Children" and I believe that. Children of all ages.

That's why one of the most important times in my life is Christmas Eve at home. All my friends are invited and they bring their gifts for everyone. Then we put them all under the tree until it's time to open them. I pass out everything to everyone and enjoy their pleasure at being surprised. And when all have opened their gifts, then I open mine and give my guests the pleasure of seeing my surprise.

The truth is that I'm preparing for Christmas all year. As I travel around I'm always sort of shopping for interesting things. I enjoy shopping. And when I see something I know one of my friends would care to have, I get it and put it away for Christmas. Of course, sometimes I can't wait till Christmas. I'm just a compulsive giver. Sometimes what they consider my generosity embarrasses them. But there's nothing I can do about it. It's the penalty they have to pay for being my friends. To show you what I mean, here's a letter I received a few years ago from Seymour Heller. It may be immodest of me to include it but I happened to think it was very funny when I received it and I still think so. I mean, who ever heard of anybody making the kind of written request this letter of Seymour's makes? It's dated December 28, but there's no year. That, however, doesn't matter.

Dear Lee,
    This is to thank you, again, for the overwhelming gifts you gave Billie, our kids and me this year, as in so many years past. They were, as always, unusual and magnificent. And because I know you

so well, I know how much pleasure you got selecting them and being on hand to see the expressions on our faces when we received them. Now there is one request I have to make. It's for next Christmas. Please don't send us anything. And that also goes for my birthday, Billie's birthday, our anniversary and all the other gift-giving occasions. I know this is a strange and ungrateful sort of request to make, so here's why I'm making it.

As you know Billie and I take great pride in our home and are thrilled when guests compliment us on it. But then, as they ask where we got one precious item after another, and each time we have to answer proudly, "Liberace gave it to us," it becomes embarrassing. It's embarrassing because they think I'm kidding. I've managed, as you well know, some of the biggest stars in the business before we got together over twenty years ago. Not one of them ever gave me anything.

Oh, yes, one of them once gave me a small vase. I know you can't be like other artists and I'm glad of that, but let me tell you this story: After showing some new friends around the house and proudly telling them about all the gifts from you, one of them asked Billie, "Did Liberace give you everything?"

Billie said, "No. Only the things we value most." I don't have to tell you how true this is. Nor do I have to tell you, I'm sure, that we'll never invite those people to the house again. You know how we hate rudeness. As they were saying good night the man asked me what time it was. I glanced at my watch and he said, "That's a handsome watch. Where'd you get it?"

I said, "Liberace." He shook his head and said, "He must think an awful lot of you."

"He does," I said. "And I think an awful lot of him."

It's not easy to write this kind of letter. You know how much I value our association and our deep friendship. But there comes a time when it just had to be said. Please stop showering us with gifts.

Billie and I love you.

That's one of the most wonderful letters I've ever received. Because I feel that in order to have a successful business relationship, there must be more than business involved. There must be a deeper understanding and mutual admiration. For that reason I decided to keep that letter among my most valued papers and pay no attention to it whatsoever.

Because Christmas is such a special event to me, I take plenty of time preparing for it, decorating the house, wrapping gifts. These are things I like to do. I find that my family, my friends, most everybody, enjoys getting gifts that obviously have some personal thought behind them. Those that are carefully selected, personalized, handmade or hand-decorated are usually most appreciated.

Since I like to fool around with artist's materials—brushes, pens, paint, ink—I often personalize the things I give in one way or another. I love to get involved with Christmas wrapping and often invite close friends over to spend an evening helping and doing little chores in preparation for the big day. I call them my "Brownies." The Heller family is, of course, always in on this sort of "doings" and Seymour once told me he could book me into the May Company's gift-wrapping department anytime I wanted to pick up a little extra change.

This fascination with the preparation as part of the celebration of Christmas is the reason why for the past ten years or so I've arranged to take no bookings whatever during December.

This amounts to a kind of Christmas gift from me to myself, as some of the most lucrative offers come during the holidays, and I refuse them so that I can devote myself wholeheartedly to making it a Merry Christmas for all.

In Southern California it's easy to reach out to everyone on Christmas because it's the custom—and it's catching on all over the country—to decorate the outside of your home. And this is something I take great pleasure in doing.

One year I had an animated Santa Claus with his sleigh and reindeer, on top of the Hollywood house. He was playing the piano and it gave the illusion that he was floating in the air. (Actually he was suspended from hidden wires and high poles that were blacked out against the night sky.) My Santa could be seen for miles because the house is high on a hill, surrounded by over a hundred tall Italian cypress trees hung with multi-colored Christmas lights.

The decorations attract many visitors. There is always a steady stream of cars passing my place during the Christmas season. They take pictures and they write me wonderful letters. I get them from people in all parts of the world who have visited in Hollywood at Christmas time, telling me how much they appreciate the decorations. If it brings pleasure to these people, it gives great joy to me too, and each year, for that reason, I try to give them something new, to top myself.

Inside, of course, besides all the decoration, there is usually plenty of partying. One year I gave a huge party twelve days before Christmas. I asked each guest to wear something spectacular and announced that prizes would be awarded. Naturally I eliminated myself.

I appeared as a solid gold Santa Claus. I spent three hours on the makeup and costume, and it was so successful that even my Mother didn't recognize me. The guests did pretty well, too. Some of them overwhelmed me with the originality and design of their outfits.

One lady came as a living candelabra, completely electrified. She was followed around all evening by her husband who kept plugging her into the nearest light socket. Naturally she won a prize. It was the first time I didn't mind that a lady got lit at one of my parties.

Another lady came as a completely decorated Christmas tree with a star worked into the top of her glittering coiffure. The men came in costumes ranging all the way from matadors to British Beefeaters. One man even came in a sparkling beaded and jeweled outfit. I asked him who he was supposed to be and he said, "You."

It was quite an affair with over 200 guests and entertainment that included everything from the Mitchell Boys Choir to my friend, the comedienne who has been on tour with me many times, Fay McKay. She came as a Partridge in a Pear Tree. As all who have seen her know, Fay is no sprite. And because she, herself, makes fun of her weight I knew she didn't mind when I said it was the first time I'd ever seen a two-hundred-pound partridge.

Then, as Santa Claus, I played the piano, joined in the community singing and gave out the prizes for the best costumes. It was certainly a far cry from the early childhood Christmases in Milwaukee. Maybe because of those, my Christmas parties always seem to feature food. One year I drained and covered the swimming pool and put a high circus tent over it. The tent was more than three stories. Inside it was all decorated with trimmed Christmas trees, poinsettias and colorful set tables, where I served a sit-down dinner for 300 people. But it wasn't like most such dinners. All the food was personally prepared in our own kitchens. I seldom go in for catered parties of any kind. They have a tendency to become rather commercial and impersonal. I like to be able to divulge the recipes for the food I serve, and you can only do this if you fix it yourself. Then you really know what's in it. And even though I have wonderful help, at a time when I know that's hard to come by, I find myself personally planning menus and preparing dinners at Christmas time, sometimes for as many as 25 or 30 guests each night.

Mother always used to like to make the dressing for the turkey. She won a prize—a blue ribbon—for her turkey dressing at the Wisconsin State Fair some years ago. Angie is great in the baking department and comes up with goodies that are loaded with calories and beat anything that ever came out of the Johnstone Cookie Company. And that explains why between the middle of December and the first of January I manage to put on ten pounds or so. But this doesn't worry me.

I find that when I'm on the road, eating usually becomes a rather dull necessity. So I manage to get down to my right weight very quickly and stay there by sticking to small quantities of food that are high in energy-giving nutrients.

This Christmas, if all goes well, I'll be happy to give everyone of my friends a copy of this book. And it will be a Merry Christmas and Happy New Year for me because the book has been a project I have long been working on and trying to complete.

21

Not long ago one of the guests at a party in my Palm Springs home was raving about California. She had just moved from the east where she'd lived all her life in an apartment. "But," she said, "you just can't imagine what it's like to move the stuff I had in that place."

"How big was it?" I asked.

"Ten rooms."

"Did you have a lot of very valuable pictures or glassware or china?"

"Oh, no. Just the usual household things we'd accumulated through the years."

While that kind of stuff is priceless in a personal sort of way, I had to smile to myself when I looked around me and wondered what that dear lady would have gone through if she'd been faced with moving me and my treasures. It frightens even me. That's why I've fixed it so I never have to go through any moving.

I've arranged to have my homes left just as they are and maintained as museums. This will happen when I get too old or too tired to enjoy them. In the meantime, I'll continue to fill them with whatever beautiful things strike my fancy. The cost has ceased to be of much importance. After you've passed your first million, there aren't a lot of things you can't afford.

When I discovered the French desk that belonged to Czar Nicholas of Russia in a museum in Pensacola, Florida, I not only bought the desk, I bought the whole shop. I figured if they had one such wonderful piece who knows what else they might have, and I didn't have time to stay in Florida long enough to check it all out.

I guess it was my love for the music of Chopin and Liszt and Mozart that got me interested in old world charm, customs, culture and the arts and artifacts of their day. And, as soon as I had enough money I began to buy period pieces that I liked and could afford. Many of them were actually only copies of real antiques. But they were excellent copies and very beautiful. And just from buying pieces here and there to put in my home, I quietly became a collector.

Naturally the house was soon filled with these items of furniture and art. Then as my fortune continued to improve I began weeding out the pseudo-antiques that I'd bought in my early enthusiasm for anything that looked old, and replacing them with genuine antiques. Some of the pieces I replaced I gave to friends who were refurnishing their homes or had admired them. Others I just put in storage.

Before long it got so that I was even putting some of the real antiques in storage, because I no longer had room in my homes for them. Then someone suggested, since I was so interested in antiques and had so many of them, that I open an antique shop as an outlet for the things that I'd bought but couldn't actually use. It was argued that my name would attract customers. And the more I thought about the idea, the more it intrigued me.

Finally I opened my first little store on Melrose Place in Los Angeles. That's in the area they call West Hollywood and it was just a little way from North LaCienega, where all the art galleries and antique shops are lined up until LaCienega crosses Third and the antique shops and art galleries give way to the wonderful eating places that are part of Restaurant Row.

Things went so well that in a short while we were able to enlarge and move right onto LaCienega where all the other important antique stores were located. But the novelty of being a storekeeper, meeting customers, talking to them and being able to please them with a beautiful piece of some sort, soon began to wear off, particularly when I had to go on the road and couldn't be in the shop. People would come in and ask to see me and if I wasn't there they'd go away saying they wanted my advice on something.

Business began to fall off because of this. There was also another reason why business got worse and worse. Everytime I'd come back to the shop, I realized more strongly that my hobby had turned into a business that I didn't really and truly want to be in. The reason for this was that I hated to sell the things because I loved them. So I'd go around the showroom hanging "Sold" signs on everything I wanted to be sure that the articles would be given the tender loving care I could give them and not fall into the hands of people who bought antiques just because it was the stylish or chic thing to do, not because they really appreciated them.

Finally, after running the shop for a little over five years in that crazy way, I closed it and put all the items in a warehouse where they'll stay until I can find a proper home for each one of them, either in one of my houses or with someone who I know will treasure it. Naturally, the pianos that I collected here and there, I kept for myself. I have seven of them in one home, three in another, four in another and one I keep permanently in England for when I go to play concerts in Britain or the Commonwealth.

They range in variety and style from the concert grand Baldwins (it's one of these that's in London) which I use in my performances, to a unique instrument that has two keyboards. With it I can play two pianos at once on one piano. Then there's a very wonderful old instrument from Leipzig, Germany and a piano that dates all the way back to Chopin. I've had it completely restored and it's in excellent playing condition, not only beautiful to look at but beautiful to listen to. For laughs there's my "jeweled" honky-tonk upright that I sometimes use in my shows. And I didn't even include my two pipe organs, the gold one and the one that also has a piano keyboard, so I can play organ and piano at the same time. So if the big organ isn't eligible for inclusion in my collection of working pianos, at least the second one is half eligible.

You notice I said "my collection of working pianos." I have another collection of miniature pianos. Some can be made to give off sound, most are just artistic little replicas that I have picked up here and there or that people have given me. They are made of almost every conceivable material from amber to zinc. Some are very delicate, others are almost gross. Others are sort of caricatures that have me sitting at them in some funny outfit or other.

I keep this collection in specially built cabinets so they can be seen and enjoyed and taken out and examined. I don't even include in my piano collection the watch that like my candelabra ring, attracts so much interest wherever I am. This is piano-shaped and the numbers are diamonds and rubies under a cover that works something like the old "hunter's cases" that the early watches had. Mine is encrusted in diamonds. Naturally the jewelry is a collection all by itself and a lot of that is on display everytime I walk onto a stage.

Collecting is lots of fun and you don't really have to be rich to become a collector. You just have to find something to collect that you can afford, like paper matchbooks or chopsticks imprinted with restaurant names. But the secret is to find something to collect that nobody else is collecting. This makes it more fun and also makes your collection grow in value with the years because yours is the only one of its kind. But you have to have some kind of real interest in what you decide to collect or pretty soon you'll become bored with the whole idea. I know I'd never get much fun out of collecting, say, old hockey pucks from famous games.

I not only love to collect and own my beautiful art objects, I love to use them. And that includes even the most precious items in my collection of china and glassware. One of my latest additions to that collection is an absolutely fantastic set of Czechoslovakian Moser crystal glasses. There's only one other set like mine in the entire world. It's owned by Queen Elizabeth. I don't know where she keeps hers, but I keep mine in Palm Springs and I use it.

There is, of course, one slight difference between the two sets. Underneath the crown on hers there's the initial E. On mine there's an L. As I said, I use mine, but only on very special occasions. My Mother's eightieth birthday was one. And I can assure you that when we drink a toast with them, I warn everyone in a loud clear voice that there'll be no clinking. And no flinging them into the fireplace or any of that sort of nonsense, when the toast has been drunk. I must say they seem to make the wine taste better, the champagne more exhilarating. I honestly don't know whether I'd be able to keep my cool if one of those glasses were to be broken. They're entirely handmade and hand engraved and it took the better part of a year to make the four hundred individual glasses in the set. Replacing one would be very difficult if not entirely out of the question.

Because this Moser crystal comes from an Iron Curtain country it cost me $3,000 duty to bring it into the United States. But I think these restrictive tariffs on works of art will recede as our relations improve between China, Russia and the countries of the Communist bloc. Actually I've found that Communist-made articles are beginning to show up in American stores.

In addition to the wonderful Moser set I also have some Stewart Crystal from Czechoslovakia. From Ireland I have some beautiful Waterford crystal and some fine Webb crystal from England. And then there's my prize set of monogrammed china from the John F. Kennedy estate. It was put up at a charity auction, and I bought the set from the people who got it at the auction. Like the Moser glasses these plates are used, but very seldom and very carefully.

Some of my friends who are more politically minded than I am sometimes question my use of the Kennedy plates. Some feel they're too sacred to eat from, others act as if they thought the plates were poison. Personally, I think both reactions are inexcusable. I hate to think that things of great beauty created by master craftsmen must have a political connotation. I feel the same way about music and books of certain countries being banned. I don't think genuine works of art, music and literature are capable of doing harm. I don't think beauty and politics mix. The former depends on dreams, the latter on realities.

Many of my guests are surprised to see so many dogs, particularly in my Palm Springs home. They're surprised because dogs are seldom given the run of a place so full of expensive and fragile articles. Yet my dogs are perfect ladies and gentlemen and take just as much pleasure in playing host as I do. Each has his own individual personality and gives love wherever he finds it. Any dog fancier can easily wind up with one or two of my dogs in his lap.

But my guests are told never to feed the dogs. They each have special diets that keep them healthy and happy. And these diets do not include hors d'oeuvres and nibbles from the bar. You never saw dogs that are really pets in better condition than mine. They have special grooming, special exercise periods, sound teeth, lovely silky coats and act, because that's the way they're treated, as members of the family.

Let me introduce them to you. There are three poodles, Jacques, Michi and Bonaparte. I have a special place in my heart for poodles because they're born performers; they're all hams like I am and I think we hams have to stick together. Then there are two schnauzers. One is Prego, which is Italian. The reason for that name has completely slipped my mind. But I know why the other schnauzer is named Elke. It was given to me by a Sommer of the same name. Then there's the Welsh corgi that came from an English kennel that has since moved to Australia. This one is a direct descendant from Queen Elizabeth's Welsh corgi, and so she is named Liza. Then there's my little keeshond. Ever hear of that breed? Nobody seems to know how or where it got started but keeshonden were used, I guess they still are, as ratters on the canal barges in Holland. People who know about things like that have told me that the word "kees" is from the Dutch and means "terrier." So the fact that they were ratters is explained. "Hond," I suppose is Dutch and is like the German "hunde" or English "hound," only it doesn't just mean any dog, it means *little* dog because "hond" also means "hand." That's too complicated for such a little animal that looks like, but is a little larger than, a Pomeranian. What keeshond really means, I guess, is small terrier. They wouldn't have room for a big one on a canal boat.

I call this little one Ciao, which is the word Italians use the way Germans use "auf Wiedersehen" or the Spanish, "hasta la vista." Ciao is used when you don't want to say anything as final as "good-bye." I wrote a song called "Ciao," which I use at the end of my concerts. Because I truly don't, as the word means, ever want to say good-bye.

In the Los Angeles house where my mother lives, she has two dogs, which she adores. They're great company for her. One is a schnauzer named Hildegarde, even though she hardly ever plays the piano with gloves on as Hildegarde once did. Incidentally, Hildegarde, the entertainer I mean, not my mother's dog, is also one of Milwaukee's contributions to show business. Mom's other companion is a miniature poodle named Mitzi. Hildegarde and Mitzi are always at my mother's side.

Another member of my family is a marvelous cockateel that sings and talks and has a wonderful vocabulary. It can whistle recognizable tunes and my mother taught it to say, "Good morning, Liberace." Isn't that great? I couldn't pronounce the name till I was thirteen. Now I have a bird named Timmy who can say it flawlessly. I've had him for six years.

With the exception of two of the dogs, which I got when they were puppies, all were given to me by people who, for some reason or other, could no longer keep them. I've adopted them, and as I've said, they've turned out to be the best behaved housedogs I've ever seen. They are allowed anywhere and they respect my rugs and furniture better than some people I've entertained.

Naturally, people who don't respect my belongings never get a second invitation. Generally they were uninvited the first time. But there's nothing you can do when someone you've asked to dinner, or for an evening of music, says, "May I bring my house guest?" or sometimes it's just a friend. There is a Yiddish word for this kind of nerve. It's "chutzpah" pronounced with a glottal fricative on the first "ch." It's fun to say, and there's no other word that is quite as good to describe the kind of insensitive nerve some people have.

To tell you the truth I cringe at the thought of having people I don't know visit me. Although I'm always polite to them when they're there, I look on them more as intruders than guests. Maybe this is a flaw in my hospitality. I like to think that it's just that I don't want people around me who may be unsympathetic to my love for the beautiful and delicate things that are part of my way of life.

I think when you entertain a guest, he or she becomes temporarily part of your life. You are responsible for him in every way including his safety. So I don't like people dropping in on me unexpectedly. Even a dear friend and business associate like Seymour Heller wouldn't think of stopping by to see me without first phoning. That's what made it so ironic, one afternoon, when the bell rang, and there on the doorstep stood a woman in her middle fifties, surrounded by a collection of rather tacky looking luggage.

Fortunately I had not answered the doorbell myself, as I sometimes do, because as I said, we never have unexpected callers. The lady asked to see me, saying, "I was at one of Liberace's shows in Fort Wayne, Indiana, and he said, 'Don't forget, when you're in California you must come out and see me.' Well, here I am." It was a sad moment and we finally straightened the whole thing out by paying the lady's fare back to Fort Wayne. I'm more careful what I say on the stage and on TV as a result of that little incident.

Maybe I can explain in another way how personal everything is in my home. I like to arrange furniture and rearrange it until I get it just the way I feel it is unquestionably right. Today I don't do it so much because the rooms have become bigger, the furniture has grown heavier and, I guess, I have too. But when I had my first little place in California, the biggest item in the living room was, naturally, my concert grand piano. I couldn't move the furniture around without being forced, sometimes, to change the position of the piano. When friends would come over and see the changes I made they'd ask who helped me move the things. When I said I moved them myself they'd say, "Sure. But who moved the piano?"

I'd say I did and they just wouldn't believe me. Even those friends who knew that I exercised a lot and did weight lifting couldn't see me moving a concert grand single-handed. I had to do it to show them how. I'd put a pillow on my back, crawl under the piano, lift it a little and move it two or three inches. Then I'd rest a while and do it again until I got the instrument in its new position.

If I didn't like it, I'd move it back. I wish I could do that today.

I guess the one collection I have that surprises more people than any other is my collection of automobiles. I'm probably the only guy in the world who owned and has driven across the desert in a jeweled dune buggy. If you've never driven one, even if it isn't jeweled, give it a try. It's the same kind of fun that a snowmobile is, only not so chilly.

But dune buggies are for the younger generation, so I sold mine to the son of a friend who bought it under ground rules that I laid down. These were that he had to earn and save every penny of the cost himself. He did. Then he made his own stipulations. He had me remove the diamond-studded candelabras for two reasons: One, he considered them too showy and, two, he couldn't afford them.

I didn't even learn to drive a car until 1949 when I bought my first—an Oldsmobile 88 convertible. Today it's considered almost un-American not to know how to drive long before you're eligible to get an operator's license. But I was busy learning how to operate a grand piano.

My next car was given to me by a bank. That's a switch. Most musicians have their cars taken away from them by a bank—the bank that loaned them the money to buy the car. But this bank was my television sponsor in Cincinnati.

The car was a 1954 Cadillac Eldorado convertible designed by a man named Barris. It was the first of the so-called Celebrity Cars that he designed. He did one for Elvis Presley I know. And he turned out special cars for television personalities to use in their TV series—cars of unique and instantly recognizable design such as in the Batman series.

My Eldorado had upholstery that featured black and white piano keys worked into the leather along with candelabras and other such personal trademarks. The bank gave it to me in appreciation of a promotion they ran that was successful beyond their wildest dreams. It was simply that they "gave" away one of my albums "free" to anyone who deposited over $100. This resulted in $11,000,000 in new deposits. So they invited me to Cincinnati to make a personal appearance and receive the Cadillac.

From then on I was hooked on fancy automobiles although I sold that first one, which they told me was worth about $25,000, to a young car enthusiast for a mere $2,000. He gimmicked it up (even more than it was). He gold plated the chromium and put in mink carpeting, which enabled him to take the car to various auto shows for around $500 a week. The car was billed as Liberace's Personal Cadillac Convertible. For all I know he may still be making the rounds, which suggests to me now that he might be less "a young car enthusiast" than "a young promoter."

I guess the actual start of my interest in *collecting* cars was born when I opened at the Internationale Room of the Las Vegas Hilton. It's the largest show room in Vegas so I saw that it was possible for me to make my first grand entrance in an automobile. Naturally it had to be something special, and my people really came up with just what the audience wanted to see. It was a black and white Rolls-Royce. But not just any old Rolls painted black and white. It was a custom-designed Phantom V Landau Limousine of which only seven were ever made. Queen Elizabeth II has one of them; John Lennon, formerly of the Beatles, has one; and some Middle East oil sheik has one. I have the fourth. I wish I knew where the other three are, or if they still exist. For car buffs, it has a James Young body and a deVille extension. It's now worth over $60,000.

As soon as I saw the car I knew I had to have a costume designed to go with it. You couldn't step out of such a Rolls in just any old thing. So I settled for an ankle-length ermine job trimmed with diamonds, over white kid. It's been over a year that I had that coat made, and I have still to see another like it on the street.

Having opened the show with a Rolls I felt I should also close with a car. Since the closing number was a nostalgic look at the Charleston period of flappers and finale-hoppers, I could think of nothing better to contrast with the elegance of the Rolls than a fire-engine-red Model A Ford roadster with a rumble seat. To go with it I wore the jeweled red knickers that were so classy for men. I never dreamed, when I was in knee pants, that when I grew up I'd be wearing bright red knickers with jewels sewn on them. Incidentally, the license plate of that little old Ford is I M CUTE.

For my second act entrance I acquired a silver-blue Excalibur designed after the 1934 Mercedes. It has ivory-colored upholstery and an ivory landau top. Chromium pipes jut out from its long sleek hood, which is held in place by a silver jewel-encrusted leather strap. It's really something. To go with it I wore a matching blue jumpsuit trimmed with mink to make me look like a mechanic. A very rich mechanic. I guess they're all very rich judging by the bills I get.

Another nice old car in the collection is a 1900 open-air Oldsmobile surrey in perfect operating condition that can attain the unbelievable speed of 25 mph.

To balance this off I have "a car of the future," a Bradley GT. It's bright metallic gold and the side windows are part of the roof, which hinges upward, like butterfly wings, so you can get into the front seat. There is also a back seat. It's upholstered in gold crushed velvet and can do about one hundred twenty-five. But not with me driving. The fastest I've ever driven is between eighty and eighty-five, which I don't like to do.

Besides these there is a white custom-designed Lincoln Executive limousine in white leather and blue velvet interior and a couple of Cadillac limousines, one of which is a two-of-a-kind car. The other was designed for Ladybird Johnson. The only difference is that mine isn't bulletproof. But both limousines are equipped with television and bar.

I also sometimes use a black and white Buick station wagon with piano keys painted where the simulated wood usually is. Its license is I PIANO.

Then there are the usual "off-the-rack" cars, ranging all the way from a Mark IV Continental to a panel truck that's used to haul the furniture and antiques I pick up from time to time.

But the car my guests get the most kick out of is the one I use to meet them at the Palm Springs airport. It's one of those great 1957 Austin taxis, like they have in London. The kind of cab a man can get in and out of without taking off the gray topper he's wearing to the Derby. I've had it painted black and white houndstooth. It has a deep red carpet and the working meter ticks off in shillings and pence just the way any proper British taxi meter should do. This way I'm never embarrassed by any of my guests trying to pay me for the ride. But I accept tips.

22

S hortly after my career began to develop momentum, a lady by the name of Kitty Pastori came to me while I was playing in the Empire Room at The Palmer House in Chicago and asked if I'd mind if she organized a Liberace Fan Club. I told her I'd be flattered.

As things began to get better for me, and then when television flashed me suddenly into national fame, people from all over the country wrote, asking if they could form a Liberace Fan Club. By this time a second Liberace Fan Club had been started in Chicago by Ms. Maxine Du Cray. Then Kitty and Maxine merged their clubs.

So whenever we got a letter from anywhere we referred the writer to Kitty and Maxine in Chicago. They'd either invite the person to join their club or tell her how to go about starting one of her own. Before I knew it these fan clubs were springing up all over the country.

This is very good for a performer. It's good for his ego and it's good for his business, since the whole purpose of a fan club is to promote the performer's name and try to get people to attend his shows. This is especially valuable when you're traveling around the country as I do. It's nice to know that there's a group in every town waiting to welcome and help you.

As the number of clubs began to mushroom, I decided there had to be some sort of control exercised over them. After all, if they were going to use my name, I didn't want them misusing it in any way.

I wanted the clubs to become more than an ego massage for me. So I insisted that they all have some sort of charitable orientation. I made it clear that I wanted all the money any club raised through the sale of autographs or photographs or any of the little articles I'd send them to auction off, like ties, gloves, record albums, cuff links or maybe an autograph album . . . to go to charity.

So what happened was, they'd go around to hospitals and find out what the shut-ins needed in the way of record players, radios, TV sets, books and magazines and then, within the limits of the money raised, they'd try to supply these items so necessary to the morale of anyone who is hospitalized.

Some clubs just gave the money in a lump sum to the charity of their choice. Sometimes they asked me to select a charity for them, and I'd do that, trying to spread the money around among the many worthy charities. It was never a lot, you understand, but every little bit helps. As the song says, "light one little candle."

On a little larger scale, once, a girl in one of the Chicago clubs was stricken with polio and I gave her a message of cheer one evening on television. Well, this got things started and her fellow club members were able to collect from her friends, and from their friends, and friends of their friends, enough money to assure proper treatment, care and comfort for her. They were even able to make her life a little less confined by getting her a portable iron lung. I was very proud not only of what the club did, but also that the first time the iron lung was used the girl came to see my show.

For a while in the late fities and early sixties we held a Liberace Fan Club Convention. A story about one of these held at the Palmer House in the Chicago *Tribune* told what it was like and what it accomplished better than I could. It is headed "Lee's Fans."

"When he knows we're in the audience, he has little ways of signalling that he recognizes us," said Mrs. Maxine Du Cray of Chicago, president of the local Liberace Fan Club. "For instance, he might give a special little wink or a wave."

She was attending a Convention of the International Liberace Fan Clubs in the Palmer House. Mrs. Du Cray said she didn't know whether she should tell this or not, but she guessed that she would. "I was in the Empire Room," she said, "and Lee got a little thirsty. He came over to the table and took a drink out of my glass of water.

He gave me a little pat on the hand. Little things like that, that no one else knows.

"Sometimes," Mrs. DuCray said, "little jealousies came up, like when one club thought Lee was paying more attention to another club." She didn't think he ever did, and she said, "He always has time to talk on the phone and he knows two hundred of us by our first names."

There is no squealing when Lee's fans encounter him in person as he does not tolerate this sort of thing. And should someone try to rend a pleat off his shirt, this member's papers are taken up and she is cashiered out of service.

Mrs. Rushmore, of Toronto, Canada, was present. The girls sent her down to find out why Lee doesn't sing more.

They got to talking about where next year's convention should be and a delegate said, "What difference does it make where it is, I'll be there!" Another said, "Let's watch those bookings or we might get to someplace he won't be. Then no one would come."

"Why not have it in Alaska?" someone asked, and the girls laughed a little, but Mrs. Roberts said, "You might think that's funny but we have a fan club there." Somebody else said, "He's got friends in Africa, too."

There's more to the story, but you get the idea. We don't have the fan club conventions anymore, because they got a little out of hand, and if you can't manage things like that properly it's better not to let them happen.

But Kay Durant, who has been president of my fan club in Great Britain ever since she founded it seventeen years ago, still holds a Christmas party every year, and they always have a party on my birthday. They're really a fabulous group. If anybody writes anything nasty about me in the paper, he hears from them. They really do a great deal to promote my career in England.

Like everything else I do, my fan clubs, and their activities on my behalf, have been heavily ridiculed. In fact the very idea that I should help the press to know about and write about me is made fun of, as if I were the first performer to ever send out advance publicity ahead of an appearance.

A columnist named Paul Herron, for instance, wrote in the Washington *Post*, "Show business biographies have arrived for Liberace who opens tonight at the Lotus Club. The thick manuscript contains the title of every Liberace record, his philosophy of life, including, 'to attain wealth one must value wealth' and complete directions for squeezing every ounce of publicity out of his appearance. An index would help."

Well, we wrote Herron a letter of thanks and the next advance publicity contained an index. I'm the first to admit that if it weren't for the help we give the press I wouldn't get nearly as much publicity as I do, nor would I, as a result, get the kind of audiences that fill my concerts to capacity. And if Mr. Herron thought the idea that "to attain wealth you must value wealth" was funny or obvious or untrue, he's wrong on all counts.

You can *make* money. But unless you *value* it, you'll waste it, buy worthless things with it, and so you will not attain wealth. You'll wind up as broke as when you started.

But to get back to my fan clubs. I'm truly indebted to them for some wonderful scrapbooks they've prepared for me. These make nice records of my various appearances in different cities from year to year, and sometimes one of these scrapbooks will contain a whole review of one of my concerts such as this one written by Marian Thomas of Melbourne, Australia. I wish all the reviewers who came to my shows wrote reports like this one.

> Festival Hall began to fill up. We could hardly believe our luck when we were led to two seats in the second row right in front of the black glass-topped piano. Everyone seemed to be talking at once. I checked my watch. The time was 8:12 P.M., the show being due to start at 8:15. Suddenly a voice came over the loudspeaker system. There was complete silence. Was this the great moment? "Would the owner of Holden JMG 449 turn his lights off or he'll have a flat battery." A sigh and signs of exasperation flowed through the audience, which soon turned to excitement when the famous candelabra was placed on the piano and the orchestra started to tune up their instruments. 8:18. He was three minutes late. Again came the voice. I felt myself grow tense with expectation. "Would the owner of STV 623 turn off his motor, please?" This time a groan could be heard from the thousands of people gathered together to see one man, and as the tension mounted the man at the other end of the speaker became immediately the most unpopular fellow in Melbourne. 8:20. We all knew he had a lot of clothes to put on but he had been doing that sort of thing for fifteen years; couldn't he be a little quicker? The incessant rustling of papers and murmuring began to annoy me. I looked around. Everybody seemed so calm. I wondered if they were in such a turmoil of emotional excitement and impatience as I was.

All at·once an ear shattering roll of drums sounded. Dr. Gordon Robinson, immaculately dressed in black tuxedo, walked onto the stage to conduct the orchestra in a jazz arrangement of "I'll Be Seeing You," his theme tune. It was twenty-five minutes past eight. Again that supremely irritating voice. Or was it? Did another car need attending to?

"Ladies and gentlemen, Crawford productions have great pride in presenting"—the lights dim—"that man who is famous throughout the world for his candelabra"—a roll of drums—"and his piano"—a blue spotlight flashed upon the stage entrance; all eyes turned to it—"the best dressed man in show business, the star of our show, Mr. Showmanship . . . LIBERACE!"

Finally! He was on stage. I almost breathed a sigh of relief. For the duration of approximately three seconds total silence reigned, and then such a thunderous applause rose that, while gazing at him, I pictured the roof lifting off with the sheer pressure of the sound. From the moment he walked before the mass of people he had one and all in the palm of his hand. Sighs and gasps could be heard. Dressed in full length maxi blue coat, fur trimmed with solid gold epaulets, overflowing with happiness and personality, he could be described as nothing less than spectacular. With "a smile as wide as his piano keyboard" he bowed and walked across the stage, waiting until he could be heard above the tremendous ovation. When, at last, we ceased clapping (mainly due to rather sore hands) he launched into the type of jokes that have become so much a part of his act, so well known by anyone who has any interest in Liberace, and yet which were still so humorous when he delivered them. "Well. Look me over. I didn't get dressed like this to go unnoticed. Do you like this one?" We did, of course. We'd love him in anything. "It was made for me when I had the honour to play a Royal Command Performance, and would you believe it, out of all the performers there, I was the only person with one like it!" Not impossible to believe. Taking this off, he revealed a golden waistcoat and white, puffed-lace pantaloons. After recovering from this outfit, he asked, "Well, are you ready for music?" What a question! Amid still more sighs and the voice of a woman behind me murmuring, "He's too good to be true," (I agreed entirely) he infused his amazing musical ability into the beautiful melodies of "Theme From Love Story," "Raindrops Keep Falling on my Head," "Close To You," following these contemporary tunes with the masterpieces of the great composer Chopin.

One could hear a pin drop in that theater. He then relinquished the stage to a young boy of ten years; the youngest professional juggler in the world. I don't know if Liberace needed the rest but I certainly did. I was feeling emotionally pulverized.

[May I interrupt this glorious review to say that the lad's name is Albert Lucas and he is certainly the most phenomenal juggler of any age I've ever seen. If he weren't the greatest, would I have him on my show?]

However, Liberace rushed back within five minutes in an outfit of pink silk with a jacket made of a thousand little mirrors, all of which dazzled the eyes as they reflected the light of his candelabra all around the building. Then Liberace virtually achieved the impossible—he bridged the generation gap by swinging into a medley from *Hair* to the enjoyment of all ages. He refused to play it in the nude ... judging by the number of unhappy "ohs" this seemed rather a disappointment to some people. So after sending us through the universe to the star Aquarius, he played and narrated "The Impossible Dream"—the song by which he wished to be remembered. I'll remember him by it and every time I hear a lovely piece of music, or hear the note of a piano, I'll remember him.

The perfection slipped a little as he missed a couple of words, but we didn't mind. He only seemed more human and we were so intent on the sound of his voice, his expressions, his sincerity, that even before he'd finished playing the last few bars, the applause could have been heard a mile away. It was almost like an impossible dream to realize the effect this wonderful performer had on all those around him.

Intermission came and I tried to relax. The only topic of conversation was, of course, Liberace. I listened to such phrases as: "He's magnificent, fantastic, he plays the piano as if he's part of it," and my favorite from a gentleman just in front of me, "My God! I wish I'd brought my sunglasses—with him you need 'em." And he was virtually right. Especially in the second half of the show, when Liberace stunned the audience by bounding on wearing red, white and blue hotpants, twirling a diamond-studded baton and laughing with us until everyone, including himself, was in stitches. As he mentioned, he certainly made the NBC peacock look like a plucked chicken.

Two costume changes later, after playing everything from boogie-woogie in double time to a Gershwin medley, he announced the end of the show. We thought differently. Amid the cries of 8,000 anguished fans yelling for "more" he decided to give it to us, as he "was in no hurry to go if we weren't." We weren't. In fact, we would just not let him go.

[Again I must interrupt to wonder why my young friend in her enthusiasm forgot to mention that the wonderful comedienne, Fay McKay, who really

rocked them in Australia, was in the second half of the show. Do you suppose
Marian Morgan could have been jealous? Or maybe she was just careless. I'm
sure no fan of mine would be catty!]

A thrill swept through the audience when Liberace bent over the stage, showing his fabulous rings, and inspecting those of others. He played seven encores on demand, his last being a beautiful song called "Ciao," one which was most appropriate, to say good-bye. Many tears could be discovered in many eyes. The lights dimmed for the last time as he switched off his candelabra. But with Liberace there had to be a spectacular ending to a truly spectacular show. In complete darkness, suddenly his suit lit up so that he resembled a miniature Christmas tree. The lights then blazed on, revealing Lee on stage laughing and every member of the audience giving him a thundering, standing ovation.

We all rushed to the stage to shake his hand and after a few bows, winks, smiles and waves, suddenly, like a breath of magic he was gone, taking a little part of Melbourne with him. We all sat down again, reluctant to move. It took an hour to fully clear the hall.

I believe that everybody felt as I did. We wanted to linger in a place where we'd been privileged to see a man who not only loved his work and his music but also loved his audiences. In his way, amid the glitter of clothes, candelabras, pianos and success he radiated personality and love. In two hours and forty minutes he'd brought to us a wonderful kind of magic, a magic we wanted to keep, as we would keep always, the memory of the magic of that night.

His last words to us were, "You've been just wonderful. God bless you all." And I think that everyone there blessed Mr. Wladziu Valentino Liberace. In a world that seems so prejudiced and talks so easily and frequently of war, Liberace has the ability to make millions of different people happy and that is perhaps the greatest gift that one human being can give another.

Do you get the idea from that review that Marian likes me? I'm glad. Because I'm going to Australia in the spring of 1973, and I feel that there'll be at least one person in the audience.

23

Sometimes I do things that, in retrospect, make me wonder how I could be so idiotic. Among these probably the most insane was to try to do my own cleaning. The day and date are unforgettable. It was November 22, 1963, the day President John F. Kennedy was assassinated. I, too, almost died on that day.

I didn't generally try to do my own dry cleaning, in fact I'd never tried it before. Bob Fischer usually looks after every detail concerning my costumes, but he was away on some important errands. I noticed that a few things seemed just slightly soiled around the collars and cuffs. I called the hotel valet, but he said he couldn't get the work I wanted done in time for me to use the clothes in my show that evening. So I went out and bought myself a gallon of dry cleaning fluid, brought it back to the hotel and went to work. I suppose I should have had the window open in the room, but it was awfully cold in Pittsburgh that day. In fact, there was a raging blizzard.

We were to open that night at a club called The Holiday and Gordon Robinson was, as usual, rehearsing the band at the club, when the awful news about President Kennedy broke. One of my managers, Seymour's associate, Dick Gabbe, of Gabbe, Lutz and Heller, rushed in to tell me about the tragedy. I immediately asked if there was going to be a show. I said I didn't think there should be, but of course, it was up to the management. If they decided to give a performance, I would be in breach of contract if I didn't give one. So Dick rushed right over to see the manager of the club and I lay down on the bed overcome with sadness. I just felt so awful I didn't know if I could give a show. I don't know how long I lay on the bed, but I must have fallen asleep.

Of course, when Dick arrived in the room where Gordon Robinson was rehearsing the music, the first thing Gordon asked was the same question I had asked, "Will there be a performance?"

Dick said he'd laid the matter before the management and they were thinking it over. Gordon, like me, didn't think there was anything to think over, but he too, was tied up contractually. So he told Gabbe that he thought the best thing for him to do, until he got positive word of a cancellation, was to go on getting the orchestra ready in case we were forced to do a show.

While he was rehearsing, Gordon told me later, a man came charging into the empty night club room where they were running through my music. He was yelling, "Stop! Stop that music! How dare you play that kind of music at a time like this! Don't you know that the President has just been shot? It's sacrilegious! It's totally profane! You should all be shot as traitors!"

It wasn't until that last outrageous remark that Gordon realized that he was not only dealing with a fanatic but a drunken one. However, he was just great at handling people in difficult situations. His motto was, "Always be nice to them." This is the approach he used on this man with whose feelings, if not the way they manifested themselves, he was in agreement.

He told the man that there was no question about the fact that it was a tragic day, that it was no time to be playing frivolous music. But he had just heard about the awful event, and the management was at that very moment deciding whether or not there should be a show that night. Then he went on to explain about the contract, and so in case there was a decision to do the show, he had to be ready.

It must have been a masterful job of handling a rough customer in a peaceable way. But the man continued his insane tirade until finally Gordon had to signal someone to go out and get help and he had the man thrown out. It shook Gordon up a lot because he doesn't like to do things like that.

This incident on top of the natural sorrow that the shooting of President Kennedy brought to everyone, made for a very listless and dull rehearsal and the strangest aspect of the whole controversy over whether or not to do a show was the fact that when

Gabbe came back to Gordon with the news that we had to go on that night, he called off the rehearsal. When Dick asked why, he told him that the men would never get any better than they were up to that point; that feeling the way most of them did, they'd probably get worse. I'm sure Gordon was right.

When Dick came back to my room to wake me up and tell me about the decision I just couldn't believe it. We talked for a little while about Dallas and then he said, "How can you stand the smell of that stuff?"

It didn't seem bad to me. I'd gotten used to it and said, "Oh, I was just cleaning a few things I have to wear tonight." Dick said, "Great! You're not making enough money. You have to do your own cleaning! I'll bring some of my ties over. How much do you charge?" I explained why I was doing the cleaning, and he said what he did to break the tension a little and change my mood which was very blue.

After he left I lay down to rest again because I really didn't feel very well. The tragedy of the day had gotten into my heart. I just couldn't understand how such things could happen. Thinking about this I fell asleep again.

When it came time to do the show I still felt a little lousy. I thought it was due to too much napping in the afternoon, which I don't generally do. And, of course, to the turmoil going on inside of me at being forced to do a show. I suppose, thinking back on it, I should have refused. But I was sure it would mean a lawsuit and I didn't want to go through anything like that. It's just too hard on me. It affects my performance and my health.

As might have been expected, when we came to do the show, there was a very small audience. Nobody was really in the mood for any kind of entertainment that night of November 22, and I remember wondering just who those few people who showed up were, and what they were thinking.

By the time I got through my first number, everything began going in circles. I became nauseated. I had never felt so terrible in my life. I rushed offstage. They could see how I felt and they re-routed the show to put on one of the other acts while I tried to pull myself together. It felt as if I were vomiting up all my insides. I was even too sick to be frightened. Then, for a few moments, I thought I felt better and tried to go on again but about three-quarters through another number, it was clear that I was finished for the night. As it turned out, I was finished for almost a month. I was almost finished forever.

They called an ambulance and rushed me to St. Francis Hospital in Pittsburgh, where a team of nine doctors began making all manner of emergency tests and examinations. From the symptoms they had some idea of what the problem might be and this led them to the diagnosis that my kidneys were seriously infected. They said it was uremic poisoning caused, the tests seemed to show, by carbon tetrachloride. They asked me if this were possible, if I'd been exposed to the fumes from it.

Then I realized what had happened to me. It was the smell Dick Gabbe had complained about and I'd gotten used to. I'd been breathing carbon tetrachloride almost all afternoon. When the doctors found this out I was immediately placed in intensive care and put on a kidney machine. My personal physician, Dr. Frank Taylor, took the first plane to Pittsburgh.

It's interesting that the doctor who headed the team at St. Francis Hospital was specializing in internal fluids and particularly active in trying to get certain chemicals, extensively used in household products, such as carbon tetrachloride, banned. I think he succeeded in winning his point on the stuff that almost killed me. He was also very active in trying to get information around that would teach people to read the labels on the stuff they use before they start to use it. That's very important and a lot of progress has been made in that direction in the past ten years in telling people what to look out for and even getting it printed on product labels.

For the first few days everyone was all phony smiles, and although I remained hooked up to the mechanical kidney and both I and, I'll bet, the machine were feeling worse and worse every day, optimism hung over my room like a thunder cloud. Doctors are lousy liars. The ones in the hospital and Dr. Taylor would tell me I was improving while glancing at my chart and shaking their heads involuntarily. Their faces always told the medical truth that their love for me would not let them say. Finally it was Dr. Taylor who had the hard job of telling me the truth.

He said that he and the hospital staff had just had a long consultation, and everyone agreed that the way things were going, he felt I ought to be told that I should "put my house in order." That's the expression he used. You hear it all the time. It's a funny way to tell a man to get ready to die. It's a bewildering piece of news to be given. It takes a little while for it to sink in. First you feel a terrible shock. Then a benign sense of inevitability and sadness at the thought of all the people you love whom you will see no more. It's strange. You mourn for your friends before they get a chance to mourn for you.

Of course, if the doctors were wrong for some reason and you survive, time turns the whole incident into some kind of sardonic joke.

Two years later, when I was playing the unctuous coffin salesman in *The Loved One*, I found myself remembering '63 and wondering which box my loved ones would have picked out for me to cross the River Styx in. And what they might have been saying. Maybe it was these thoughts that somehow made me wring out of the New York *Times* critic, "Chalk up a good performance for Liberace." Clearly he was surprised.

I've always wondered why so many people are surprised when I turn out to be good at what I do. I could tell them why. It's because I work very hard to be good.

But back to my big death scene. I sent for a priest and had him administer the Last Rites. Then I did just what the doctor told me to do. I began to put everything in order so I'd make a minimum amount of trouble for my accountants, my attorneys and my heirs. I asked how much cash there'd be left after all the conditions of my will were fulfilled. And after giving that a going over with the adding machines—computers were not yet such a big deal—they told me there'd be about $750,000.

Since all the charities and everything were taken care of in the will, I decided to give out a few presents, remember my friends and relatives with a few things to remember me by. I had charge accounts opened at Cartiers, Tiffany's, Saks Fifth Avenue and all the other good stores, and the nursing sisters at the hospital each day would phone in what I wanted ordered and where to ship it. My stage manager of seventeen years and dear friend Ray Arnett stayed in Pittsburgh and visited me every day if even for a few minutes. It's then you realize how wonderful it is to have loyal friends. He shared my ordeal and made each day in the hospital a little more cheerful for me with his presence. Making people happy with things you know they need or love is not a bad way to spend your last days, if you've got the means.

The gifts ranged from a house in Beverly Hills for my sister to a mink coat, pearls and jewels for my Mother, and a boat for a member of my staff which numbered twenty-eight people. The men got everything from cars and motorcycles to gold jewelry, the women, diamonds and furs. It was wild. If you think a drunken sailor spends money carelessly, you should get a load of a rich piano player when he thinks he's dying.

Then in the midst of this orgy of giving, a nun I'd never seen before came into my room and sat next to my bed and said softly, "St. Anthony has performed many miracles. Pray to him." Then she touched my arm gently and left the room.

Her words had a tremendous impact on me, and I began to pray. I don't know how to explain this, and I don't know if I ever want an explanation. But almost immediately I began to feel better. Doctors smiled, feeling that their work had finally begun to take effect. I'm willing to believe that. But I also have to believe what the sister said and what happened as a result of it.

I tried to find her around the hospital. I described her to the other sisters who were helping me. None recognized her from my description and none remembered seeing her enter or leave my room. I found out about St. Anthony. He was the Saint who was thought of as "The Doctor of the Church" and credited with many miracles. I read about him in a book called "The Treasury of St. Anthony." No one will ever know, least of all me, exactly what happened. Maybe the doctors did something right. Faith? It never hurt. Perhaps it is just that the body has a way of curing itself.

As for the sister, maybe I was heavily sedated. Perhaps I was hallucinating in the fever of crisis. Whatever it was, that sister will always live in my heart. She was the herald of what I choose to believe was another miracle of St. Anthony.

When the doctors confirmed what I already knew in my heart, by saying, "Don't ask for any scientific explanation but you're goint to make it," I didn't ask. I broke down and cried. I had brazened the whole thing through. Then, just as twice before when I felt death was certain, the full impact hit me only after the danger was over.

I had the same sort of after-shocks that I'd experienced the time I was left floating in the Mediterranean, and it took blankets and hot bouillabaisse to pull me through; the same awful feeling inside that gripped me hours after the near crash at Buffalo airport.

Then came the dawning, the warm and wonderful glow of how glorious life is. Just as my numerology chart had said, the firing squad had not been allowed to fire. I was told I would be home for Christmas. I immediately called my friend Bob Fischer in California and told him to go all out on the Christmas decorations at my Hollywood house as I was coming home. I gave him a budget of $25,000 to work with (which was about all the cash I had left after buying all those expensive gifts) and he decorated the house inside and out like it's never been decorated before or since. It was a Christmas I will never forget and I've never been closer to heaven literally and figuratively.

From that moment on I knew I'd appreciate life a little more,

24

I suppose that as long as I remain a bachelor people are going to ask me why I have never married. It's one of the questions that pops up in every interview I have. And I'm sure it will continue to unless I get married. Then I'll probably be asked why I changed my mind and why I picked the woman I did. The second half of that question, should it ever be asked, would be harder to answer.

Not many people know this, largely because it's none of their business, but I come from a family of divorces. My mother and father were separated. I sometimes give as an excuse for not marrying, the bitter truth that my brother George "has been happily married five times, and I'm waiting to see how it turns out."

Everytime I've come close to marriage some incident made me know, gave me a warning, that it wouldn't work.

Mother tells me that my first love was a little girl who lived in our neighborhood in West Milwaukee. We were very close. She lived next door. The rumor is that her name was Rose. I was about nine and she was about seven. Clearly she'd be too old for me today. I have no idea why we drifted apart, but we did. Whatever the reason it should have taught me a lesson, but it didn't. The lesson—don't ever fall in love with neighborhood girls.

The first house I owned in California I bought from a wonderful character actress, Lurene Tuttle, who later appeared with me in *Sincerely Yours*. It was not only the first house I owned in California, it was the first one I ever owned anywhere. And like the homes of so many ambitious young newcomers to Los Angeles, it was in San

Fernando Valley. But that was before "The Valley" became, as it is today, mountain-to-mountain houses. Then it was still kind of country and western, still sagebrushy enough to inspire the hit song that told the story of a man who was going to "settle down and make the San Fernando Valley my home." As everyone who has watched Los Angeles grow knows, hundreds of thousands of families did just that.

Not far from this house lived a little girl I didn't meet for several years. I think the reason I finally met her was that she grew up. Little girls have a way of doing that as Maurice Chevalier reminded the world.

This little neighborhood girl did just that. She grew up in a *very* lovely way, so lovely that she became one of the beauties in the chorus at the Moulin Rouge, one of Hollywood's most glamorous night clubs in the days when Hollywood had night clubs. However, we did not meet at the Moulin Rouge. We met at our parish church and became very good friends. I brought her to the house for dinner. Mother liked her and her father liked me. He was Eddie Rio, one time head of AGVA—the American Guild of Vaudeville Artists.

Everyone thought ours was one of those matches made in heaven because we met in a church. There was a lot of sideline cheering from both our families trying to push things along too fast. For a while Joanne and I became what the gossip columnists of the day called "an item."

Since I had just become, overnight, the season's hottest new television personality, our "romance" got much too much publicity. I don't know why I put the word "romance" in quotation marks unless it is because there is the romance of infatuation, which doesn't last, and the Romance that is born of true love. Sometimes one can become the other. Neither Joanne nor I minded very much what was printed about us. Maybe Romance, with a capital "R" is more private than "romance" in quotation marks. Anyway, the serpent of publicity got into our temporary Garden of Eden.

A very ambitious syndicated newspaper reporter talked Joanne into collaborating with him on a nationally syndicated series that was called "My Dates With Liberace." These pieces contained many intimate details, confidences and personal confessions that two people share when they're in love (or think they are). When these are set down in cold print they tend to make both parties look somewhat ridiculous.

These intimate stories followed me all over the country and became the source of a lot of kidding. They caused me a great deal of embarrassment.

But what finally hosed me down and cooled me off was the discovery that Joanne had been paid a tidy sum by the newspaper syndicate to let them publish the details of our romance.

I guess the only thing you never learn by experience is how to control your emotions. Not long after my split with Joanne I became involved (they tell me it was "on the rebound") with a lovely young heiress named Frances Goodrich. Her family owned a number of large citrus ranches in the Los Angeles area. And it looked for a while as if this romance were going to develop into the real thing. Then the strangest conflict of interest started to divide us.

Frances, influenced no doubt by her family, tried to talk me into doing something so completely opposite to what I would ever want to do that it amazes me. She and her folks wanted me to quit my music, concerts—show business—and take over the management of their citrus holdings.

Obviously that romance was not sun-kissed.

Then there was an interlude with Sonja Henie whose great skill as a figure skater took her to the very top of super-stardom in Hollywood. It was at a party at Ciro's. I was seated next to her, and because some things happen that way we immediately became friends. It seemed as if we'd known each other for much longer than just that evening. Why else would I have invited her to my sister Angie's wedding the following week? Why else would she accept?

She not only honored us by coming, but as a surprise to Angie, she had two beautiful ice sculptures made for the buffet table. One was a skating figure resembling herself. The other was a pianist seated at a piano. Thinking about it as I write, it seems terribly pointed. But that didn't occur to me at the time and, of course, Angie was thrilled by Sonja's thoughtfulness. The only trouble was that the buffet table seemed to be saying that it was Sonja Henie and Liberace who were to be married, not Angie and Tom Farrell.

Our sudden friendship developed into a very personal and warm relationship, and we enjoyed many evenings together either at parties or just the two of us. These private evenings were spent watching some of Sonja's movies in the projection room of her beautiful home in Bel Air. As I recall, it was not unlike a scene from the Gloria Swanson picture *Sunset Boulevard*. The two of us sat in a darkened room watching Sonja. After each reel the lights would come up; she controlled them with a rheostat right on her chair. We would then refill our champagne glasses. This, incidentally, was all she ever drank. Then we'd view the next reel of the film. I even recall some of the titles. There was *One in a Million*, in which she starred with Adolphe Menjou and Don Ameche; I remember admiring Mr. Menjou's clothes. Then there was a picture called, predictably, *Thin Ice*. I have no recollection at all who was with her in that one. And another thoroughly forgettable one was called *Wintertime*. But she was lovely in all of them, and it was easy to see why she had become so popular.

Then I had to go on tour, and we couldn't see each other as often as we had. We only met when she'd come to see me in New York or Las Vegas. This was noted by the columnists. Ours was called "a torrid romance." Everywhere we were seen together we were trailed by photographers and reporters. Finally we were labeled "America's Sweethearts." I suppose with this sort of thing going on, our friendship might have developed into something more permanent had I not left the country for an extensive tour of England.

During my absence our "hot" romance wound up on ice. I read about her new "interest" in the newspapers. He was a wealthy Scandinavian and he helped prove that this talk about absence making the heart grow fonder doesn't have much substantiation in fact.

Sonja was the kind of person who could get very lonely without constant companionship and love. She needed someone always at her beck and call. Obviously I couldn't be that person. She'd had her career. I had a career to build. I suppose that's the basic story on which half the films about show business are based.

The next time I saw Sonja a year had passed. She and her husband were at ringside the night I opened at the Riviera in Las Vegas. And there's another scene from a B picture. She looked very glamorous and was wearing jewels that were the envy of every woman in the room. I invited them both to the reception following the opening, and we remained the very best of friends.

So, you see, everytime I came close to marriage I received a warning that it wouldn't work. Of course, in the case of Sonja it was her marriage to someone else. But if that's not a warning, what is?

My philosophy of life is one of loving and giving, and I could only be happy with someone who honestly felt the same way I do, someone who loves the same things I love, appreciates the same things I enjoy and, you might say, becomes part of me. Selfish? Maybe. But it's realistic.

I don't lead the kind of life, living in the limelight, traveling all over the world, showing off, being a showman, spending money and making people happy, that can be understood, much less enjoyed, by most people. True. Everyone says to himself, "Wow! That's how to live! If I only had his dough!" But money really doesn't have that much to do with it. I'd be the same way I am if I didn't have a dime. In fact, I was. The only difference was that then I wanted to do what I'm now doing, instead of actually being able to do it. I think it must have been the *wanting* that made the *doing* possible.

Today I hear people say that I'm the toughest kind of man to make into a good husband, a confirmed bachelor. The trouble is, I have yet to experience that confirmation. Should the right woman come along, one who clearly loves me enough to take a chance on me and I feel that deeply for her, I'm sure we'll both know that "this is it." Should that ever happen it will be a happy day for me.

In the meantime I have no message for the world. I never have been able to understand why, because a man has a certain talent, because he spends a lot of time in the public eye, he is thought to be a deep thinker. I'm not.

But this I can tell you. I feel better today, more energetic than I did twenty years ago. Then my career seemed to smother me with demands that were not always to my liking. I wasn't master of my own destiny. I had to do certain things to get where I wanted to be. I had to *make*, as it were, my detiny. Now I feel I've done that.

I am now wholly in charge of my own life. I no longer have to do things for expedient reasons, to please others. I feel I've fulfilled all my obligations—any I've ever had—to everybody I've ever owed anything to in the way of help and cooperation. In short, I've reached the point in my life that everyone longs for, the point at which I am able to say, "No!"

As a result of this, I take much more pleasure in my work,

because I've spent time improving and polishing my craft. And because of this, those who come to see me have a keener appreciation of what I'm doing because I do it better than I ever did before. Without time to rest, reflect and practice, without time to enjoy life, there can be no self-improvement.

Gone are the years when I was forced to make appearances I didn't want to make, do shows under the worst possible conditions, smile when I didn't feel like smiling because I was exhausted or depressed or both. Back in the white heat of the television years, a time came when I was so completely worn out that I went to a doctor who gave me some of those magic pills to pick up my spirits and my energy. Fortunately, this same doctor warned me against this medicine and said that what I needed was a complete rest. I decided to take his advice.

That was the first time I got up enough courage to say, "No!" It took guts to give up lucrative engagements. But the truth always shines through and the truth that time was the realization that my health was worth more than the half-million dollars I was forfeiting. Having learned that lesson, I resolved never again to let my health sink so low. And I began to book my time off, my leisure, as carefully as I booked my playing engagements.

Just recently, for example, Seymour came to me with a simply wonderful offer for a series of concerts. I turned it down. He was crestfallen. "Why? Why? Why?" he asked. When I told him he thought about it and then began to laugh. The reason was that the tour would keep me away from home during the time my orchids in Palm Springs would be in bloom. If you can understand that you can understand me today.

Now, whenever Seymour comes to me with a very attractive offer for a tour he says, "Lee, you can't turn this one down. It comes at a time when your orchid trees are in the dormant season."

And this I must admit that even though I'm a bachelor, no matter how successful the tour, I get awfully homesick when I'm on the road. I miss my "children," my seven beautiful dogs who give me so much love and companionship when I'm home in Palm Springs. Just the surroundings of home give me so much pleasure that I get lonesome for them. Seymour will say to me, "You broke all records last night. Hit a new box office high."

I say, "That's very nice but I miss Palm Springs and the dogs."

If that sounds silly to some people, think of this. What else have